CHANGE YOUR LIFE WITH

FAT
CLUB

LOSE WEIGHT - FOREVER

Annie Ashworth and **Meg Sanders** are a very experienced writer/editor partnership based in Warwickshire. Their work includes features for *Homes & Gardens*, *Women's Journal*, *The Evening Standard* and *Natural Choice* Magazine, and books include activity books and encyclopaedias for Kingfisher, titles for Hamlyn and Conran Octopus, The *Trade Secrets* series and most recently *How to Beat the System* (Orion 2002).

CHANGE YOUR LIFE WITH

FAT

CLUB

LOSE WEIGHT - FOREVER

ANNIE ASHWORTH AND
MEG SANDERS

GRANADA

First published in Great Britain in 2002
By Granada Media, an imprint of André Deutsch Limited
20 Mortimer Street
London W1T 3JW

In association with Granada Media Group

Text copyright © Granada Media Group, 2002

Fat Club is an LWT Production

A catalogue record for this book is available from the British Library.

ISBN 0 233 05015 9

Typeset by Derek Doyle & Associates, Liverpool
Printed and bound in the UK
by Mackays, Chatham

2 4 6 8 10 9 7 5 3

Contents

To all the Fat Club members:
For your honesty, courage and determination.

Acknowledgements

It has been a fascinating and inspiring experience putting together this book. Our thanks to Dr Sarah Schenker, Dr Raj Patel, Professor Alex Gardner and Harvey Walden IV for their endless patience and enthusiasm in the face of a constant barrage of questions from us, night and day, in the course of our research. Thanks too to the Fat Club production team for letting us loiter during filming and for tolerating our raft of emails with good grace.

AA and MS
October 2001

Chapter 1

Hooray! Diets Don't Work!

Before you throw down this book in horror when the words 'food' and 'calories' jump out of the page, this is emphatically *not* a diet book. It is the extraordinary story of a group of overweight people who were prepared to take up the challenge to change their lives, and to do so in the most public way imaginable – on prime-time television.

We all know that diets do not work. How many have *you* tried? Perhaps you've cut out fat with Dr Atkins, boiled up dubious-smelling cabbage soups, filled up (with wind) with the F-plan? Your dieting career might even stretch back as far as the Cambridge, the Beverly Hills or even the Scarsdale diets. Millions of us have tried at least some of these strange and often unappetising eating regimes, tempted by the promise of lasting weight loss. Indeed, we have tried them again and again, and that is the point.

If diets did work, would the UK diet industry be worth £1 billion? No, that is not a misprint, by the way. One *billion* pounds of our money each year is spent on diet books, clubs and foods that are almost certain to fail. Right now one in three of us is on a diet, but within a year of reaching our target weight, we will gradually have regained 40 per cent of what we have lost. Almost all of us will be back to our original weight, if not heavier, within three to five years.

Even before we fork out the pounds to try and lose the pounds, we should stop and think. It is more than likely that within weeks of starting an extreme diet we will be gaining weight again. This is because the fat we store in our bodies cannot be lost rapidly. Diets that promise fast weight loss rely on cutting calories to an unhealthily low level. During the first week of any drastic diet, all we will lose is carbohydrate, which is stored in water. It is this which produces a dramatic effect on the scales, and we feel elated (if famished). Only after this will fat loss start, but calorie intake has to stay very low, weight loss slows down, we are hungry and lose motivation.

Don't you find that once you tell yourself you are on a diet, all you can think about is your stomach? Food begins to take on an enormous importance. Cabbage soup or liquid meal replacements are hardly feel-good foods. Also many faddy diets function by creating an imbalance to one extreme or another (high protein or high carbohydrate only, for example). Not only is this unhealthy, it can be unbearable after a while, so it is hardly surprising that when we are feeling low and hungry, we say 'what the heck', and buy a bag of salt 'n' vinegar crisps.

As attractive as these promise-all diets may be, they will not work in the long term. It is not just expensive and miserably demoralising for a diet to fail *again* – in fact the idea of 'being on a diet' suggests it is something temporary – experts now reckon that the yo-yo effect of weight loss and weight gain is actually worse for our bodies than remaining at a constant weight because, if we pursue a 'faddy' or extreme diet, we are more likely to deprive our bodies of essential nutrients.

So that is the good news: diets are a waste of time and money. Even better news is that by the time you have read this book, you will realise you will never have to be 'on a diet' again.

The state we're in

There is bad news, however, and that is that we are fatter than we have ever been before, and British people are the worst offenders in Europe. In fact, according to a February 2001 report by the Comptroller and Auditor General, Sir John Bourn, one in four of us is overweight, while one in five of us is classed as clinically obese – over 30 per cent heavier than our recommended body weight. Over half of women and two-thirds of men are either overweight or obese – and the situation is getting worse. It is reckoned that, at this rate, *half the nation* will be obese by 2003.

You probably think that ugly word 'obese' could not possibly describe you, but if you should be 10 stone and you are weighing in at 13, technically you would be defined as obese. Work it out for yourself: the ideal body weight for your height should be measured by the Body Mass Index (BMI). To find if you are in the danger zone, see page 216.

Has this epidemic come about because we are eating too much? The irony is that we are actually consuming fewer calories than we did 30 years ago, yet we are far fatter. So what is going on? You do not have to be a rocket scientist to realise that, to lose weight, you have to use up more energy (or calories) than you are taking in. The real difference between our lifestyles now and 30 years ago is that we are taking far less exercise. Modern technology has become our downfall. We sit in front of the TV with the remote control and the closest many of us get to sport is watching it. We spend too much time glued to our computers. We drive our cars and our children to school when we should be walking, and we take the lift instead of the stairs. We call out for pizza to be delivered instead of going to get it. In fact, the obesity epidemic is directly related to the increase in the number of TV aerials on roofs and cars on the road.

Modern diet, too, like that take-away pizza, is also to blame. It is a question of what we eat and how we eat it. Whereas once we ate fresh fruit and veg, and home-cooked food, our busy lives today make it so much easier and quicker to grab a high-fat take-away or convenience meal. As a nation we eat more snack foods than any other country in Europe. Not surprising really when they are so readily available everywhere – newsagents, supermarket checkouts, garages, garden centres, even – oh, the irony – at the local swimming pool!

But being overweight is dangerous

The facts:

- One in five British adults – 20 per cent of the population – is so fat that their health is seriously endangered.

- 30,000 deaths a year in the UK can be directly attributed to excess weight.
- In 1998 obesity accounted for 18 million days of sickness absence and 30,000 premature deaths.
- On average, each person whose death could be attributed to obesity lost nine years of life.

For years we have been bombarded by facts about the dangers of smoking, and even the most hardened 40-a-dayer will admit that they are well aware of the damage they are doing to themselves. The message has got through – you can't miss it, it is written all over every packet of cigarettes and advertising billboard. What we are less educated about are the dangers of being overweight. OK, so being fat makes running difficult, you may not like the way you look, and finding clothes that fit is a challenge, but would you be shocked to find out that being overweight also causes high blood pressure, asthma and coronary heart disease; that it increases death rates from all cancers by up to 50 per cent, and that it is a major contributing factor in cases of *diabetes mellitus*? And diabetes is not just a minor inconvenience; it is a chronic disease which can lead to impotence, blindness, amputation, kidney and liver failure. At worst it is a killer and it is on the increase.

Paul Trayhurn, Professor of Obesity Biology at Liverpool University, reckons that, world-wide, the number of diabetics is likely to *double* to 300 million in the next 20 years, and that is largely due to the surge in obesity. For those defined as clinically obese, the chances of developing diabetes increase 20- to 30-fold. Those whose BMI is over 40 are defined as morbidly obese, which simply means their weight is threatening their life. The bottom line is that 30,000 deaths a year in the UK can be directly attributed to excess weight.

It seems incredible, but the latest research from Liverpool University shows that in an obese smoker, more immediate health risks result from the obesity than from the smoking. There are health professionals who don't even realise this yet, so it is no wonder we are confused.

There is more to being overweight than just the physiological dangers. Fat people are rarely comfortable with being fat. If you look overweight, struggle to find clothes to fit and, more often than not, are subject to cruel comments from the people around you, it leads inevitably to low self-esteem, social isolation and even clinical depression. It is sad, but true, that obese women are nearly a third more likely to attempt suicide.

Those are the pretty scary facts. Which is why the Fat Club television programme had to be made and this book had to be written.

Is there a way out?

MAKE THE CHANGE

We already know a diet, by definition, is a temporary fix. It might do the trick for those who simply need to shed a few pounds before slipping into their holiday bikini, but health professionals all agree that the only way to lose weight effectively is to eat a healthy calorie-controlled diet and to exercise. Unless there is a genuine medical reason for it (and these are few), being overweight comes down to lack of exercise combined with overeating, so the only lasting route to losing weight and being more healthy is to change your lifestyle.

If the garage told you that your car was unsafe to drive, would you risk using it or would you do what was necessary to fix it? We hope the latter, even though it may be an effort to do so. The same principle applies to your life. If you are overweight, the way you live now is unsafe. You are taking unnecessary risks with your health, every day. Make the change.

Change can be alarming, but once you try it, it is not so hard. Try doing something now that is completely out of character. Put on the radio and dance round the room to the music. Or jump up and down shouting 'Eureka!' You probably feel a complete idiot, but you have just broken out of a paralysing straitjacket of inertia, and you have taken the first step towards doing something different. Build on it.

Changes begin with your relationship with food. All the

13

members who joined Fat Club, and indeed all overweight people, become experts at making excuses, even to the point of lying to themselves. How often have you used a bad day as justification to drown your misery in a packet of chocolate digestives? Finished off the children's leftovers 'because it's a waste to throw them away'? Eaten three bags of crisps 'because they're only small'? Ordered a king size burger because 'it's quick and only costs a bit more'? Have you heard yourself blame your size on 'my genes', your fat tummy on 'water retention', your build on 'big bones', your inactivity on 'my metabolism'?

Changes do not even have to be radical. At Fat Club, no one tells you what you can and cannot eat. (Heck, you can even eat chocolate!) It is about understanding food and making changes that count, some you may not even notice: drink semi-skimmed milk instead of full fat; eat twiglets instead of crisps, frozen yoghurt instead of ice-cream. It is a question of lowering fat and reducing calories. It is about balance.

Increased activity needs to become part of that balance. Exercise tones up your muscles (especially that rather important one – your heart), reduces your appetite and is the only way to make your body burn up fat faster. But here too you can fool yourself with excuses. Admit it: are you frightened of going to the gym because you'll 'look a prat'? You might even have joined a gym and stopped going within weeks because you are 'too busy'. Do you take the car down to the shops 'because it will be quicker'? Is it too cold or too hot to go for a walk? The Fat Club members admitted to using every excuse in the book and more, but the sense of achievement even a small amount of exercise gave each of them more than compensated for feeling foolish at the start.

No one is asking you to be Linford Christie. Incorporating exercise into your life does not have to mean state-of-the-art trainers, day-glo Lycra and a ten-mile run. It can be as simple as walking faster. Getting off the bus a stop early. Taking the stairs instead of the lift. Walking to post a letter. Even standing up to do the ironing can help. There are infinite ways you can incorporate a little more activity into your daily routine, and the effects can be dramatic.

The facts speak for themselves:

- A 10 per cent reduction in body weight leads to a 30 per cent fall in diabetes-related deaths.
- A weight loss of up to 20lbs almost halves the chances of mortality from obesity-related cancers.

Suddenly this life change business doesn't sound so hard, does it? The first step to changing anything is admitting it needs changing. By opening this book, you have admitted that your weight is a problem and you have taken the first step to doing something about it.

Who wants to be humiliated?

The original and enduring concept behind the Fat Club programme was that it should be a documentary about over-weight people learning how to make these changes in their lives. They would learn:

- about food and reducing their calorie intake, without the agony of feeling hungry
- how to increase their daily activity.

Over a period of six months, ten carefully selected Fat Club members would:

- attend one weekend a month of assessments, weight checks and workshops
- have the opportunity to be advised by a team of experts who specialise in weight problems.

This was not to be voyeuristic reality TV, but a serious exercise with a positive message for anyone battling with their weight. The Fat Club members are real people who have real issues in their everyday lives.

15

What is obesity? Obesity is the heavy accumulation of fat in the body's fat cells to such a serious degree that it increases the risk of obesity related diseases. People are considered obese if their BMI (Body Mass Index) is between 30 and 40. A BMI of over 40 is considered to be morbidly obese (in very serious danger of death as a result of overweight). See Chapter 12 to calculate your BMI.

The facts about obesity:

- 60 per cent of adults in the UK are overweight.
- 21 per cent of women and 17 per cent of men are clinically obese.
- Obesity levels in Britain have tripled in the last 20 years, and are rising faster than in most other countries in Europe.
- It is predicted that one in four adults will be classed as obese by the end of the decade, equivalent to the levels of obesity in the United States.
- 6 per cent of all deaths each year in the UK are caused directly by obesity.
- The average dress size in the UK is 14–16.
- Obesity is costing the NHS £500 million per year at least in treatments for conditions such as heart disease, diabetes, high blood pressure and osteoarthritis.
- Obese people are at the highest risk of developing hypertension and suffering heart attacks.
- Virtually all obese people develop some associated physical symptom by the age of 40.
- Obese men are 7 times and obese women 27 times more likely to develop type-2 diabetes than people of a healthy weight.
- Being overweight can take nine years off your life expectancy.
- Obesity costs the economy £2 billion per year, in terms of premature deaths and days off work for sick leave,
- According to recent Leeds University research, one in ten 11-year-old girls is obese and one in five 11-year-old-boys.
- In a recent study of severely obese children in Paris, Dr Patrick Tounian showed that obese children already have abnormalities in their arteries which may lead to cardiovascular disease. (*The Lancet*, October 2001)
- In the last five years, primary schools in Britain have cut by more than 50 per cent the amount of time allocated to PE lessons, and in secondary schools PE is allocated less time on the curriculum than anywhere else in Europe.

'In a world where appearances count, sadly it is acceptable to be fattist,' explains the Fat Club series producer, Denise Seneviratne. 'Look on the TV – the only acceptable fat people seem to be comedians. People who are fat are perceived to be stupid and lazy, and we wanted to find a cross-section of people from different backgrounds for the programme to show it is a problem across all areas of society.' By selecting a true representative sample, the programme makers would ensure that the Fat Club members represented Everyman and Everywoman. Viewers could find someone like them to relate to.

With this in mind, advertisements were placed in the press and on radio in January 2001; flyers were sent out; obesity clinics, speciality outsize clothing shops and websites were contacted, and within three months over 500 people called in to the programme answer-phone. 'We aimed to find a group,' continues Denise, 'who had tried all the well-known and the fad diets, even Xenical, the drug which helps people lose weight by reducing the amount of fat they absorb. We wanted people who had made an effort in the past and failed, and who would relish the chance to do something different.'

The enormous number of candidates who responded all had compelling stories and reasons for wanting to take part, and making the final choice was a headache for the production team. Those finally selected underwent rigorous medical tests to ensure they were in sound basic health, and psychometric tests to check they had the right motivation for joining Fat Club. The programme had to be about life change, not a vehicle for instant celebrity.

After months of phone calls, screen tests, home visits and meeting after meeting at LWT headquarters in London, the final ten were chosen and the team knew they had achieved the right mix of people from a wide age range, all walks of life, at differing levels of obesity. As if to confirm their decision was right, the experts were given a shortlist of 15 to whittle down to ten. Independently they chose the same ten.

The Experts

The key to Fat Club and the reason why it is unique among programmes about overweight people is in the help and advice it offers members throughout the six-month duration of the programme. This support came from a carefully selected group of professionals, all leaders in their particular field of expertise and chosen from over 200 possible candidates.

DR RAJ PATEL

'Some patients tell me that they're happy being fat. I'm all for informed choice – the problem is that very few people really understand the health risks of being obese.'

The serious health implications of being overweight made it essential for an experienced GP to act as coordinator for the team of experts, and Dr Raj Patel, 41, is perfect for the role. He has been a full-time GP for the past eight years in Hyde, near Manchester, and he is also a GP adviser to the Department of Health, writes a weekly column in the *Daily Express*, and has made regular appearances on the Granada Digital Wellbeing Channel.

In many ways Raj is the ideal GP, the one everyone would like to have. Softly spoken and thoughtful, he inspires confidence – and confidences. He is a good listener and deals sympathetically and promptly with the health problems of the Fat Club members. His speciality is explaining preventive measures, and he is uncompromising in his belief that a lifestyle change is the only lasting way to achieve and maintain a healthy weight. A slim, active man, Raj loves skiing and is a keen runner – an excellent example of fitting exercise into a busy life.

Like many GPs, he is encountering increasing numbers of patients with weight problems and has formulated a scheme with a local health club whereby he can give his patients 'exercise on prescription'. He tells them how many hours a week they need to exercise, and they use the gym facilities for free. This works well for patients he has seen on a one-to-one basis, but he is humbled by the positive power of the media. 'One of my patients came to see me, smiling all over his face. "I've given up smoking, doctor," he said. This was great news – I'd been on at him about it for several years and felt delighted that I'd got through to him at last. But I got a shock when he told me it was because he'd seen a doctor on the telly talking about it, and it was that which had encouraged him to make the effort! All those consultations, but the thing that finally got the message home was a TV programme!'

In the last few years Raj has taken an increasing interest in strategic public health, which he sees as a powerful instrument for change. 'The Department of Health's initiatives on smoking have had a tremendous impact,' he says. 'And there have been campaigns to inform the public on coronary heart disease and diabetes. But the root cause of these and many other chronic health complaints is obesity. That's what we really need to get at.'

Raj certainly does not underestimate the problems of tackling the national epidemic of obesity. 'In some ways, smoking is an easier target – you either smoke or you don't. But there are so many factors involved in obesity. Changing your lifestyle seems a lot more daunting than just giving up one part of it, but information is the key. No one aims to be overweight.'

Despite his experience, Fat Club has been an eye opener for him. 'I was shocked at how low the members' general level of activity was. They walked slowly; they tried to avoid using the stairs. This only contributes to the problem. I was surprised, too, at how little they knew about food. Most of them secretly hoped their obesity was caused by some medical problem, and were almost disappointed when I told them that wasn't the case. What I'm hoping to achieve through Fat Club is for the members and the general public to be better informed on the consequences of obesity and on how they can help themselves; to enable them to make positive life choices.'

19

DR SARAH SCHENKER

'There's no such thing as bad food.'

Sarah Schenker is a woman with a mission – to help people to understand and enjoy the food they eat. This is not as simple as it may sound, particularly for people who have a history of yo-yo dieting, like many of the Fat Club members. 'People receive a lot of misinformation about food and dieting, often from magazines. They reject some foods altogether as being "bad", restrict themselves to a few others they classify as "good" and end up with an unhealthy, unbalanced eating programme. Women are particularly brainwashed by the media and embark on extreme, often unhealthy, diets that are bound to fail before they even start. We need to dispel dieting myths and women's preconceptions and half knowledge about dieting.'

One of only 5000 state registered dieticians in the UK and a graduate of the University of Surrey, Sarah is currently working for the British Nutrition Foundation. She rejects the notion of dieting altogether. 'What's important is the overall balance of what you eat,' she says. 'The very term "diet" implies something temporary, unnatural and unpleasant. We all know how bad yo-yo dieting is these days. It's something to avoid at all costs. I want to teach the Fat Club members enough about food to devise their own healthy and enjoyable eating plan for life – one that suits their lifestyle and tastes; one they'll be able to follow whatever changes take place in their lives, and one that matches their level of activity to ensure they stay a healthy weight. Once they realise how simple it is to balance calories in against energy out, they have the key to healthy weight loss.'

Sarah practises what she preaches; her enviably slim figure is certainly not the result of dieting. She eats a healthy and varied range of foods. She has been a keen all-round sportswoman since her schooldays and now runs regularly, enjoys horse-riding and has competed in triathlons.

Her wide experience, including working in hospitals, conducting research trials, advising cardiac and cancer patients and devising a high-performance eating plan with Delia Smith for the players at Norwich City FC, has given her the opportunity to observe people's attitudes to food and nutrition. 'All failed dieters have a list of excuses to account for their problems – I've heard them all. I've asked all the Fat Club members about their dieting history, what's worked and what's failed, trying to help them look for patterns and pitfalls that might arise. They're pretty representative of failed dieters in the UK.'

Sarah does not underestimate how difficult it is to change long-term eating habits, but she aims to give the members wide-ranging information to help: from buying food and reading labels to low-fat preparation methods, from judging portion sizes to coping with eating out. There are strategies to help in any situation. 'Once people realise how many small changes they can make and sustain, almost without noticing, they really start to get into it. I hope they'll come to know most of their calorie counts by heart, and how to get the full range of vitamins, minerals and antioxidants by choosing enough fruit and vegetables daily – whether fresh or preserved, tinned or frozen. For some of them, it will be the first time they'll feel in control. With their dieting history, it's a revolution!'

* Sarah's recipes appear in Chapter 13.

GUNNERY SERGEANT HARVEY E. WALDEN IV

'When I met the members, I had to make some pretty swift adjustments.'

When the production crew first looked for an exercise expert to join the team, they expected to recruit a Lycra-clad personal trainer of the type usually seen on breakfast television. 'But no one was quite the type we wanted,' says Denise Seneviratne, 'so we had to spread the net fairly wide.' Finally they heard of an excellent US Marine gunnery sergeant who was based near London. Even though Harvey Walden had no previous TV experience, when the team met him, with his determination and unswerving commitment to his goals and, let's face it, a certain

21

similarity to the army sergeant in the film, *An Officer and a Gentleman*, they realised that they had hit on a gold mine. 'Harvey isn't a gimmick,' says Denise. 'We wanted someone who was immersed in being fit, and who knew how to take control of a team of people.'

Born in Chicago, Illinois, 35-year-old Harvey joined the US Marines in 1985. There was no army background in the family, and Harvey's excuse is that 'the Marine recruitment officer had popcorn on his recruitment stand'. However, that he decided to join the Marines is not surprising. They are the very top of the service professions, and nothing less would have been good enough for Harvey Walden: a man of few words, extreme self-discipline and a physique which would be the envy of Action Man.

His parents' divorce when he was just six helped mould Harvey into the self-sufficient, independent person he is 'because', he says, 'I had to be'. He self-deprecatingly refers to himself as a 'Neat Freak'. Family now is a wife in the US civil service, a daughter of twelve and a son of eight, all of whom accompanied him to England when he was posted here in March 1998.

When a colonel from the US embassy told him that LWT were looking for a trainer to appear on a 'boot-camp style' TV show, the idea of a weight-loss programme in a controlled environment appealed to Harvey. 'The extent of the weight loss was not mentioned at the time,' he says wryly, 'though one communication said overweight, not *over*weight. When I first met the members, I was very shocked. How could these people have allowed their bodies to get this way at this point in their lives?'

Harvey had to make some on-the-spot changes to his plans: 'I had a fitness regime in mind starting off with a timed half-mile run and two minutes of sit-ups, but when I met the members, I realised there was no way these people could even attempt to accomplish that. I had to make some pretty swift adjustments. I had to show them that they were able to do exercises that they had never done before, and to give them something to strive for and to improve on every month. The initial assessment results were very shocking. These people were really out of shape, but their initial motivation did not surprise me because new things for positive reasons always involve drive and motivation.'

Super fit himself (he runs every day at 4.30 a.m.), Harvey was ideally qualified to demonstrate that exercise and self-discipline are a critical part of a successful life change and weight-loss plan. None of the Fat Club members would aspire to reach such heady heights of fitness, but Harvey's uncompromising approach would at least steer them in the right direction. His praise would be hard to earn. 'Failure is not an issue in my profession,' he says. 'It's mission accomplished.'

PROFESSOR ALEX GARDNER

'There is an emotional charge with our relation-ship to food.'

Successful and lasting weight loss is about finding the right mind-set, and the Fat Club badly needed an expert to help the members work through the psychological aspects of the challenge. The choice, however, seemed to be a selection of (often American) 'shrinks', steeped in psychobabble and obscure theories. The appeal of psychologist and psychotherapist Alex Gardner was in his straight-talking, refreshingly honest Scottish charm. Highly qualified and, most importantly, experienced in working with people with weight problems, 68-year-old Alex was the perfect solution. With his gentle, sympathetic approach (he is affection-ately called 'The Wizard' by Harvey Walden), Alex could help the members discover for themselves the way out of the cycle of their weight problem.

Alex Gardner did not find his vocation until relatively late in his career. A chemistry degree followed various jobs, including five years in an RAF air crew, and he finally went to Glasgow University at the age of 30 with three kids to support. A period teaching followed until he decided to do a second degree in psychology. Alex's speciality was child guidance and he was head-hunted to teach methods of educational enquiry at Queen's College in Glasgow. From there he became head of nutrition and dietetics, teaching psychology and communication for 20 years. He has since taught psychology at Strathclyde University and now works as a broadcaster and research consultant for multinational companies, looking into people's perceptions of medical conditions, including herpes and epilepsy, for drug-marketing strategies.

For Alex the secret of working successfully with people lies in the quality of communication. 'I look at things and want to know. I totally believe in finding ways to measure the subjective experience of the individual. There is no point in making assumptions about their lives. You need to ask.'

One particularly relevant period of his extensive career was spent working for the Health Education Authority researching people's perceptions of health warnings, such as those found on cigarette packets. 'The basic model is called PRUBIC, and relates just as well to overweight people. You *P*erceive a warning, *R*ead it and then *U*nderstand it, but fat people think they understand their reality when in fact they don't or they would change their lives. Crucially they must *B*elieve the message, *I*nternalise it (or make it mean something to them), then make the *C*hange in their lives. Only once it is internalised can change happen.'

Alex's role at Fat Club would be to 'measure the way the Fat Club members see the world. I can simplify complicated stuff, and help the members work through the psychological obstacles of weight loss. The difficulty is that food has a significance religiously and socially in our lives. It's a way of saying "thank you" or "I love you". People come to your house and you offer them tea and cake as a welcome. We take food when we visit. Food is so bound up with our schemata. It makes us feel good and have what us Scots call a good "conceit" of ourselves.

'There is an emotional charge with our relationship to food,' he continues. 'Food has a texture, a sensuality, a cultural role. It can be a comfort. It is a powerful thing. I want people to reframe their current perceptions of food, and I see Fat Club as a chance to change people's way of thinking. I'll be:

- asking the members to take their own experiences and reframe them. People say "I can't diet", but the important message is that you have to increase exercise above the amount of food you eat.
- teaching the members that they need to radically change

their behaviour – that they need to find techniques to help them face the challenge ahead – aware all the time that life is not black and white.'

Many Fat Club members do have fundamental 'emotional baggage' or psychological reasons behind their relationship with food and exercise which overlap into other areas of their lives. Alex's is an onerous responsibility.

The Fat Club weekends

'At the end of the day, the main object is not losing weight. The aim is to change their lifestyle. Weight loss is a by-product.' – Alex Gardner

The ethos behind Fat Club weekends was to create a controlled environment in which severely overweight people could face their weight problem and lay strong foundations to change it and to empower them with the tools to carry out all they have learnt in the weeks between each club. The selected group of ten members would meet at a special location once a month, where they would be weighed, assessed for their fitness and taken through workshops on the implications of being overweight and how they could change their lives for the better.

By their very nature, these weekends would be intense and at times emotional. The group would be exposing themselves and their feelings in ways that could be painful and make them feel vulnerable. The environment had to be right; it needed to be comfortable but controlled, well equipped and secluded, without any external pressures, interruptions or temptations. To encourage the members to see themselves as a team, an environment of mutual support had to be created. Location, too, was a considera-tion, as the group came from as far afield as Skegness and Cardiff.

The production team chose Gorse Hill near Woking, part of the Initial Convention Centre Group, for its proximity to London and the M25. The facilities were ideal: swimming pool and gym, extensive grounds for fitness assessments, seminar rooms for workshops and private consultations, and a chef who could create calorie-controlled meals planned by dietician Sarah Schenker. The advantage of Gorse Hill was that it allowed members to be accommodated in one separate building, the Lodge, where an almost boarding-school atmosphere could be created: the production crew could control evening curfews, but an element of privacy would allow the group to unwind and share experiences away from the experts' watchful eyes.

As each member was recruited to the programme, they were issued with a Fat Club pack, which included bathrobes for the weigh-in, tracksuits, logoed T-shirts and hooded sweat tops, and an uncompromising list of rules.

FAT CLUB RULES

1. There will be no unsupervised activities.
2. No one may leave the premises without permission.
3. Members must participate in all activities over the weekend – there are no exceptions.
4. The Fat Club kit must be worn at all times during the day, but Members may wear their own clothes to the evening meal. In warm weather, shorts are permitted.
5. All Members must hand over their mobile phones on arrival. They will be given the option of one supervised phone call on Saturday evening.
6. There should be no extra food, drink or items that are unrelated to the purpose of the Fat Club, brought to the weekend.
7. The Fat Club curfew is 10 p.m. Members must not leave their rooms after this time.
8. If the panel decide at any time over the next six months that one of the Members is lying about what they are doing, or not taking the Fat Club ethos seriously, they have the right to issue the Member a warning. A second warning means the Member will be expelled from the Fat Club.

The rules were not greeted very enthusiastically. 'After the first

Fat Club it was clear the members had plans to treat it like a party,' says Denise Seneviratne. 'To discourage them from regarding the weekends as a break, the rules had to be strictly enforced. They all made excuses for having their mobile phones with them.' This was absolutely wrong for the controlled environment vital to the success of Fat Club.

THE FAT CLUB WEEKEND SCHEDULE

The weekends were to follow broadly the same pattern, but the members were kept in the dark about what each weekend held for them. They were expected to arrive at Fat Club on the Friday evening preceding a weekend, when their bags would be searched for food, mobile phones and other temptations.

Saturday

7 a.m. workout and fitness assessment with Harvey
Weigh-in and plinth shot to show changes in members' figures
Breakfast, like all meals, was to be determined by Sarah Schenker
Mid-morning workshop
Lunch, again with menus determined by Sarah
Afternoon workshop
Individual sessions with the experts to give members the chance to discuss any medical, psychological, exercise or dietary issues
Early evening workshop
Dinner, down time and 10 p.m. curfew

Sunday

7 a.m. workout or swim with Harvey
Breakfast
Morning workshop on diet, exercise or psychological issues
Lunch
Afternoon workshop
Individual sessions with the experts
Farewell meeting

WORKSHOPS

Fat Club One: May

Saturday: | First weigh-in and plinth shot
Fitness assessment
One-to-one sessions with Alex, Sarah and Raj
Gym workout (Harvey)
Laughter workshop (The power of humour – Alex)
Sunday: | Swimming (Harvey)
One-to-one sessions with Alex, Sarah and Raj

Fat Club Two: June

Saturday: | Exploring food myths (Sarah)
Circuit relay race (Harvey)
Body image workshop with distorted mirrors (Alex)
Sunday: | Swimming
Weighted jackets (Raj)
Question and answer line-up (one-to-one with Harvey)
Group gym session (Harvey)

Fat Club Three: July

Saturday: | Dance aerobics with Pineapple Dance Studio instructor
Cookery challenge (Sarah)
Relay race (Harvey)
Sunday: | Swimming relay race
Group psychotherapy session (Alex)
Penalty shoot-out (Harvey)

Fat Club Four: August

Saturday: | Drill session (Harvey)
Body fat session with artificial fat (Raj)
Salsa dancing
BBQ with dancing

Sunday: | Swimming
Temptations workshop (Alex)
'Slam man' session (Harvey)
Relay race (Harvey)

Fat Club Five: September

Saturday: | Responsibility workshop (Alex)
Iron member competition (Harvey)
Food-tasting challenge (Sarah)
In bed with Raj (exploring feelings about relationships and sexuality)
Sunday: | Tug of war (Harvey)
See yourself slim (digitally altered before and after pictures – Alex)
Trampolining

Fat Club Six: September

Saturday: | Workshop exploring the nature of hunger (Sarah and Alex) – following cancelled breakfast
Yoga with Penny Roberts
Food mountain (Sarah)
Assault course (Harvey)
Discussion about family history and being overweight (Raj)
Camp fire party and awards ceremony
Sunday: | Triathlon (Harvey)
Fat Club quiz (all experts)
Posture session with Anita Young, ballet instructor
Responsibility session and farewell meeting

HOMEWORK

Critical to the success of Fat Club was that all members could maintain what they had learnt in the weeks between each meeting. From the start they were asked to catalogue everything they

29

ate during a normal four days in the week prior to the start of Fat Club. Each member was given a personal daily calorie intake guide at the first weekend, determined by Sarah Schenker, and they were asked to keep an honest diary of their new food habits and exercise regimes. They were asked not to weigh themselves on their home scales between Fat Clubs – all scales vary – and they were also subjected to drop-of-the-hat visits from the production team to monitor their progress and to give an insight into their real lives.

THE FAT CLUB ETHOS

The route to successful weight loss could not be simpler:

Mindset: To lose weight successfully you need to commit to making long-lasting changes in your lifestyle.

Diet: You only need to balance the number of calories you eat with the amount of energy you burn, so no food is forbidden.

Exercise: Make simple changes to increase your daily activity in everything you do. You can get plenty of exercise without ever having to step into a gym.

Each Fat Club member had a different reason for coming to the Club, just as each had a different reason for their weight gain. What they had in common, however, was a pressing urge to lose weight, and they gained support from each other's struggles and experiences. Some succeeded, some failed, but each story is unique.

Chapter 2

Simon's Story

'My ambition? To be able to wear a pair of jeans and not look like Captain Pugwash.'

Simon Payne
Age: 41
Lives: Cardiff, South Wales
Occupation: House-husband and part-time college caretaker
Height: 5ft 10in
Weight at first weigh-in: 28st – morbidly obese
Waist at first weigh-in: Tape measure would not reach round

A warm-hearted Welshman, with a twinkle in his eye and an engaging, flirtatious manner, Simon is the big man of Fat Club. He is not sure how long he has weighed this much. 'I can't use the scales at home,' he explains. 'They don't go high enough, so I have to go to the Post Office and stand on the parcel scales.' Measuring his waist has not been easy either. 'My waist is too wide for a tape measure.'

Unlike some of the members who had a podgy childhood, Simon cannot remember being fat as a child. 'I was in the school football teams in my home town of Cardiff, and played rugby at high school until I was 19. I had plenty of exercise, and in my early 20s, I was 12 or 13st. When I left school, I did a job for a short time as a plasterer's mate and then, after a spell on the dole, started working for a removals company, lugging around furniture; that was when the weight really fell off.'

While doing removals during the day, Simon managed a local rock band in the evening. He became busier and soon set up a public address system business for other local bands. His interest in music led to a job with a local record company and radio station. He freely admits: 'There was a lot of booze and a lot of drugs, and, to be honest, the early 1980s were a bit of a blur! It was one long party. I moved in with my first girlfriend when I was 25 and that's when the weight started to pile on. Then, in 1986, I went on the road with David Bowie for a European tour, working on the electrics at each venue. We were working very hard, but there was always a catering van to keep us well fed. Then we'd stop at truck stops and eat rubbish. I'd come home with pots of money and go down the pub and drink it all. There was too much booze, and rock and roll "substances"!'

'My wife knows it's down to me to do something about it.'

This is not the first time Simon has made an effort to do something about his weight, and he has tried a whole range of slimming pills, including Xenical, 'but I just gave them up'. 'The idea is cockeyed,' he adds. 'You are not supposed to eat fat whilst taking them. If you don't eat fat, you'd lose weight anyway!' This is not his first encounter with TV fame either – he took part in a quick-fix diet regime on *Go For It* with Gloria Hunniford – but for any treatment or regime to work you have to show willing, and, he says, 'I was just brushing off my weight problem.'

By Easter 2001 Simon was an enormous 29st. 'I've always been aware that I was putting on too much weight, and Clare, my wife [whom he married in 1991 and is a neat size 12] always nagged me about it, and we'd end up rowing. Now she's given up. She knows it's down to me to do something.'

He admits that living life normally is a struggle. 'Everything is so much effort. Buying clothes is a nightmare. I can buy XXX-large from catalogues like Cotton Traders, but before discovering them it was T-shirts and joggers. Shirts, ties and trousers are even harder to find and uncomfortable to wear.' In fact,

Simon has an interesting point to make about extra-large sizings: 'I think that being able to buy bigger clothes is a bad thing. Years ago you couldn't buy anything over a 38in waist. If you couldn't get clothes, you couldn't afford to be fat! My ambition now? To be able to wear a pair of jeans and not look like Captain Pugwash.'

'I get depressed and then eat chocolate to make myself feel better.'

Simon's character is obsessive. Food has taken the place of the booze, fags and drugs of the past. He eats to assuage his mood. 'I get habits and then I get addicted. I get depressed and then eat chocolate to make myself feel better – give myself a fix. I'm a snacker and I eat at least six times a day. Unbeknown to my wife, I go out for a cooked breakfast at a café about four times a week, and snack in the afternoon between meals. I also drink pints and pints of milk – but at least I gave up on full-cream milk ages ago. Now it's just skimmed.'

His weight demonstrates graphically the medical conditions which obesity can bring. 'I don't know which are related to my weight, but I discovered by accident some time ago that I have an irregular heartbeat. I gave blood for a long time too, but when they started testing for Aids, it was discovered that I had hepatitis C which I must have picked up on tour abroad. The brown envelope came through the letter box with the news and it gave me a hell of a fright. I'm now tested regularly to check it is in a stable condition. My knees are shot, which is probably a result of playing rugby, but the extra weight doesn't help. I have asthma, too, and have had it all my life.' Medical issues have brought him to the stage where his doctor has suggested stomach stapling as a viable option.

Other people's perceptions are an issue too – a man of Simon's size gets stared at and in some cases ridiculed. We have all seen a very large person walking down the street, and thought 'How could they get like that?', even if we do not say it out loud. 'Children can be particularly cruel,' he says, 'and people will call me a "fat bastard" or take the mickey in conversation – and I know they think that if you are fat, you are lazy. They talk down to you. I just shut myself off from it. I even remember one child in the queue of a fish and chip shop saying to his mother, "Look at that fat man." Everyone in the queue started to squirm and feel uncomfortable. But curiously that kind of thing doesn't stop me eating.'

'God knows having kids makes you think about your mortality.'

Simon admits that in the last few years exercise just has not figured in his life – he clearly demonstrates the fact that if you do not exercise you get bigger, and the bigger you get the harder it is to exercise. 'If I do go to the pool with the children, I rush from changing room into the pool and back to the changing room, because I don't want people looking at me.'

By the time he saw the advertisement for Fat Club in the local paper in Cardiff, he had determined to do something about his weight, and had even managed to shift 14lbs. His children, Joe and Adam, if anything, have been the catalyst. 'The boys are five and three, and I find it hard to play with them – God knows, having kids makes you think about your mortality – I feel lethargic and am finding it hard to get motivated. I'm also very aware that if I don't lose weight, I won't live to see them grow up. I thought millions of people watching me on TV might help.'

Once he answered the press advertisement for the programme, he had to endure a four-week wait to hear if he had made the grade. 'I sat by the phone and was gutted each day that passed and I hadn't heard.' But when the confirmation call came through, he knew it was 'the right thing for me'.

FAT CLUB ONE

'I was finally with people who had experienced what I had experienced. No one was judging anyone else.'

Like all the members who were selected for Fat Club, Simon had an initial full medical examination with Dr Raj. Many men of

Simon's weight would by his age be beginning to show the signs of the damage caused by obesity – high blood pressure, high cholesterol, even early warnings of diabetes – but Simon's results were encouraging. 'I think [Raj] was amazed,' he says, 'that my blood pressure is normal and my basic health is good.' But Raj was concerned: 'Simon is a walking time bomb, a heart attack waiting to happen. The heaviest of the whole group, he has a Body Mass Index of 57 and needs to lose half his body weight to be within acceptable and healthy limits.'

Simon passes Alex's psychometric testing with flying colours – though possibly misunderstands Alex's role as a key motivator in changing the way the group control their lives, regarding him as a shrink. 'I enjoyed talking to Alex, because I enjoy talking!' he laughs, 'but I don't think I've got any emotional baggage and I don't think he revealed anything.'

Simon is an important member of Fat Club – his irrepressible good humour helps to break the ice with this disparate group of people thrown together for the first time in these strange circumstances. As they meet for their welcome chat with the experts, Simon is the one who laughs first when Raj tells them they are there because they are all fat. Of the group he is the most direct and open, readily agreeing with all the pearls of wisdom he is given but, as time will tell, one wonders if his words about wanting to see his children grow up come from conviction or if it is a question of saying what he thinks the experts want to hear.

What brings him up short, however, is the first weigh-in. 'Suddenly my weight was there for all to see. There was no denying the fact that I was 28st and to illustrate it graphically, I had to be weighed on a different set of scales from everyone else. I was putting myself up for ridicule and I finally admitted I was going to do something about it. But I realised I was amongst people who were supportive, and most impressive was Tony Curley showing his psoriasis – that took some courage.'

For one so unused to exercise, his first encounter with Harvey comes as a shock too. 'I thought he looked like an overgrown boy scout,' he says, recovering from the assessment session early Saturday morning. 'I don't think any of us enjoyed the exercise routine. In fact the exercise makes my knees hurt more than ever.

I was surprised that we were made to jog. The ground wasn't firm and I got a rash all over my arms from the bushes we had to run close to.' But his response to Harvey, despite drill-sergeant shouts of 'Are you motivated, Simon?' is positive. 'I like him. He's the enforcer, and the persona he initially gives out is tough and merciless, but I realise he has a soft spot for me. He's inspired me. You can ask him anything.'

At the first workshop, Simon baldly admits this is the last chance in his life to lose weight, and the expert who holds the key to Simon's success is Sarah Schenker. She is the one who has to find the catalyst to make Simon readdress his whole relationship with food. After a one-to-one chat with her, he is riveted by her message: 'The food discussions are interesting. Fat Club is not a diet, it's a lifestyle. I've realised that chocolate and sweet or unhealthy things are like a drug. Her message is that it's all about cutting out fat. She says we can eat what we want, but we need to balance it out.' To control his hunger pangs, she recommends Simon eats cereal if he is hungry and he leaps on the information that 'there is less sugar in Ricicles than in Special K'.

Sarah also goes through the BMI to explain it to him and points out what it means for him to be at 57 and morbidly obese (ironically a word Simon has trouble getting his tongue around). 'It was new to me, although I suppose my doctor has explained it before, but it hadn't hit home.'

With his jocular manner, Simon is the lovable clown of this motley group, and is soon friends with everyone. 'There has been a lot of laughing, and I think the production team has been taken aback by the smiling and laughter in the group. In fact I'm sure they don't think we are taking it all seriously enough. It has more to do with the fact that we are having a great laugh.' In the boarding-school atmosphere of the Lodge, there is the inevitable fun and games before bedtime curfew. 'We tried to see if we could all fit on one bed (and break it – which we didn't!), and we even all got into the wardrobe together.'

Simon leaves Fat Club fascinated and claims he is armed for the next few weeks. But though he is hearing new and exciting facts about food, the experts are not convinced that he is absorbing the fundamental message that he has to cut down and control his diet. What they are interpreting as lack of commitment is simply relief at being with people who understand what it is like to be fat.

FAT CLUB TWO

Date: June
Weight at weigh-in: 27st (378lbs)
Weight loss since last weigh-in: 14lbs
Total loss: 14lbs
Waist: 59in

'I won't stop until I achieve what I want to achieve.'

But perhaps it is too early to judge Simon and accuse him of not absorbing the messages of Fat Club. Since that first trial by fire, already his life is beginning to change: 'Since joining Fat Club,' he says in the weeks before the next weekend, 'I have stood up proud, and been to the swimming pool with my kids and no one has batted an eyelid. Without Fat Club, I wouldn't have gone because I would have been afraid of what people would say. My outlook and my confidence have changed.'

He attributes this volte-face to the power of the positive messages of the first weekend. 'We all had such a good time meeting people who had been through the same experiences. I think it had a lot to do with finally acknowledging I was doing something about the weight too. Alex gave us all small fluffy pink toy pigs last time, and asked us to name them. They were to help us remember our goal and to remind us not to feel downhearted but to stand tall. I called mine Alex Harvey – for obvious reasons, and also after the fantastic Scottish musician who I admire.'

Already the bonding in the group is strong, and encouraging phone calls are exchanged. Simon seems at pains to prove the experts wrong. 'I do have will-power. I've stopped smoking and drinking like I used to, and if I have a fag at the pub, the next day I don't need another. I can take it or leave it.'

Working for the council part-time, Simon has the privilege of a subsidised membership card for local leisure facilities in Cardiff. It allows him to use the pool as often as he likes, for just £14 per month. But never backward in coming forward, he persuades the powers that be to allow him to use all the facilities, including the multi-gym, until Christmas at no extra charge. 'They heard about Fat Club and the efforts I was making, and I think they will let me go on longer,' he says.

So that is the exercise sorted. As far as food is concerned, Simon is in the ideal position as house-husband to be in control of what goes into the family shopping basket. He admits to barely giving the fish and yoghurt counters a second glance in the past. In would go pasties and pork pies, chocolate desserts and cakes. But Sarah's food messages have hit the mark. 'I'm getting better at shopping and I've even been more careful with what the children eat. I think in the past I was guilty of giving them what my wife calls "rubbish" too often – chicken nuggets, waffles, that sort of thing. Now I am buying more fish, we're all eating low-fat yoghurts and I haven't bought a pork pie, pasty or steak and kidney pudding since the last Club. The reduced-fat foods available are getting better and better and the prices are more reasonable than they were too. A packet of reduced-fat Custard Creams used to be 10p more expensive than the normal ones. I've taken up sushi too in a big way – Chris from the production team put me on to that – it's lovely. Friends have been really supportive and encouraging, asking me how much weight I've lost. I'm pleased with myself.'

The group meet up at Shepperton Studios for publicity pictures, and fall on each other, thrilled to be together again. They roar with laughter, tease each other and Simon is the recipient of cuddles all round. They share the changes they have begun to notice already and Simon is delighted to report that, when he is in the car, he does not have to put the seat back so far. He drives back to Gorse Hill keen to see what else he can learn.

The facts show that he has lost a stone, and at last the tape measure will go around his waist, but the reality of Simon's weight comes home to him in a dramatic and rather hilarious way. He takes up the story: 'It has been lovely weather this week-end, and we have been swimming in the pool after the intensity of the day. The pool had a certain amount of water taken out for safety reasons because there isn't a lifeguard on patrol. There are ladders that go down into the pool and one of them wasn't very secure. I stood on the top step and crack! I went falling backwards. Everyone roared with laughter, which was embarrassing. Today [Sunday] we went back into the pool after the workout. I jumped in and swam, but when I came to get out I stood on the (unbroken) bottom step. Of course it broke! There was a 2ft gap between the top of the water level and the top of the pool. How was I going to get out? Harvey rolled up a towel for me to grab, and Tony and Stuart pushed from underneath. Donna shouted 'Stop, you'll graze your stomach' and laid out a towel on the side of the pool. By the end, six or seven people are pushing one end and pulling the other to get me out. It has to be in the top ten of the most embarrassing moments of my life, and I wasn't even pissed!'

The group sympathise, but it is not the first time they learn the problems of severe obesity, at Simon's expense. At the session with Raj on Sunday morning, he intends to show them the pressure extra weight can put on the heart. Simon is given a heart monitor and his resting pulse registers 80. He is then loaded with four extra stone in a weighted jacket, and is asked to take as brisk a walk as he can with this extra load. His pulse rate reads 160 beats per minute. Raj then asks Stuart to carry a jacket weighing eight stone, which will not even take him up to Simon's weight. Stuart's resting pulse rate is 75, but by simply wearing the jacket, without moving, his heart-rate monitor registers 126 beats per minute. A short walk up and down some steps and it increases to 160. Breathless, Stuart is stunned. 'I really feel sorry for you, Simon,' he gasps.

Simon sounds nonchalant: 'Now you know how it feels when I have to run.' It seems that the message really has been driven home for him this weekend. He is deeply affected: 'Every fat person should be made to put on that weight jacket and experience it.'

39

FAT CLUB THREE

Date: July
Weight at weigh-in: 25st 11lbs (361lbs)
Weight loss since last weigh-in: 17lbs
Total loss: 31lbs
Waist: 54½in

> *'I want to lose 11lbs so I can get on the same scales as everyone else – that's my target.'*

The group has been in close contact, and Donna, Kelly and the two Tonys have all been over to visit Simon at home in Cardiff. In the excitement of seeing them again, Fat Club 'went out the window'. 'We went to the pub and we weren't going to stand there drinking orange juice! But the next day we exercised all day and ended up with a swim. In fact we even got Tony Curley into the pool. He was nervous about his psoriasis and what people would think, but no one batted an eyelid.'

Simon has found swimming to be his 'ideal' exercise, and now he has overcome his own fear of exposing his body at the pool, he has taken to it with gusto. Despite all his enthusiasm for low-fat shopping, however, food is still an issue. 'I need help with it from Sarah,' he admits. 'I still need to sort out portions, and what I can and cannot eat. My life is very irregular – I'm in and out of the house all day and it's hard to plan. If you can plan, you can work out the calories. All I can do is watch the fat content.' He adds, 'I don't mind if I haven't lost weight at the next weigh-in. I'm more interested in the inches. People look at how you are.' It is an alarming statement, and the experts wonder if he has really got his food intake under control.

As ever he is enthusiastic about the upcoming weekend, refreshed after a holiday in Tenby, but perhaps the honeymoon is over; perhaps the members have become wise and confident enough to challenge the rules of the Club. Whatever the cause, Fat Club three is a tense one.

'The main reason is Harvey's bag search,' says Simon. It is an aspect of the weekends which the group has tolerated thus far, but which suddenly seems petty and intrusive. Simon has also brought a stick of rock for everyone from his holiday, and is annoyed that these are confiscated. By Saturday night he has had enough. 'I've felt bad all day. I didn't enjoy the dance aerobics or anything all day. We thrashed out issues like the bag search that annoyed us with the production team a short time ago, which made me feel a lot happier, but I am tired.'

To add to it all, Simon is selected to take a sleep apnoea test to check the effect obesity has on his breathing during sleep. 'It involves having straps on your waist, monitors on your chest and on your finger, things up your nose, wires everywhere. I couldn't cope with it,' he says the following morning. 'After an hour and a half the equipment was all over the place, and by 4 a.m. I turned it off. I haven't been very happy about my weight loss either – after all I only managed 2lbs a week, which isn't a lot.' It is actually the recommended weekly weight loss, but by this point nothing would have sounded right to Simon.

Sunday morning, however, and despite a bad sleep, things look more positive. 'We have had an excellent relay race in the pool, and done some excellent stuff with Sarah about the calories in different types of food. This has been great for me as I had struggled with the food issue. I hadn't really known enough about calories, and it's great news to hear you can eat a CocoPops bar like a chocolate bar and it's less than 100 calories. That has helped me with choosing snacks to eat.' (See Chapter 12 for more low-calorie snack ideas.)

He is relieved too that he has made the target on the pedometer given to them the previous weekend by Raj. With kids to run after, 10,000 steps was a doddle for Simon. 'The message about lifestyle change has really hit home. Will I reach the 6lb loss target set by Raj and the team for next Fat Club? I want to lose 11lbs so I can get on the same scales as everyone else – that's my target.' Simon leaves the weekend resolved: 'I still feel as motivated and my waist line is now 55in, a drop of over 4in.'

Harvey admits that he had got Simon all wrong. 'I had a very bad impression of him at first. I thought he just wanted to be comical and the clown of the group, but he is never a problem at the assessment and takes it all seriously. He is really dedicated to losing weight, and I have had to tell him to ease back a little after reviewing his exercise diary. He has great motivation.'

FAT CLUB FOUR

Date: August
Weight at weigh-in: 24st 13lbs (349 lbs)
Weight loss since last weigh-in: 12lbs
Total loss: 43lbs
Waist: 54½in

> *'Though I am eating the right food, I'm having problems with the quantities.'*

Harvey was right – again. In Simon's passionate desire to reach this self-imposed target, he has overdone the exercise. After a rather over-enthusiastic weekend at home with a swim, game of badminton, followed by a circuits session in the multi-gym with weights and bench presses, he sits down and cannot move for about 48 hours. 'I feel as though I have been beaten up,' he says.

He arrives at Fat Club – and success! The Saturday morning weigh-in shows he can finally be weighed on the same scales as the rest of the members, and has shifted the target 11lbs, but the motivation had been so strong and the strain so great that during the 7 a.m. training routine he experiences chest pains and feels faint.

The experts are alarmed. Raj gives him a thorough examination and discovers that Simon has not been using his Beclar Forte preventor inhaler for his asthma, under the misapprehension that, because it contains a steroid, it would make him gain weight. 'Raj has put me right and says it is very important I continue with it.'

He is depressed, however, that he has made no headway in losing inches around the waist. Harvey has an explanation. 'Unfortunately, I don't think Simon has been really honest with his food which will contribute to lack of loss on his waist – and I mean things like beer and other foods that will cause him to not lose inches on his waist. This is one of the biggest problems with men and why some have beer guts. You can eliminate this by simply increasing your cardiovascular exercise, which is the case with me. I love my pints, but I know swimming alone won't keep my gut off. Also if he is not doing cardio workouts that target that particular area, then he has missed out as well. You don't do press-ups every day to improve your running. You don't run every day to improve your freestyle swim.'

Simon admits he is struggling with the food/exercise balance: 'Though I am eating the right food, I'm still having problems with the quantities. I get hungry and rather than grab chocolate, I will have a bowl of cereal. But in one day I might have three of them, as well as meals.' Resisting snacks is going to be the greatest test of Simon's will-power. 'When you come home in the evening, you don't really want to munch an apple,' he admits, a sentiment shared by a million people struggling with their weight, and in private he admits, 'At times I just think "stuff it!" and I get the urge for fish and chips.'

But Raj's fat workshop provides a powerful message for him. Each member is encouraged to touch and feel 5lb blocks of arti-ficial fat, which bear an alarming resemblance to the layers of fat inside our bodies, 50 per cent of which are around our vital organs. The concept disgusts Simon to the extent that during Alex's temptations workshop on Sunday, in which he makes them hold their favourite food, Simon admits: 'I just can't do it. I have this picture in my mind of the lumps of fat Raj had made us hold yesterday.' When Alex then asks them to put some chocolate in their mouths, he cannot do that either. 'I would be sick.'

Afterwards at an experts' meeting, Simon is one member they are all keen to discuss. Alex is genuinely impressed with Simon's achievements: 'He has now lost almost 8 per cent of his body weight since the start of Fat Club. He is, I believe, very conscious now about his health and wants to grow old to see his children grow up.' He has reservations, however, about his ability to stay with the diet and exercise plans, but he has shown great moti-vation in the last three months. He will have most problems with eating management in social situations, but in the workshops he shows a growing sense of control and understanding. This may have been a result of the fat workshop. The concept of "ugly fat" made great impressions on him. If he retains this image, he can use it as a motivator to maintain control.'

Food may be becoming easier to control, but Simon's exercise routine is still a cause for concern. His pains during the morning training session gave Harvey a fright: 'During the week he is always pushing himself to the limit and I am still wondering if he might be over-training himself. Despite his knee and elbow injury, he still gives it his all.' Raj agrees: 'We have finally managed to weigh Simon on the same scales as everyone else and I am pleased with his weight loss, though he was gutted that his waist measurement had not changed and he felt as if he had failed. He is still relying too much on exercise and not enough on diet and he is pushing himself beyond his limits.'

The results this weekend show that despite all his enthusiasm, Simon is still not getting the important balance of food and exercise right.

FAT CLUB FIVE

Date: Early September
Weight at weigh-in: 24st 8lbs (344lbs)
Weight loss since last weigh-in: 5lbs
Waist: 54in
Total loss: 48lbs

> *'This is not a rehearsal. Your health is so important, the clock of life ain't gonna wait for you.'* – Harvey

> *'I can't imagine how my wife can like me as I am.'*

When the offer came at the end of the last weekend to take home and use a video camera to record moments in his day, Simon jumped at it. Though he thinks it is a great support during the down moments, he decides not to take it with him on a night out with friends. He admits he succumbed to several pints of beer and a T-bone steak and chips. 'I didn't feel guilty eating it for a second – in fact I was so looking forward to it and it was lovely, but I know now that I have to balance out meals like that with better and less food the day before and after.'

For Simon Fat Club Four has been a powerful turning point. He interprets his understanding of getting the balance right as a feeling of being in control of what he is eating and doing with his life. 'I'm not going to pretend I won't and don't eat McDonald's because I do, but not every day or even every week. I'm enjoying eating more fruit than I ever did before, and am eating strawberries and nectarines that I would never have even tried. I feel very positive that I will be able to cope when Fat Club is over. If I binge I will sort myself out through the week. I think I always knew what I needed to do to lose weight, I just needed the motivation and a bit of help.' For Sarah this talk of binges and making up for them is dangerous and a troubling weakness. 'He still has a dieter's mentality and that will spell failure.'

But the lessons from overdoing the exercise are hitting home. 'I'm doing about 50 lengths of the pool each day – not the swim, circuits and badminton I was doing in 12 hours before – but I'm trying to get my timing up. I'm four stone lighter than I was five months ago and if someone had told me then I could be, I would have bent over backwards to make it happen. Now I want to be 22st by the time we finish.'

The physical changes for Simon have been very positive, but he has some reservations about the psychological ones. 'Looking after my children all day, I am amongst women all the time. When you are fat you can laugh, flirt and make jokes and people don't take it the wrong way. They feel safe (and so do their husbands). If I said the same things and I was 15st, I'd be taken the wrong way, and I don't really want to change my personality. And I don't want the women who I spend so much time with to feel inhibited when they are chatting in front of me.'

He has noticed women behaving differently towards him already. 'I've been propositioned twice over the last weekend, and it's a new thing for me now, but it used to happen when I was younger. I feel uncomfortable with it – perhaps because the temptations for the male ego are enormous – and I have to learn to take looks and comments as compliments and just feel better for them.' He is an extrovert, prone to saying outrageous things and usually raising a laugh when he does. It is curious that he feels safe being flirtatious at the size he is or was.

It is all part of what Alex has been trying to teach the members about their perceptions of themselves. 'I like myself on the inside,' says Simon, 'but not on the outside. I can't imagine how my wife for example can like me as I am. But I suppose after 15 years there must be something she likes!'

The team of experts decided to focus this penultimate weekend on 'handing over the locus of responsibility' to the group. 'It is all very well when there is someone taking over the control for you,' says Alex to the group, 'but what happens when that support is gone? We need to bring you back up and off on your own.'

This message is never more important than in the case of Simon, who reveals he is still struggling with the food issue. A couple of setbacks (the deaths of a close friend and a GP in his local practice) and, as Sarah feared, Simon finds himself gorging 12 Galaxy ice-cream bars in 24 hours. 'I was greedy and I had time on my hands,' he admits at the opening session of the weekend. Boredom can often be a factor in overeating, especially for women, and Simon is unusual in his role as a house-husband. For a man who finds will-power difficult, however, it is potentially disastrous.

'I put the wrappers in the bin at first, then thought to myself "that is two or three days' exercise gone in a few minutes". But once I'd done it, I'd done it and there was no point in hiding it, so I took the wrappers out of the bin.' Alex is very positive about Simon's actions: 'I think that is a very powerful thing that you have done.' But Simon is humble. 'I think fat people do make excuses. I was annoyed with myself. The ice-cream was a fix.' To Raj's reminder that 90 per cent of weight losers fail, Simon is adamant: 'I really feel now like I did in my early 20s. I'm just not going to go back to struggling to climb stairs, get out of a chair or the bath.'

Alex has taken a lot of trouble preparing his 'see yourself slim' workshop. Using computer graphics (PowerPoint), he has taken images of the members in their bathing costumes, as they were at the first Fat Club, and manipulated them to produce slimmed-down versions. The result is striking. First he projects the 'before' images on to a screen, and gives everyone a copy of the picture to hold. There are audible gasps, but he does not allow anyone to evade what is coming. In his customary gentle but persistent way, he asks the question the members do not want to ask themselves. 'What are your feelings when you look at these images? This might be painful, hurtful, but it needs doing. Listen to one another. Share your feelings.'

Simon gazes wonderingly at his image. 'That's how I still see myself,' he says resignedly. But Alex challenges him: 'Is this picture saying to you that you have to stop kidding yourself?' 'Yes,' Simon reckons. 'I can't forget the past because there are lessons there. I want to keep the old photo so I can put it on the landing at home where other people can see it too.'

Alex's message to Simon is a positive one: if he carries on losing weight at this rate, he will have lost nearly half his body weight by next summer, June 2002. At the farewell meeting, Harvey is less forgiving. In words clearly directed at Simon, he says: 'If you think you can feed your face for three days, then take violent exercise, you have learnt nothing. This is not a rehearsal. Your health is so important, the clock of life ain't gonna wait for you.' Sarah feels as strongly: 'Don't put obstacles and excuses in the way of a better eating programme. Life will always throw things at you. You have to learn to cope.'

In the privacy of the experts' meeting the mood is merciless. Harvey's belief is that Simon lacks self-discipline: 'He comes here and gives 100 per cent, but goes home back to his old ways. He's fat and he always will be.' Raj agrees: 'I do worry that it is only Fat Club that is keeping Simon going.'

Back home, and after a long summer with the children, college term has started again and Simon is busy working 28 hours a week as caretaker at the local Community Education Centre. 'I'm on my feet a lot,' he says, but he has managed to fit in an eight-mile charity walk for the British Heart Foundation. 'I would never have done it in the past,' he admits. 'I wouldn't even have given it a second thought, but I saw it advertised and thought it could do me good – and with my heart murmur, it's a charity which interests me anyway.'

He has learnt from his mistake before the last Fat Club of weighing himself on the post office scales, which showed a weight gain and upset him terribly until he found out the scales were inaccurate. He laughs about it ruefully now, joking that perhaps the post office scales overestimate weight so they have an excuse to charge more for parcels. He has upped his swimming quota to 64 lengths – a mile – and admits that he has been finding the first 50 easier and the extra 14 knackering.

Life is looking better for him after a low following the last weekend. Sarah, disappointed with most of the members for their poor weight loss, strongly believed many had overeaten, then starved themselves in the days leading up to the weigh-in, and she challenged Simon directly. 'I was very pissed off by criticism from Sarah of my eating. She told me she was very disappointed in me and accused me of having starved myself.' But their argument was patched up in a phone call from Sarah. 'She'd been given the wrong information from somewhere. I could never starve myself – if I could I wouldn't be so fat!'

Now Simon is approaching the weekend feeling positive and 'bubbly'. 'I haven't binged at all – though I did have a cooked breakfast at a café one day – and I feel confident about that. I'm trying to set myself up to cope when there is no Fat Club and I am well chuffed that eating less and exercising over the last few weeks hasn't been difficult. I'm getting over hunger pangs with fruit or a bowl of cereal and, though I have missed the cup of tea and the packet of Custard Creams I used to enjoy, I have replaced it with one Go Ahead bar from McVitie's. I bought two boxes of them about two weeks ago and I have at least six left.'

'If someone had said to me a few months ago that I could be five stone lighter by Christmas, I would have bitten their hand off. The way I'm living now is sustainable. I don't want to binge and the thought of it makes me feel quite sick. I keep thinking about that fat workshop with Raj.'

FAT CLUB SIX

Date: September
Weight at weigh-in: 23st 9lbs (331lbs)
Weight loss since last weigh-in: 13lbs
Waist: 50in
Total loss: 61lbs

> *'These foods aren't unhealthy. An excess of these foods is unhealthy.' – Sarah Schenker*

Simon's colossal weight loss this month – 13lbs – means he beats Tony Curley's overall loss by one pound and bumps up the group's monthly weight loss to 58lbs. It is a remarkable achievement and gives him a well-deserved confidence boost. With great glee he says he has taken up tap dancing at the community college where he works. After the Saturday morning yoga session at the Fat Club gym, he is keen to recommend the college should offer that too. Teacher Penny Roberts takes the group through the basic yoga moves, and explains how yoga is ideal for toning up muscle, but the subliminal message affects Simon most strongly. She asks them to imagine themselves looking in a mirror, and picking up a pen and rubbing out their reflection, redrawing it as they would like to be. It is an image that appeals to Simon.

The posture workshop with the ballet instructor is less successful for him as the exercises are difficult for a man of his size. He talks it over later at lunch, and as he leans over the table, it becomes obvious that the message of good posture has had little impact. 'I took on board the basics of what she said,' he concedes, 'especially how important one's feet are, but frankly when you are my weight it is more comfortable to slouch.' A glance around the table shows that all the members are bent over as they eat.

Surprisingly, Simon is least affected by the production team's contrived decision to delay Saturday breakfast to prove the point of the power of hunger. 'I don't generally eat breakfast until mid-morning anyway,' he explains, 'so it's not a problem.' But the food mountain workshop after lunch contains strong messages for Simon to take on board for the future. The members are faced with a huge pile of food on the table in front of them – pizza, biscuits, beers, burgers – and Sarah Schenker explains that this represents 50,000 calories, just one quarter of the extra 200,000 calories Simon and Tony Curley have cut from their diet to achieve their weight loss.

Simon is astounded. 'It's so embarrassing,' he says. 'To think you could eat normally plus four times this. I eat well now, but I can't believe I ate this extra too.' 'Food is there to be enjoyed,' Sarah stresses. 'But if you don't get the balance right, that's when the weight goes on again. Keep your eye on the ball. You know now that you don't have to feel guilty if you eat a bag of crisps or a piece of strawberry cheesecake, but don't do it all week every week. These foods aren't unhealthy. An excess of these foods is unhealthy.'

From the start Simon admitted motivation was a problem for him, and among the raft of lessons he has learnt is that he can achieve results if he takes that extra step. This is shown strongly during the triathlon, which involves a short bike ride. Simon has not sat on a bike since a clairvoyant told him years ago that if he carried on riding anything with two wheels, he would end up in a wheelchair. He refuses to get on. Harvey calls him over, and Simon anticipates a telling-off. He is surprised. 'If you believe that kind of nonsense, you have more problems than being over-weight,' says Harvey angrily. 'Do you realise that you are very inspirational? You have to get on that bike.' He offers to run alongside if it would help, but Simon has already realised that he has to lay this ridiculous ghost to rest and off he cycles.

Simon's overall weight loss over the six-month period has been a staggering 4st 4lbs. When once a tape measure would not even go around his waist, he can now fit into size 48 trousers. He is excited that all his clothes now fit him, and some are so large it is funny. If he carries on like this he will need a new wardrobe, and 'a sponsor to pay for it all'.

He modestly admits: 'The bigger you are the easier it is to lose weight,' but there can be no denying that, for a man whose life was in danger, the experience of Fat Club has been immensely important. 'I'm so delighted that I was able to become a member.

We have been given information on food and health issues that will be in my mind for the rest of my life, and I can walk past the supermarket aisles loaded with chocolate without a second thought. Harvey's exercises have been great, too, though most of that stuff I wouldn't do. You have to do exercise you are happy with – for me that is swimming or riding an exercise bike – but the important thing is, I am exercising.'

For years he ignored his weight gain, and chose not to listen to warnings from health experts. Now he has strong words of counsel for others like him: 'You have to be honest with yourself – otherwise you are only lying that you are overweight. You can make excuses until you are in your grave. There are plenty of people who are there to help. I have surprised myself, but when you are feeling down and tired, and then you push yourself that little bit more, you think "It only took half an hour. I'm glad I've done that" and you feel good inside.'

His targets are modest. 'My ideal weight would be 18st and just under 40 on the BMI scale. Another 4st and I'd be under the 30; 15st would be perfect. I'm going to do it because I still aim to be able to walk down the high street and buy myself a pair of Levis, pay the money and walk out. That is what I really want to do.'

Sarah: 'Simon does not have a healthy relationship with food and it will always be a battle for him, but hopefully he has learnt some lessons.'

Harvey: 'Simon has all the heart and drive in the world to move mountains and overtake skyscrapers. He has a threshold for pain that most POWs and hostages would kill for. During my sessions he has overcome so many obstacles and hurdles it is unbeliev-able. He has jumped rope for the first time in his life. He has ridden a bike after some fortune-telling Nazi giving him a reading that if he ever got on anything with two wheels he would die. Well, he can tell her to go pound sand and shove it where the sun don't shine, because I got him on the bike and he is still very much alive. However, this strong individual lacks the essentials he needs to be able to lose all the extra weight and live a healthy

Chapter 3

Donna's Story

'I wanted some sort of control in my life and by binge eating then making myself sick, that was the way to do it.'

Donna Norris
Age: 40
Lives: Somerset
Occupation: Calf rearer
Height: 5ft 6in
Weight at first weigh-in: 15st 2lbs – obese
Waist at first weigh-in: 40in

Donna is a gorgeous-looking woman with a mane of long, thick, dark wavy hair, an impish face and a wicked sense of humour. She is popular, funny and outspoken, attributes which are all the more remarkable in the light of her unhappy childhood and early adult life.

'Food has always been a problem. In my early teens I was 7st 4lbs. My weight yo-yoed like crazy, and from 1984 until 1995, I was bulimic. I wanted some sort of control in my life and by binge eating then making myself sick, that was the way to do it. I always felt guilty and by being sick, I was somehow purging the guilt.'

Donna's guilt is very deep-seated. Her mother left the family home to live with another man when Donna was four years old. Her father, a dustbin man, was left to cope with five children and a cousin who came to live with them, and he brought them up the best way he could. For the next ten years Donna's mother would intermittently come home to escape the domestic violence in her new life, and 'Then,' says Donna, 'just when we would think everything was fine, she'd go again.' The family was poor, and she describes living like 'a street urchin, but with a house. Everything we had – clothes, bedding – was supplied by the Women's Royal Voluntary Service, and school uniform was supplied by a cheque from the Social Security.'

'I was a fighter and the only contact I had with people was with my fist.'

Donna's childhood was a roller-coaster of trouble – she remembers on several occasions being brought home in a police patrol car – with periods spent in foster care and eventually a children's home. 'I was a fighter and the only contact I had with people was with my fist. I was an aggressive tomboy, and was eventually put into foster care at 14 after being caught shoplifting.' Throughout this traumatic time, Donna was subjected to sexual abuse by family friends and carers, which started when she was just six years old.

Like many children who are victims of abuse, she believed it was somehow her fault, and so began the cycle of guilt. 'Why was it happening to me?' she asks now. When she became a teenager, her feelings about her sexuality became confused. 'I was a well-developed young girl, and when boys started looking at me physically, I couldn't understand it.' She had never considered herself to be attractive, indeed had rarely looked in the mirror, discouraged by her father, who thought it 'vanity'.

A troubled marriage to a soldier followed and Donna's life was out of control. Her weight yo-yoed dramatically. She made what she calls 'a cry for help' attempt on her life in the mid-1970s, then a more serious attempt after her daughter was born, in 1986. She was referred for psychiatric care again in 1987, then once more in 1988 when, overwhelmed by bulimia, she was discovered by a neighbour sitting on the kitchen floor eating cat food.

By the mid-1990s Donna's weight had swung the other way

and she was very overweight. She explains her battles with diet and her misery in moving poems written at intervals throughout her life. 'I must get thin or it'll break my heart,' she says in one, and in another, 'I'm making progress and striving on/No matter how I try something always goes wrong.' But ironically it was during this time that there came a turning point in her life. She met Tony, whom she married in 1996. For Donna it was love at first sight. 'I couldn't stop looking at him,' she says now. 'Tony changed my life. He turned my legs to jelly. For the first time, having sex became something that is tender and loving. The past has come out in bits and pieces, but he loves me and it has never bothered him.' It is indicative of her complete lack of confidence and self-loathing that she still cannot believe he asked her to marry him. 'I couldn't get my head around that.'

Now she has a real family for her three kids, all of whom treat Tony as 'dad', and two small grandchildren. 'Life is more focused, less stressful and it has more meaning,' she says. In her contentment, she admits she is enjoying too many of the foods we all find irresistible: chocolate, pork pies, lashings of butter melting on jacket potatoes, Danish pastries, donuts, 'anything with icing or custard' and her particular favourite, pecan and maple twirl, 'to die for'. But the weight is getting her down. 'At first I thought, Tony loves me, what does it matter?' But now she realises it is time to tackle the body she is not happy with.

She admits to fad eating regimes with impossible promises and even worse side-effects.

The focus of Donna's self-loathing is her breasts, and her ambition is to have a breast reduction. However, when she consulted a plastic surgeon five years ago, she was told that first she would have to lose two stone. Weight loss has never been hard for Donna, who once went from 16st to 10st in seven months – 'I could lose weight even without the diets,' she says – but the way she has tackled it in the past has always been wrong and the weight simply returned. She admits to cider vinegar, cabbage, fruit and egg diets, all dramatic, fad eating regimes with impossible promises and even worse side-effects. 'I turned into the nasty bitch from hell,' she laughs, 'because I wasn't getting the right nutrients. I thought I was in control, but I wasn't. I wasn't eating properly.'

Donna heard about Fat Club from an advertisement on her local radio station in Somerset. Quick as a flash she rang for more information. It sounded like the answer to her prayers.

FAT CLUB ONE

> *'Harvey looks like Yogi Bear's ranger, and I'd been told it was a health farm.'*

Donna is not experienced in staying in a hotel-like atmosphere and the first weekend at Gorse Hill is a revelation to her. 'I am overwhelmed,' she says. 'I've never seen anything like this place, and for the first time in my life I have my own room and bathroom. The staff too don't look down their noses at me as has happened in the past, especially at school and from blokes.'

The reality of what she has let herself in for comes as a shock though. 'The first weigh-in has made me aggressive and angry because I see it as a form of abuse.' In order to assess the change in physique during Fat Club, part of each assessment includes a 360° film shot, taken on a revolving plinth with each member dressed only in a bathing costume. For Donna it is a step too far and she cannot do it with the crew and other members watching It is agreed that the set will be closed with the minimum of people present. 'I have a horrible feeling I haven't felt for 30 years. It is bringing up the past and I don't know how to deal with it. I want to go away and scrub myself clean.' She goes very quiet and, feeling nauseous, bolts back to her room to be sick.

This violent reaction comes as no surprise to Raj, who noted after his first meeting with her, 'Donna is a very warm and open person, but I am concerned about her participation in Fat Club because of the emotional baggage she carries, the history of bulimia and self-harm.' The experts can only hope that now that she is at last in a secure and happy marriage, her clear reason for wanting to lose weight will see her through.

For Donna, the shocks keep coming. At the first meeting with Harvey Walden for fitness training at 7 a.m. on Saturday, he reads the riot act: members must wear Fat Club kit at all times, must not leave the premises, must be in their rooms by 10 p.m. and are allowed only one supervised phone call. 'One warning,' he states menacingly, 'and we launch you like a scud missile.'

'I thought they must be taking the piss,' says Donna, as she recovers from the session. 'He looks like Yogi Bear's ranger, and I'd been told it was a health farm. Then he started! Well, I had been told that fat people shouldn't jog, so I said just that. I was arsy. Then when we had to swim, the pool was so cold and dirty – my husband's water troughs for the farm animals are cleaner and warmer. I've been cold in my life, but never as cold as that. I don't want to be a soldier, and there was Harvey making us get in the pool. It was all I could do not to push him in! I was shivering in my towel and when he asked me how I felt now I had achieved my goal, I said "Cold!" '

With a typical lack of faith in herself, Donna tries to second guess Harvey's opinion of her. 'He thinks I am the type who will do the bare minimum, but I'm not like that – I only don't do things if I think they aren't right. I couldn't believe that as free-thinking adults we are doing this. Harvey obviously thinks, "I'll have to watch her." ' She is wrong. 'My first impression is that Donna has an attitude problem,' he admits, 'but her motivation is good. I think she'll do well. She's determined and very strong-minded. She just needs discipline in her life.'

Despite the bad start, Donna quickly begins to relish all that Fat Club has to offer. Good friendships start to be forged with other members, especially Stuart and Tracy. Throughout the weekend she is keen to glean advice from Sarah Schenker on her calorie intake. Sarah sets a target of 1500 to 1700 calories a day for Donna, quite high but necessary in view of the energy she needs to do her job on the farm. Donna accepts with enthusiasm the calorie sheets and low-fat food advice she is also given. 'Now I know I can eat a bar of chocolate, but know I've got to work hard to work it off.' She laps up Harvey's words about exercise and the importance of the fat burning zone (see Chapter 12 to calculate yours) and absorbs everything Dr Raj and Alex Gardner can teach her about self-monitoring and having the right attitude.

Her resolve is firm. 'I am going to do this. I've tried all the rest of the diets, but they don't work. When you want to lose weight, you'll believe anything, but the only way to do it is not to eat too much fat and to burn off food. If one person watching Fat Club on TV or reading this book can relate to any of our lives and make a decision to lose weight, that's good. Until I came to Fat Club I was horrible when I think about it, but I am leaving here thinking "Here were four professional people interested in doing something about it." '

For Donna an active life is not a problem, as she busies herself on the farm with the cattle and raising the calves, and she is often to be found walking the dogs on the hills around Shepton Mallet. But since the weekend, Donna has fierce determination and promptly transforms her dining room at home into a mini gym. She finds an air walker at the local tip, which she picks up for £5, and invests in an ab-doer, a chair stomach-exercise device. She tackles the food issue stage by stage, at first cutting out butter, then a few days later rejecting pork pies and pastries. Later still she waves goodbye to the sausage rolls. 'It has taken a couple of weeks, and I will still eat chocolate, but I know nothing is really forbidden so long as I eat sensibly.'

FAT CLUB TWO

Date: June
Weight at weigh-in: 14st 9lbs (205lbs)
Weight loss from last weigh-in: 7lbs
Total loss: 7lbs
Waist: 37in

> *'If I don't do anything about myself, I'll be carrying that extra weight around forever and my forever won't be as long as everyone else's.'*

But a dose of 'flu descends in the meantime and, struggling with a very painful mouth ulcer and feeling lousy, Donna is on the verge of skipping the weekend. It is only Tracy's and Stuart's persistent phone calls and persuasion that convince her to take the plunge again. They are confident that, because she has been able to eat only mashed banana because of her sore mouth, she will have managed to lose a lot of weight.

As the group meet at Shepperton for the photo session, Donna is as bubbly and vivacious as ever. Considering she has been ill, she is looking radiant, transformed under the expert hand of the studio make-up girl. She admits later that for the first time she sneaked a look in the mirror, and for a fleeting second, admitted that she just might look good. 'Basically I think that I am an ugly person. My ex-husband used to say, "You're so fat, miserable and unattractive no one else would ever want you" – and that was even when I was 8st. I'm not miserable, but I still think I am fat and unattractive. "Sticks and stones may break my bones" is a cockeyed saying. Name-calling is the thing that hurts. The only time I've thought perhaps I wasn't ugly was that split second I looked in the mirror at Shepperton. Then I thought "Nah!" I couldn't believe it because I am always looking from the inside out.'

Battles for Donna are on the inside. She has no difficulty embracing the ethos of Fat Club, and takes the rigorous house rules in good heart, even teasing the inscrutable Harvey at the Friday-night bag search. 'It just makes me laugh,' she smiles broadly. 'The bag search doesn't bother me – I've been married to a soldier – so I've put my vibrator in my trainer. I am desperate for him to see it.' She plays the whole situation with aplomb: 'Here are my bags, Harvey, and these are my bras!' She's not fazed because her admiration for Harvey is growing at each meeting. 'I think Harvey is excellent. I know the bag searches bother some people – they see it as a violation – but it makes good TV. But really it is not necessary. If I was going to cheat [with food], I could have done it the week before.'

As willing to learn as ever, Donna enthusiastically enters into the spirit of the weekend. The weighted jacket session with Raj is the turning point for her. She is overwhelmed by the effect the extra weight has on her heart rate and the experience moves her to tears. She has managed early on in the programme to internalise the message of weight loss, a point so strongly made by Alex. 'It's the switch,' she says. 'It has been almost spiritual, the physicality of it all. I had three stone on my back and I jogged up the circuit. It really blew me away. It made me realise that when you are overweight your heart is working at least twice as hard before you have even got out of bed in the morning. And when the weight is taken off, it is like being kissed on the forehead by an angel. No one can take that feeling away from me.'

The effect is far-reaching for her. 'I realised that if I don't do anything about myself, I'll be carrying this extra weight around forever, and my forever won't be as long as everyone else's. No amount of shouting would have done it. I had to experience it for myself.'

Her image of a switch inside her head is a good one, and she has been lucky that she has understood the physical importance of weight loss so early in the proceedings. The battle for her now is with her self-image, but she is not ready yet to take on board Alex's messages about the importance of liking oneself. She talks about Alex's laughter workshop. 'It has been about dealing with emotions,' she says, 'and I'm not very good at them. He asked us about incidents in which we had felt humiliated, and I remembered sports days and mothers' race at my children's school. I simply couldn't take part because I didn't want to embarrass myself. As we talked, I remembered too people saying to me: "If you lost weight, you'd be really pretty," which is such a back-handed compliment.'

She struggles when Alex asks them to look in the mirror and tell him what they see. 'I can't look,' she says. 'Because I might like what I see and then I'd feel bad and guilty about it again.' Donna is only just starting out on her journey of self-discovery.

FAT CLUB THREE

Date: July
Weight at weigh-in: 13st 12lbs (194lbs)
Weigh loss since last weigh-in: 11lbs
Total loss: 18lbs
Waist: 35½in

'I want to be feminine and feel like a girl.'

For production reasons, there has been a delay between week-ends and Fat Club Three is tough for everyone. Donna has been working hard exercising at home and is keen to get back into the swing of things, but everything is held up by Jacey's failure to arrive at Fat Club on Friday evening. Donna is candid: 'She could have phoned and we'd have known she was not coming and could have got on without her. She is wasting my time now. To have everything working around her is selfish. She had seven weeks to say I'm not coming back.' The stress of the uncertainty as to whether Jacey will arrive and the subsequent delay in starting the weigh-in affect Donna deeply: 'I've thrown up because my routine is shot,' she says, as though this reaction was something quite normal, 'but though I loved the dance aerobics and relay races, the whole weekend has been stressful and emotional.'

The weigh-in, when it eventually happens, however, reveals a staggering 11lb weight loss and affirms how effective sensible eating and exercise can be on her life. She has set herself a treat for when she reaches her target weight, something she is determined to do. 'I'm going to go up to London and have my hair and make-up done, and sit on the Millennium Eye. I can't think of anywhere better to do it. That would do me I think.'

The experts, however, are still providing support for her, and she is not yet ready to fly on her own. 'Though we're not supposed to, I do jump on the scales at home, but I have never had the nerve to look. I'm like that man off *The Vicar of Dibley*. 'Yes, yes, yes ... no!' I only believe Raj when he tells me how much I weigh at the weigh-in.' She invests a great deal of trust in Harvey as well, saying: 'It's great that someone is interested in my life – not just for dirty reasons.' And he too is noticing the changes in her. 'You can tell she is impressed with her look. She walks with such confidence and poise now.'

As for Alex, many of the group have never encountered a psychologist before, but for Donna the whole routine is familiar. 'I've had lots of therapy. I think he is trying to make me like

61

myself and I don't know that I am ready for that yet. I don't know if I could cope with liking myself. I've always coped with the past by blaming myself and I think I would feel guilty.'

She is wary too about opening up her feelings. 'In the past, I didn't talk about it. I was 14 [and at the care home] when all the abuse first came out, and the person I told about it abused me. The care home was subsequently under investigation, and it was only the police therapists who were constructive when I was interviewed about it. They told me it wasn't my fault and I believed them.' But for all her strength of personality, any confrontation with those she cares about is hard for her. 'It physically hurts. It goes to my soul.' For this reason she is unsure about addressing eating disorder issues with Alex. 'People say I have coped well, but if I ever did anything horrible, it was because I was a "horrible person". A session with Alex worries me, though I would like to talk to him. I feel safer talking with the cameras there because I'm frightened that I might say something to Alex [in private] I need to think about.'

Even without a face-to-face meeting, Donna is beginning to emerge from the façade of self-loathing behind which she has hidden for so long. 'I do make more of an effort now than before I began Fat Club. I've started to buy hair mousse – I've always liked my hair and it seemed a good place to start – and I've tried make-up. On the train up to the weekend this last time, women were talking to me as if I had something to say.'

Fat Club is providing lessons for Donna way beyond the remit of weight loss. That for Donna will be a bonus. 'If my experience helps one person, not even necessarily a woman, then it has been worth it.'

FAT CLUB FOUR

Date: August
Weight at weigh-in: 13st 10lbs (192lbs)
Weigh loss since last weigh-in: 2lbs
Total loss: 20lbs
Waist: 35in

*'I feel I have much more spark and energy. My skin
is different and people keep saying I look younger.'*

Donna puts down the success of her endeavours to the fact that
Fat Club is different from anything she has tried before. 'Then
weight loss was about food, and this is not just that, but about
exercise too.' She has become almost evangelical in her enthusiasm for it, but the experts worry that she is overdoing it and, sure
enough, Donna injures her neck during the weekend's circuits
session and feels dizzy and nauseous. 'It is partly my own stupid-
ity,' she admits afterwards. 'I discovered from Harvey that you
have to replace body fluids when you exercise with isotonic
drinks and I had just drinking water. Water flushes out elec-
trolytes in your body, which are essential in fluid control and the
muscles when you exercise.'

She has learnt her lesson and now keeps her sports drink close
to hand. In fact she admits she is not exercising as manically as
between the first three Fat Club weekends, but is using the Ultra
trainer, a gift from her husband for her 40th birthday, three times
a week.

The weigh-in is a disappointment – just 2lbs – but Donna is
encouraged by the considerable change in her body. Harvey
advises her not to panic, because the changes are a result of
muscle development and muscle is heavier than fat. 'I have less
than 10 per cent of the cellulite that I had. My bum is smoother
than it was before, because I have worked off the fat from the
inside, but if you don't eat fat you don't get fat. And I've been
shopping, and bought a size 16 top when once it was size 20.
Even my feet were affected when I was fatter. I'm a size 7 and
I've even had to wear a size 9 in the past.' The original issue –
her bust size – has also shown a change, and she is now 38F
down from 44. But her determination to have it reduced is still
not resolved. 'I can firm it up, but at the moment I still want to
have a bust reduction, though I don't know whether I will still
want it when this is all over. I call that a year from now. That's a
realistic time scale for a new way of life.'

And for Donna this is a new way of life. 'I've learnt that if you
starve your body it shuts down and says, "Hello, we'll store this

weight." I should have a healthy balance of all sorts of foods. Sarah has been so good. She's dispelled all the stuff about eating late in the evening being bad for you or that pineapples speed up the digestive system. It's all a crock. My attitude to food has changed. I never used to fry anything and I did try to eat healthily' – despite a penchant for pastries – 'but now I don't use butter and I don't use salt at all. I even use skimmed milk powder to make custard. I don't make as many sponge cakes as I once did, and I make crumbles with oats and honey. Some techniques I've learnt from Fat Club and some from Rosemary Conley's *Low Fat Cook Book* which Sarah gave each one of us. It has taught me different ways to cook.' Much of what Sarah has taught her she already knew, but she has put it into terms that Donna can understand and apply.

Alex contrives an interesting temptations workshop during the weekend, to test out the members' resilience to a food they have said they love. He asks them to hold a dish of it, then to scrape it into the bin. Donna is handed a plate of chicken korma – something she has admitted in the past she 'loves and can't resist' – but throwing it away is not as much of a strain as she had anticipated. Lessons have clearly been learnt. 'I still eat korma at home, but now I don't buy it from the Indian take-away. I buy a low-fat korma sauce rather than have to forgo it altogether.'

When Alex plays devil's advocate again and asks them to hold chocolate in their mouths, Donna disobeys and swallows it fast, but, she reckons, chocolate has never been an issue for her. 'I shared a bag of honeycomb chocolate pieces with my nieces when we went to a soft play centre recently, but I did so much running around. And that's another thing. I would never have gone into one of those play places before. They have squeegee rollers you are supposed to squeeze between. Before Fat Club, I couldn't have got through.'

Throughout the four Fat Club weekends, Donna has proved to be a catalyst in the group, asking questions and challenging issues. She uses one session this weekend, during which Alex asks them how they perceive themselves, to address difficulties she is experiencing at home. 'I want to know whether the others have noticed a change in their sex lives since losing weight or whether I am the only one going without. Perhaps like me they have tried to lose weight in the past and failed. This time there is a whole body change and a whole life change.'

She asks this because her focus, now that she has really grasped the ethos of Fat Club, has moved into her personal life and her marriage, and she finds a soulmate in Tracy who is struggling with similar experiences. 'Since being at Fat Club, the physical contact between us [Tony and her] just hasn't been there, and he cannot bring himself to compliment me on my achievements. I feel shell-shocked. It has been hard and personal. I've come to the conclusion that he is worried I'm going to take on a whole new persona, or that he is going to lose me. But we've had words and he knows he is going to have to make some adjustments. He's got to meet me halfway. Tony is quite vain and suddenly I'm the one being told to look in the mirror. I can understand some of his point of view – I'm changing which must be alarming – but I am still his wife and I should get the same amount of respect as I give him.'

Support from sons Brett and Adam has been the opposite: ' "Cor, Mum, you look like a bit of a chick," they say and that makes me feel good. I'm learning to take compliments better. When I get looks from men I still think they are a bunch of lecherous bastards, but indifference from people that are important to me like Tony – that upsets me the most. It's hurtful, and I hope that if the boot was on the other foot, and he was having to lose weight, I'd be encouraging.'

Matters come to a head, and she has a confrontation with Tony after the Fat Club weekend, both on camera and privately at the kitchen table. They talk frankly about how she feels, and after much heart-searching, things begin to look better. 'Hopefully today will be a step in the right direction to talking like we used to.'

Her growing confidence helps to change her attitude to talking to Alex, and a session with him is pencilled in for the next Fat Club meeting. 'I'm not sure I can separate the demons of the past from the weight issue, but I hope to work that through with Alex. I just want to hand it over to someone and say "You have it!" '

Harvey is thrilled by Donna's development. 'She is still looking toned and fit,' he says in his report, 'and her weight loss does not compare to how well she is looking since the beginning. Despite her neck injury in the gym session, she still wants to work out with 110 per cent. I'm still very impressed with her and her attitude.' Raj, however, is more concerned: 'Her weight loss has slowed down. She is relying too much on exercise, and her recent neck injury may cause further problems with exercising.'

Alex also has his worries. Though he acknowledges that Donna is well on target, despite her enthusiasm to eat the chocolate offered at the temptations workshop, her self-image is more his concern: 'She still can't believe she is a good-looking woman, and has problems in thinking of herself as a person of value. As we've seen with Tracy, her husband married her as a fat woman and he is frightened of what she will become. She has also become almost obsessional about exercise. When she showed some signs of injury, this prevented her from doing workouts and upset her badly. If she has developed a dependency on exercise as a means of weight loss, these sort of restrictions will be a problem to her.'

FAT CLUB FIVE

Date: Early September
Weight at weigh-in: 13st 9lbs (191lbs)
Weight loss since last weigh-in: 1lb
Total loss: 21lbs
Waist: 35in

> *'I have the greatest respect for you, Donna. You have taken on a demon and it's gone.' – Alex*

> *'I have a nice gap inside me to fill with positive thoughts and experiences.'*

Donna has news. After years of little contact with her dysfunctional family, she has spoken to her estranged sister, Christine. In a remarkable step forward in her confidence, Donna decided to bite the bullet and call after her son met his aunt in town. 'We talked for about an hour, and we talked about our childhood. Then she started a conversation about abuse – she's in an abusive marriage herself and she thinks of herself as a victim. I found myself saying to her, "Dad had some perverted friends didn't he?" and we both started reeling off names of people who had abused us. I'd say one and she'd suddenly mention another. Though I wouldn't have wished my experiences on anyone, it has helped me so much to know that she has been through the same. I wasn't alone, and now I am in a unique position to help her.'

But the weigh-in removes all Donna's positive feelings when it is revealed that, despite all her hard work, she has lost only 1lb. Like Tracy, she leaves the room and bolts for the Lodge, 'to beat the crap out of the pillows and bed'. She is fuming. 'When Raj told me the weight, for the first time I felt negative, but I must have learnt something here because I would normally have eaten something and gone and thrown up out of anger.' But she is still incredulous. 'I just can't understand why I'm in smaller clothes and smaller bras and only 1lb lighter. I feel fitter and stronger now than I have done in 20 years. I'm hoping that I'm toning muscle too much or something's wrong, but I'm not coming back next time unless I've lost 6lbs. Sarah has told me that 1500 calories is the healthy amount to eat, but I'm going to cut that down ...'

As she rants, other members of the group come to join her and, once she calms down, she brings out photographs taken at the first Fat Club. They amaze everyone – they have not noticed the changes in themselves. Stuart thinks positive and admits that his face looks brighter and fitter. Donna, dispirited, is at pains to point out the 'rolls of fat' in a shot taken at New Year 2000. Her fears are eventually laid to rest by all the experts who reassure her again that it is her muscle tone which accounts for the lack of weight loss.

This self-image dilemma comes home to roost in Alex's appearance workshop, see yourself slim, when he shows the group shots of themselves at the first Fat Club and digitally mastered images of how they could be. 'The "before" picture makes me feel sick,' says Donna, horrified. 'It makes me feel sick that I let myself be like that. That I could do that to myself.' Alex explains the point of the session: 'A button has to go off inside yourself that says you want to change the way you think and live. You cannot allow yourself to go back. It's got to change. I want you to start thinking differently. If you are going to change you have to forgive yourself. You have been guilty, but I want you to tear up the picture of you big. That is forgiving yourself. Now think ahead.' 'I do feel in control,' she says tearing up the picture. 'I'm not going to let that happen again. I've learnt to respect myself.'

As the group chat and marvel afterwards, Donna sits quietly to one side and as if to reaffirm the changes she has made to herself, she frantically tries to piece back together the torn-up pieces of the picture like a jigsaw.

In spite of the weekend's setbacks, she has made the leap. Donna, the self-loathing abused little girl, seems to have finally come to like herself – probably the biggest step forward in her life. At the promised one-to-one session with Alex she talks like a new woman: 'I had trouble with mirrors, but now I can look at myself naked and see bits I like. I'm not all the way there yet, but I've come such a long way since the first Fat Club. A few days ago I wrote down all the people I liked on one side of a piece of paper, and thought, "If all these nice, intelligent people like me, there must be something there to like." So I started writing down the parts of me I like on the other side of the paper, and each day I look at it. I've discovered I'm lovable and I'm getting love without abuse.'

This realisation has shifted Donna from the role of victim to supporter. Referring back to her phone conversation with her sister, she says: 'When she told me that she thought she was unlovable, I could give her all the advice I had been given here.'

Alex admits that her words give him a 'tingle'. 'I have the greatest respect for you,' he says. 'You have taken on a demon and it's gone. I respect you for that.' He does, however, confront Donna with issues about her changed relationship with her husband. She freely admits that Tony finds her confrontational attitude difficult, but she justifies it by convincing herself she is not going to bury her feelings any more. Alex has a lesson to teach her. 'Out of the love that you have for yourself, you'll have to learn to tolerate it when things don't go the way you want. Don't blame yourself if you don't get the moon.' He talks about the difference between expectation of people's behaviour and the more realistic approach, anticipation. Donna owns up to expecting Tony to behave a certain way, and being disappointed. 'Would you feel threatened if I expected something from you?' Alex gently probes. For Donna the penny drops.

Of all the members in Fat Club, it appears that Donna has absorbed the message the most effectively. She seems to be taking exercise and watching carefully what she eats and, without question, Fat Club has taught her to value herself. She has even accepted the 1lb weight loss.

Disaster strikes, however, just after the penultimate weekend when an over-affectionate cow on the farm knocks Donna off her feet and on to her elbow, reawakening an old injury.

For a week she is weighed down in plaster, but a sympathetic surgeon, after hearing her pleas that plaster would interfere with her exercise routine, concedes and offers her a state-of-the-art foam and Velcro arm support which she can remove. 'I'm still able to go on my air walker and do floor exercises, but not the ultra toner, which is driving me potty.' Misguidedly, however, she has reduced her calorie intake from 1500 per day to between 800–1000 to make up for the lack of activity. Sarah is horrified. 'It's a mistake,' she says, and advises Donna that she must eat plenty of protein to help the healing process.

Regardless of the strapped arm, her self-confidence is coming on impressively. 'I now have a pair of button fly Levi 501 jeans, size 14 – the last time I was a size 14 was in 1976! – and some very trendy clothes given to me by my sister-in-law. I can look at myself in the mirror and be critical, not mortified. I'll say "That looks good, but that could be better." It's like sculpture. I'll target areas that need work.'

Her relationship with Tony is improving too. 'When he says something now it's noticeable and he's saying things that perhaps he wouldn't have said before. The door is slowly creeping open. I think he has realised that I haven't changed in my feelings towards him. I showed him the "before and after" pictures from the last Fat Club, and asked him which did he prefer, the slim Donna or the fat git. He said, "I have never seen you as a fat git, I fell in love with *you*." When I told him I didn't want to be thin and lose him, he responded that I wasn't going to lose him. He just didn't want me to think he had ever thought I was fat.'

This sort of confrontation would have been unthinkable six months ago. 'My approach to my life has changed dramatically since Fat Club. Now I say what I think and won't let things fester. I want to talk things through. It all has to do with growing self-confidence. After work when I've had a shower, I'll put on clothes that fit, rather than hang off me. I'll leave an extra button undone. It's part of liking my body. Jacquie Marsh gave me some great advice. She said you have to look in the mirror and like what you see. Find something and build on that. I have always liked my hair, so I worked from there. I've got the tools thanks to Fat Club to succeed. Now if I have a bad food day, I know I have to follow it with a good day. In the past I'd have said "what the hell".'

With this change in her life, the future does not scare her. 'I'm not worried about being responsible for my own self-control. I have learnt so much from all four experts and what they have said is always with me. When I did my arm, I thought what would Harvey say? I could hear him "Now come on, it doesn't mean the rest of your body can't function."

'Fat Club has really worked for me,' she says, and she believes confronting the past has gone hand-in-hand with solving the weight issues. She chooses a rather ironic metaphor: 'After all those years of being abused, I had become like a chocolate éclair sweetie. Hard toffee on the outside, but soft inside, when everyone had disappeared and gone home. I was trapped in this hard shell, but I know now that the abuse wasn't my fault, I didn't like it, but I had no control. But I'm not having any of that any more. I've dumped it all with Alex. I don't get emotional about it, when in the past I was raw and choked. Now I have a nice gap inside me to fill with positive thoughts and experiences.'

FAT CLUB SIX

Date: September
Weight at weigh-in: 13st 4lbs (186lbs)
Weight loss since the last weigh-in: 5lbs
Total loss: 26lbs
Waist: 33½in

'Fat Club was a once-in-a-lifetime experience – I'm so pleased I was able to do it.'

Donna's injured arm was always going to make the weekend difficult, and a Friday evening meeting with Raj confirms this. He is not happy with Donna doing any exercise that involves having to put weight on it. For Donna, so enthusiastic about her exercise, this is a tremendous blow and starts off the weekend on the wrong foot. 'It's broken my heart. I don't like upsetting my routine, and even though sometimes I can be stupid, I know about looking after my arm. I am being sensible. The orthopaedic consultant even said to me that he had been concerned about sending me home without plaster, but he has been amazed by how well I have done. I have understood from Harvey when pain is good and not good, and that has helped to not overdo the exercise.'

Though she is buoyed up at the Saturday morning weigh-in by her 5lb weight loss, the production team's decision to cancel breakfast for the group as a means of exploring the nature of hunger, is a disaster for Donna. 'We have been taught that we should eat breakfast – I don't understand it,' she says bemused and anxious.

Of course, this is the theme of the hunger workshop later in the morning. Sarah Schenker explains the reasoning behind the no-breakfast strategy: 'We are demonstrating how powerful the sensation of hunger is. It's not a bad feeling, but how you satisfy it is important. Leave it too long and you might be tempted to satisfy it in the wrong way. Be organised – have food around (in your bag even) to take the edge off hunger that you won't feel guilty eating.'

This lesson is not new to Donna, but she has missed her mid-morning banana she might have had at home. When she eventually eats lunch, familiar feelings of nausea come flooding back and she runs back to her room to vomit. 'I feel so disappointed. It is the same sensation I had when I was bulimic: as if my stomach was saying, "You're hungry but you are not allowed this food." ' She shudders. 'I'm not going down that road again.'

The production team and the experts are distressed to learn that incidences of Donna being sick were happening up until a month before she started Fat Club, but Donna is keen to point out that this is not sickness from putting her fingers down her throat. 'I had been warned by the community psychiatric nurse who cared for me when I came out of hospital in 1988 that I could become nauseous with anxiety, and when I am upset, it translates itself into sickness.' The last six months have had a radical impact on her. Donna is emphatic: 'If this incident had happened six months ago, I wouldn't have been able to cope with it. Now I know it is because I got too hungry and I don't let that happen any more. I have the tools.' The experiment of skipping a meal may have worked for some members. For Donna it could have been disastrous, but the subliminal messages of Fat Club have helped her through a crisis.

She also copes well with a potentially difficult moment with ballet instructor, Anita Young, who misjudges Donna's smile and places a stick down her back to demonstrate the importance of posture. Donna is upset and Anita is quick enough off the mark to apologise. She is intrigued by the session, but admits afterwards: 'I was really distressed. It was a combination of the physical pushing and pulling me to put me into the position she wanted – and the commands, telling me what to do as if I was a child. Straight away that was like a no-no. I have triggers and she was on the edge of pushing one of them. But if she had done that to me at Fat Club Two, I would have hit her. I gave her a look and she realised she had overstepped the mark.'

The final weekend is coming to an end. Donna has managed to overcome the disappointment of not being able to throw herself into the exercises. She reflects on the last six months, and has not forgotten that she came to Fat Club with a determination to lose weight in order to have a breast reduction. It is an operation she still wants because, although she has gone down in bra size as she has lost weight around her back and rib cage, her cup size has actually increased to a G, probably as a result of the toning exercises she has been doing. 'I wasn't expecting a dramatic change in shape,' she says, 'because in the past when I have lost weight on faddy diets, I still had big boobs.' She is not going to wait the year she had promised herself. The minute she hits 12st, she says, she will be knocking on the plastic surgeon's door.

But she leaves Fat Club with so much more than she came with. The woman who had tried so many faddy diets that she could have written a book on the subject has suddenly realised how wrong they are. Now she is the group nutrition expert: 'I've realised weight loss is so simple, but you can make it so complicated with all the diets on the market. Newspapers and magazines are full of "eat protein, don't eat carbohydrate", "flatten your stomach in four weeks". Sarah has dispelled all those myths about dieting. Losing weight is all about calories in and calories out. 'Fat only burns in the flame of carbohydrate,' she quotes one of Sarah's favourite phrases. 'You cannot burn fat if you don't eat carbohydrates.'

She's learnt too about the power of the right exercise. 'I had never exercised properly before, and Harvey showed me how to do it right. Fat Club has been so powerful for that, and I would do it all again even though I hated him when I first saw him! I ended up loving him. He's an amazing man.'

Above all, for Donna more than for any other member of this disparate group, Fat Club has been a life-changing experience because it has enabled her to look at the past and come to terms with it. 'The fat thing and lack of self-esteem have gone hand-in-hand and I have faced things that I haven't been able to before. I was grief-stricken and now I have changed all that. Making things up with my sister Christine had to be done, because it proves to me how much I have altered.'

She knows she has a way to go to achieve her weight-loss goal, but she is adamant that she can carry on. 'Fat Club was a once-in-a-lifetime experience – I'm so pleased I was able to do it.'

Alex is thrilled by her development: 'The strength of character she has shown in being resilient after all these traumas in her life confirms she is a remarkable woman. I still think Donna needs to work out some of the issues from her past. The difference this time is that she is now much more confident about herself and she may be able to confront old ghosts with a lot more conviction. When she can, there will be a whole new world there for her.'

Harvey, Donna's hero, is full of encouragement for her: 'Donna is still looking toned and fit, and her weight loss does not compare to how well she is looking since the beginning. It is so unfortunate that she got injured because she is definitely a winner, and I personally believe she got the message of leading a healthy lifestyle. She has been a real go-getter since Fat Club One, and has given a 110 per cent even when injured. She is full of motivation and very strong-minded. I think she will definitely stay with it and do very well in the future. She really looks great.'

Donna's Fitness Assessment

Fat Club 1

Run	Sit-ups	Press-ups
2.25	23	40

Fat Club 5

Run	Sit-ups	Press-ups
2.05	23	50

[Donna damaged her arm and was unable to participate in the Fat Club Six assessment]

Chapter 4

Jacey's Story

'I want to lose weight before starting a family.'

Jacey Eze
Age: 32
Lives: South London
Occupation: Pentecostal Minister and charity worker
teacher
Height: 4ft 11in
Weight at first weigh-in: 18st 2lbs – morbidly obese
Waist at first weigh-in: 42½in

Just reading about the pace of Jacey Eze's life is enough to exhaust most people. Her days are busy as a project manager in a voluntary organisation for disaffected teenagers based in South London, and during her evenings and weekends, she is involved with her work as a Pentecostal Minister, with three services every Sunday, and meetings and bible study during the week.

A bubbly, vivacious woman with an engaging laugh, Jacey comes from a big Afro-Caribbean family, where she is the only daughter, with three brothers. She reckons the weight started to creep on after her mother died from breast cancer. 'I was thin as a child, but when I left secondary school I started to put on weight. I was 18 years old at the time of her death, but can't be sure it affected my weight gain. Then I left home and lived on my own, and soon I was up to size 30–32.' Jacey's lifestyle does not help. As she rushes from one commitment to another, meals are often snatched, the wrong things eaten at the wrong time.

'I want to lose weight to gain weight.'

Unlike many of the other members of Fat Club, weight for Jacey has never been an issue. 'I'm an energetic person. Weight hasn't bothered me until now. I never weigh myself,' she laughs. 'I use the bathroom scales for weighing suitcases.' Her motivation for wanting to lose weight is a positive one, though: in April 2001 Jacey married Emmanuel, whom she met at a church conference in Nigeria, and though her weight does not bother her new husband – he calls her his 'beautiful shapely wife' – Jacey is keen to start a family. 'If I didn't want a child, I wouldn't have joined Fat Club, but I think it is fate at this point in my life. I want to lose weight to gain weight,' she laughs. Jacey is also concerned that her children would be teased if they have a fat mum. She has discussed pregnancy with her doctor, and has been advised of the risks to herself and her baby if she was to become pregnant while so overweight.

High blood pressure (pre-eclampsia) can at worst endanger the life of both mother and baby.

The side-effects of obesity in a pregnant woman can be serious, not only for her but also for the unborn baby. Not only are obese women three times more likely to have problems conceiving (as hormone levels change and in turn alter the ovulation process), they are more than twice as likely to need a Caesarean section (a serious operation made more complicated in a woman with layers of excess fat), and they often produce larger babies. Antenatal care can also be difficult because it is harder to measure the size of the uterus in a very overweight woman, or to get good ultrasound images.

The medical conditions which concern doctors most, however, are diabetes mellitus which can appear during pregnancy and endanger the baby, and high blood pressure (pre-eclampsia), which can at worst endanger the life of both mother and baby. A recent study in America has also suggested that obesity might increase the chances of birth defects.

Whether these facts have struck home remains to be seen, but

Jacey is showing enough determination to shift her weight. She found out about Fat Club as a result of her weakness for lingerie. 'I just love matching sets,' she beams with her broad, friendly smile. 'If you have nice foundation garments you feel good.' A friend of hers, who owns an outsize lingerie shop, had been contacted by the programme, and suggested to Jacey that she might like to give it a go.

FAT CLUB ONE

'I believe it is my destiny to have a baby and be reasonably healthier.'

The fact that Jacey has not put herself forward for the Fat Club regime worries Raj. Despite her avowed intention to be in good enough health to have a baby, he finds her evasive at their first meeting, and is not fooled by her engaging character and contagious laugh. 'She is horrendously overweight, but does not have a strong enough motivation and I really wonder why she is here. She wants to have a baby, and her statement "I want to lose weight to gain weight" worries me.'

From the onset Jacey is uncomfortable with the concept of being on TV. She is a woman who knows her own mind, and does not cope well with the inevitable stage-managing that is part and parcel of making a documentary. She describes her arrival at the first Fat Club weekend as being 'cloak and dagger stuff'. 'It all seems so secretive. Everyone has arrived separately and we won't meet until Saturday morning.'

The anxiety of meeting a new group of people under such artificial circumstances is heightened by the fact that it coincides with the fitness assessment with Harvey. 'It was tough,' she says later. 'And very emotional. I think I was in tears at one point. It wasn't because we hadn't exercised, but that we'd been thrown in at the deep end. We all thought it would be a softly, softly start.' She correctly reads Harvey's mind: 'Our size is new to him. He had built up a quarter-mile circuit and hadn't realised who he was dealing with.'

Unimpressed by his dictatorial manner, Jacey calls it 'a bit of a culture thing'. Curiously he is gentle with her, but perhaps he has sussed her out already. 'If he'd shouted at me, I'd have shouted back,' she says.

Culturally, diet is a problem for many Afro-Caribbean people. 'We eat a lot of food cooked in oil,' she says, and one of the first lessons she learns over the weekend is from Sarah: 'I told her to use a spray oil, so as little as possible is used. Olive or rape seed are preferable to other oils as they are monounsaturates so have a better effect on blood cholesterol levels: they help reduce LDL cholesterol (known as bad cholesterol), but do not lower HDL (good) cholesterol and are also less prone to oxidation. Polyunsaturates such as vegetable oil, sunflower oil and nut oils lower both LDL and HDL and are oxidised more easily.' Sarah also suggests Jacey poach meat instead of frying it. 'I've never poached chicken,' admits Jacey, 'and it has taken some convincing that I can cook yams and plantain like that.'

The laughter workshop with Alex, during which he teaches the group the importance of laughter to feeling good, is nothing new to Jacey. 'I think I could run this session myself,' she says. 'That's me. Regardless of the situation, I laugh. I think it's important, especially in marriage. There's not a day when we don't laugh.' During the session, each member is given a small pink pig to name and keep. Jacey decides to call hers 'Destiny', because 'I believe it is my destiny to have a baby and be reasonably healthier.'

By the end of her first weekend, Jacey is exhausted. By her own admission, the experience has been 'awful', full of 'scare tactics to frighten us to death and get us to do well next time'. But she admits she is leaving feeling motivated. 'I really think Fat Club is for me.'

She goes home and promptly ditches the contents of her kitchen cupboards. She is now enjoying basmati rice, vegetables such as broccoli and spicy meat and has replaced fatty snacks with low-fat crisps, and half-fat biscuits. 'The biggest problem,' she says, 'is learning to eat on a regular basis – not always easy when life is as busy as mine. Ironically, I have never eaten as much as I am eating now, but it is all better food.'

FAT CLUB TWO

Date: June
Weight at weigh-in: 17st 12lbs (250lbs)
Weight loss since last weigh-in: 4lbs
Total loss: 4lbs
Waist: 44in

> *'When I look in the mirror, I see personality, beauty*
> *and strength. I feel at peace with the size I am.'*

Despite the motivated beginning, the cracks in Jacey's resolve are already beginning to show. Her weight loss between the first two meetings has been just 4lbs, and at Alex's appearance workshop, Jacey produces a photograph of herself in a glamorous gold dress, but taken when she weighed more than she does now. Alex asks all the members how they feel when they look in the mirror. Words like disgust and loathing come from the other members. Tellingly Jacey replies: 'I see personality, beauty and strength. I feel at peace with the size I am.'

Though she is working hard to put into practice in the privacy of her home the lessons about food preparation she has learnt from Sarah Schenker, she is showing difficulty is accepting the ethos of Fat Club. 'It is difficult to be told that you are eating the wrong food, that you have done it all wrong.' Exercise, too, never her favourite pastime, is proving a struggle. When work permits, she is putting in an hour-long aqua-aerobics class each week, and a weekly gym workout which she describes as 'a bit of cardio vascular, circuits and weights'. It is not enough.

During the weekend she misses the swim, something she did at the first weekend, pleading a bad period as an excuse, and takes to her bed with migraine. Feeling too ill, she packs her bag and leaves Gorse Hill early. The experts are confused. 'Is she playing games with herself?' wonders Alex. Harvey is less forgiving: 'We need to tell her to stop this trash, and get her butt into gear.'

From then on Jacey hits trouble. She packs up to fly off to

Nigeria to complete an immigration interview so new husband Emmanuel can return with her to London. It had been ten weeks since they had last seen each other, and she describes the meeting as being 'giggly and silly like before we were married'. There was the added excitement of meeting her new family once again and seeing the house he had created for them both in Nigeria. 'The *pièce de résistance* was the bedroom,' she says. 'He'd done it beautifully, and had put a fan in the bedroom just like I'd asked – I was freezing!'

Two weeks later the couple return to London and a typical English summer, a shock for Emmanuel, used to African heat. The airline contrives to lose Jacey's luggage, which contains her wedding dress and wedding presents. To add to the stress, the next day Emmanuel is rushed into hospital with a serious strain of malaria which can, at worst, she is told, cause kidney and liver failure. Jacey sits with him for the 16 hours he spends on a trolley in Accident and Emergency, and for the next five days while he undergoes treatment in hospital. Once he is home, it is up to Jacey to nurse him back to health.

Fat Club issues, she admits, go out of the window. On their first night home she buys Kentucky Fried Chicken and ice-cream, and in Emmanuel's delirium, she claims he insists she 'eats the top of the carton while he eats the bottom'. She continues to prepare traditional Nigerian food as carefully as possible – taking the skin off the chicken, for example – but all her best intentions are taking second place to her new husband's needs. This all sounds laudable, but the experts are suspicious. To Harvey and Sarah especially, Jacey is simply seeing problems as insurmountable obstacles.

FAT CLUB THREE

Date: July
Weight at weigh-in: 17st 10lbs (248lbs)
Weight loss since last weigh-in: 2lbs
Total loss: 6lbs
Waist: 44in

'I feel pressure being the only black person on the programme.'

By the time the next Fat Club comes round, Jacey admits she is under pressure at work and at home and by Friday feels she 'hasn't got a grip of things'.

Her failure to turn up at Gorse Hill until Saturday morning affects everyone. The reasons for it are ambiguous. 'It has been just bad timing,' she says, 'but I have had my period each time there has been a Fat Club weekend, so I was worried before I even got into the car on Friday afternoon. The last thing I wanted was Harvey going through my bag and saying "Oh, well I guess you're not swimming this time again." ' She sets off from home, armed with her mobile phone, awaiting a call from Raj to discuss her menstrual problems – it has been suggested that she might have polycystic ovaries. Circumstances conspire against her. Her mobile battery runs out, she 'gets lost' on her way to Woking and turns around, but by the time Raj finally manages to make contact, she is tired, miserable and in bed at home in South London.

By the time Jacey eventually arrives at Gorse Hill to join the other members, she has delayed the weigh-in by two hours and things have gone awry. Alex has words with her about the reasons behind her late arrival, but she is not impressed. 'He wants to put meaning into everything. I used to be a very aggressive person, but now I deal with things a bit at a time. Alex is advising me to confront issues now, but I'm not ready to do that.'

Her weight loss is poor – 2lbs in seven weeks – and she is told she will be sent an official Fat Club warning: improve or leave. Later Harvey goes for the jugular: 'I'm not at all impressed with her,' he says between sessions. 'She gives excuses for everything. I think we must not entertain them and get more firm with her across the board. She's awesome at the PT sessions, but when she is away from me she plays a different role, wanting attention, sympathy and compassion. If we don't buckle down on her she will not do well and will come up with an excuse to leave.'

As the weekend progresses, Jacey admits privately that she is not as committed to Fat Club as she was before. 'I am more unhappy now than when I first started. My priorities have changed. I can take Fat Club or leave it. Only losing 2lbs in weight went right over my head, and I realised it was not about me, it's about the viewers watching. I'm a black face going through all this. I feel pressure being the only black person on the programme. Fat Club hasn't helped me as an Afro-Caribbean person. I wanted to learn more about cooking cultural food in a good way, but I've had to work that out for myself. I can't afford the membership to a gym, or to spend a fortune on food. My shopping bill has doubled since starting out.' This is the sort of statement which infuriates Sarah – buying and cooking healthy food should cost no more than the members were spending before (see Dieting myths in Chapter 12).

Indeed Jacey admits to feeling ambivalent about the future. 'I don't know if I'll come back next time, and the only reason I am here now is because I have spoken to Emmanuel and he has said, "Yes, we're doing this, so you've got to stay." But Fat Club is not as important as other issues right now.' And the crux of the change in her outlook emerges when she says: 'There are larger people than me having babies every day.'

Despite her dwindling resolve, Jacey joins in the events of the weekend, though reluctantly at times (her face during the dance aerobics session registering less enjoyment than she might have had at the dentist), yet she is thrilled to win the cookery competition with Jacquie and Tony Curley with their inspired summer pudding. But overall the strain is showing. She has a short and inconclusive meeting with Alex, but feels pressured. 'If I have issues, I talk them over with God,' she says. From the start the concept of being on television has been an uncomfortable one for her, but in the context of her faltering acceptance of the Fat Club challenges, it reads more like lack of motivation.

After the warnings dished out on Saturday, on Sunday the group members are asked one by one to make a commitment to Fat Club. Kelly pinches Jacey to encourage her to make a commitment. 'I have already made a commitment to myself, but I don't want to let the others down. It has been quite relevant throughout that I was happy before and only want to lose weight for one reason, but I feel I can't let down the team.' It comes to her turn to speak, but she cannot say the words. 'I'm not going to be rushed.'

Raj comes back to her at the end. It is a tense moment for everyone, and after a long, painful silence, Harvey butts in: 'Stop talking about how there will always be obstacles in your way. Don't beat about the bush – make your decision.' Jacey's reaction is ambivalent. 'OK,' she says slowly. 'I'm committed to my goal of wanting to lose weight, to have a baby.' But the experts want more. They want a commitment to Fat Club. Even at this critical moment, Jacey will not bite the bullet. 'When Fat Club gives me 110 per cent, I'll give it 110 per cent,' she replies, placing responsibility squarely back with the experts, 'I don't think I'm getting it either from Alex, Raj or to an extent Sarah. I want to make sure it's two-way.'

Alex's reaction is blunt: 'If you employed us to help you lose weight, we would cost you £500 a day. If you make a commitment, show evidence that you are.'

So reluctantly Jacey makes a commitment along with the rest of the group to progress with the regime. She comes away 'feeling fine, looking forward to the next time and ready to meet the 6lb loss per member challenge. I do have other factors too though,' she adds, and claims again that eating healthily is hard on a small budget. 'I'm not going to go bankrupt because of Fat Club.'

It is clear that Jacey is either not taking on board fundamental messages about the importance of exercise and that food does not need to cost more – the choices just need to be healthier – or that it is a sign of another nail in the coffin of her commitment. Alex is hopeful that by making a commitment to stay with Fat Club, she has taken the responsibility on herself. The other experts are less optimistic. Raj's concern is that Jacey is 'trapped in Fat Club for other people and not for her own reasons. Part of me feels I have let her down, and she appears to have lost trust in Alex and me. Does she genuinely want to lose weight or does she have another reason for wanting to be at Fat Club? Is she really crying for help, or does she just want attention?'

FAT CLUB FOUR

Date: August
Weight at weigh-in: 17st 12lbs (250lbs)
Weight gain since last weigh-in: 2lbs
Total loss: 4lbs
Waist: 44½in

> *'I told them the timing was not right for me, and that I was going to leave.'*

In the three or so weeks between Fat Club sessions, Jacey works hard; she takes more care than ever with her food, does some sessions at the gym and plays football with a friend's kids. But the seed has been sown that, as she perceives it, Fat Club is impinging on her life. She has missed the point entirely. Fat Club is about life change not an extra burden to tackle in an already hectic schedule.

Then the letter arrives at home in South London saying that her weight loss is disappointing and that she is being given an official warning. She should not be surprised as she was warned at the last weigh-in, but Jacey interprets it as a kick in the teeth. 'Emmanuel is very upset by the letter and I feel very discouraged,' she says. 'For me it is another nail in the coffin.' Once again she shifts the blame from her own lack of motivation to the experts. 'Before this letter I was working towards the next Fat Club. But this is a hindrance. I've made the decision to resign, but to come to Fat Club Four and say goodbye to everyone.'

Jacey refuses to do the Saturday-morning exercise routine, but knows that once the weigh-in reveals a weight gain of 2lbs, a 'Harvey shouting session was on the cards'. She is right. 'You've let [the members] down,' he thunders. 'You've let us down and you've let yourself down. You're wasting our time. I believe you have nothing to say.' 'It didn't faze me,' says Jacey afterwards, revealing nothing will motivate her in the final analysis, 'because he doesn't faze me, but I'm glad it was me on the receiving end, not any of the others. As a child I would cry before I threw a right hook, but I just felt calm. I told them the timing was not right for me, and that I was going to leave.'

Jacey's explanation for her failure is that it is not the right time in her life. The experts argue that no time is the right time. She interprets migraines and, she now reveals, bouts of stomach upsets as her body's way of reacting to stress. The experts see them as excuses.

Ironically, Fat Club may not have been a waste of time for her although her antics have wasted a lot of time for the others. The nutritional information from Sarah, Jacey now feels, was 'brilliant' and she has changed the way she buys and prepares food, but she is disappointed that the other lessons have not told her anything she did not already know. Or if there were things to be learnt, she has not absorbed them. 'If I become pregnant before I lose the weight,' she admits, 'I'm still going to have the baby. I don't regret Fat Club at all – especially as I had the chance to meet nine great people, and we'll keep in touch.'

'You have to accept there are outside issues in your life.'

'I hope people are inspired by what they see, but also realise that they must not beat themselves up if it doesn't work for them. You have to accept there are outside issues in your life. A girl at work barracked me recently for eating a slice of pizza. Well, a slice of pizza never killed anyone and when people start to pressure you, that's when diets become stressful. Also in the week before the last Fat Club, I wasn't home before 11 p.m. on any evening, so that the last thing I could do was go to the gym. This all has to fit around other areas of your life. I don't think I have failed myself at all.'

Jacey's departure from Fat Club has been a great disappointment for the experts. Raj is realistic. 'No one including the members was very surprised at Jacey's weight gain. I feel that Jacey's presence was adversely affecting Fat Club morale and her departure may improve motivation.'

'I don't think Jacey has grasped the nettle of becoming pregnant and the dangers of being so.' – Alex Gardner

Alex feels a huge loss of opportunity. 'It's a great pity she has gone,' he says, 'because I really think we could have done something for her. But I don't think she was motivated from the start. She likes to do things her way and she has a high level of self-deception. Her social circumstances at this time really do make life difficult for her. In her failure, she blamed everyone and everything else, and it was not in her interest to have self-control.'

He is concerned about the dangers ahead for her. 'She tries to show a well-collected face to the world and appears to be quite happy about her weight. Her husband likes her the way she is. Health risks for her are high though, and for her own sake she must get down to tackle the problem. I really don't think she has grasped the nettle of becoming pregnant and the dangers of being so.'

As usual Harvey is tougher in his analysis: 'Her leaving is long overdue and a blessing for me. She was never committed and a waste of all our time. She sat there with a smirk and a smile on her face as if she didn't care the members failed in their overall weight-loss target because of her weight gain. She didn't give a rat's behind about losing weight and she knew it from the beginning, but she let the team fail at the target goal.'

The only regret Jacey has weeks after leaving Fat Club is the day she left. 'It was very inconvenient to go to Gorse Hill but I wanted to tell everyone to their faces. Emmanuel was fit to knock Harvey out, but the only thing that stopped him was the fact that he saw how calm I was. I had chosen to come to Fat Club one last time and all Harvey could do was ask if I had apologised to everyone.'

She is not convinced that she can achieve weight loss on her own, but knows that she could not do it to fit around the schedule of a TV show. 'If it had happened before the wedding it would have been good, but after the wedding it was a very stressful time. I kept being ill, and even my doctor told me I was stressed out. Weight loss has to happen when I want it to.'

Her lack of concern about the dangers of pregnancy is still a worry. 'There are women out there who are bigger than me who have healthy babies, though it is harder,' she says. It is all the more worrying because, as she leaves Fat Club for the last time, she is already pregnant, though she has not yet realised it. Conception was not planned, but, as she says later, 'We weren't actively trying, just not not trying.'

Let us hope the next few months go well for her, and she defies the risks. In herself she is content with the news. She refers back to the laughter workshop of the first weekend. 'Not being happy with weight loss can be as damaging as being unhappy about weight gain. I'm concerned for the group that they are happy with losing that weight and love themselves. Alex is trying to teach them in six months what it can take a lifetime to learn. Whatever, Fat Club cannot take my joy away. I have always loved myself. That is so important.'

Jacey's Fitness Assessment

Fat Club 1

Run	Sit-ups	Press-ups
3.47	17	35

Fat Club 4

Run	Sit-ups	Press-ups
3.20	26	30

Chapter 5

Tony Upson's Story

'I used to joke that I'd become twice the man my wife married, but she didn't see it that way.'

Tony Upson
Age: 47
Lives: Cheshunt
Occupation: Sales executive
Height: 6ft
Weight at first weigh-in: 23st 7lbs – morbidly obese
Waist at first weigh-in: 58in

Intelligent and direct, Tony has immense charm and a nervous vitality. He is confident, ultra-organised, very determined and focused, particularly on his career. A perceptive man, he has great insight into his situation and is not afraid to speak from the heart, yet still gives the impression of being ruled by his head. He is divorced with three daughters, one of whom, Emma, lives with him.

His brother was 20st as a teenager, but Tony's weight gain came later. At 22 years, he was just 9st, and was known as 'bony Tony'. His activity levels were high. He was keen on football, trained frequently and rode a bike everywhere, but by the age of 28, his weight had almost doubled, to 17st. 'Looking back on it, I reckon that my weight gain played a big part in the breakdown of my marriage. My wife used to complain about it, and she made me feel bad. I used to joke that I'd become twice the man she'd married, but she didn't see it that way. I think I became someone different during my marriage. Thank goodness, though, my relationship with my three daughters is great.'

At 42 Tony stopped smoking overnight, from a 60-a-day habit, but after the breakdown of a four-year relationship, his weight ballooned again and he reached a high of 26st in November 2000.

His weakness is food, all food. There is very little Tony will not eat, and eat in large quantity, especially fry-ups. His job presents difficulties too, as he spends hours on the road sitting idly in a car, often stays in hotels with tempting menus and even keeps a plate in his car for all too frequent take-aways. He is a regular at the local pub where he enjoys his ale, and he has little time or inclination for exercise. 'My weight's causing problems now in lots of areas – I'm even finding it difficult getting in and out of the car.'

What galvanised him into action was a video taken of him playing drums in his band for his daughter's 21st birthday party. 'My brother invited me over to see the tape, and when I saw myself I couldn't believe it. I couldn't stop watching. I looked terrible. I was waddling around like a penguin. I looked ridiculous. I didn't know that's what I looked like and I couldn't stop thinking about it, all that night, all the next day. I went to the doctor, but I still don't think I really accepted that I had to take responsibility myself. I just wanted him to sort it out for me.'

His GP swiftly referred Tony to an obesity clinic, but even then he imagined they would 'wave a magic wand'. 'In a way they did, putting me on Xenical, a supplement that reduces the amount of fat your body can absorb from food. I lost 2st.'

It was the secretary of the obesity clinic who told Tony about Fat Club. 'I thought it sounded just what I need, and I want to try and do it without the Xenical, so I'm giving it up. I'll never have a chance to have so many experts helping me again.'

FAT CLUB ONE

'I don't know how I'm going to fit exercise around everything else. Still, I've got to try, haven't I?'

Raj brackets Tony's weight problem along with Simon's, Tony Curley's and Tracy's: 'I'm concerned because Tony has a lot of weight to lose. People who are less overweight tend to be more successful.' However he is encouraged by Tony's commitment in trying Xenical. 'I hope we can continue a steady weight loss.'

Positive from the outset, Tony goes into the first weekend with a receptive and co-operative attitude that is to become his trademark. 'I'm a bit nervous – I'd be lying if I said I wasn't – and I don't know what to expect at all, but I'm keen to get going. I'm here to lose weight. I've got to do it. The Xenical helped, but I'd much sooner do it on my own so, anything they ask me to do here, I'll just get on and do it.'

Tony's open friendly manner helps to get everyone chatting in the tense opening moments as the group meet for the first time, and he soon finds he has a lot in common with Tony Curley and Simon. Kelly, too, looks as if she will become a friend.

The second heaviest man, Tony has a BMI of over 44 and a long way to go before he can consider himself anywhere near a healthy weight for his height. 'I know my job works against me, and because I eat out a lot of the time, my diet's a mess, so that's one thing I've got to change. But I don't know how I'm going to fit exercise around everything else. Still, I've got to try, haven't I?'

At the first fitness assessment, he impresses Harvey by getting on with the exercise without making a fuss – not something that can be said for all the others. 'He's a very mature and level-headed guy who seems to be very determined to lose weight as well as get fit. He really got into the PT session and tried very hard at the exercises.' Praise indeed from Harvey! But although Tony's time for the quarter-mile run is a creditable 2 minutes 39 seconds, he can manage only 18 sit-ups and a paltry 15 press-ups. Those hours spent driving all over the country have taken their toll.

In the one-to-one meeting with Alex, it soon emerges that Tony loves to feel in control of his life, to the extent that he plans his every move at work in a meticulously kept diary. It is encouraging news to Alex, 'This will definitely help Tony to monitor his food intake and exercise, and he can turn his ability at planning to organise healthy meals in advance when he's on the road.

With his businesslike approach to life, I've encouraged him to use SWOT analysis, a business technique that aims to identify Strengths, Weaknesses, Opportunities and Threats, to help keep him on track.'

Alex and Sarah both suggest Tony can overcome the problem of erratic eating by calling ahead to the hotels he will be staying at to order healthy, low-fat meals in advance. Tony can see the logic of this straight away and, once he leaves Fat Club, wastes no time in putting it into action. It works even better than he anticipates. 'I've called a hotel where I'm going to be staying for a couple of weeks and had a chat with the chef there, and I'm picking up menus from all the places I stop regularly so I can go over them with Sarah at the next Fat Club weekend.'

But Tony knows that exercise is what is really going to make the difference for him. 'Obviously I've always eaten, although I have been eating the wrong things a lot of the time, but exercise is the new thing for me. I haven't done anything much for years, only a bit of swimming. So starting to exercise is the lifestyle change I have to face. Also there's a bit of competition going on between me and Tony Curley – we're both about the same weight so we're egging each other on. We've got a bet on as to who can lose most weight each time. That'll keep me on course too!'

FAT CLUB TWO

Date: June
Weight at weigh-in: 22st 4lbs (312lbs)
Weight loss since last weigh-in: 17lbs
Total loss: 17lbs
Waist: 54in

'What a start! ... We're on our way.'

When the members arrive at Fat Club on Friday evening, a shock awaits them. Harvey is going to search through their bags for concealed alcohol, food and mobile phones. Some of the members are outraged, but Tony is as pragmatic as ever, and brushes it off with typical good humour. 'As far as I'm concerned, it's just another thing we have to go through to get the help we need. If that's the price we have to pay for being here at Fat Club, I'm prepared to pay it. If I lose weight, it'll be worth it.'

He does not escape a ticking off, however. 'I've just had a pint of lager on the way here and Harvey could smell it on my breath; he wasn't happy with that. And he found the plate I carry around for all those emergency take-aways. That took some explaining!'

Saturday morning is particularly nerve-racking because it is the first opportunity the members have to see if they are all losing weight. Unlike some of the others, Tony has not been weighing himself but is quietly confident that he has done well. 'My robe's fitting better,' he jokes. When Raj announces a weight loss of 17lbs, Tony's face is a picture of delighted disbelief. 'Bloody hell! Brilliant! Wonderful!' he beams, but he's typically generous towards the other members. 'Between all of us we've lost 7st, and I lost the most. I don't expect that to continue every time, but what a start! I'm surprised, really. Surprised but very pleased – we all were really, but we're well on our way.'

Tony Curley has to pay up for the bet they have started, but the rivalry is friendly, and works well for them both. They have a similar amount of weight to lose, and both are very determined.

In the afternoon Harvey supervises a two-minute phone call for each member. Even the unflappable Tony is showing signs of irritation. 'I just think it's unnecessary, that's all.' The experts justify this ban on phone calls home because they want the members to rely on the experts for advice and on each other for support, without outside reference. Tony can see the logic but he still does not like it. 'I think they've underestimated us,' he says.

On Sunday afternoon, Harvey and Raj run the workshop that shows how much strain extra weight puts on the heart. Tony puts on a weighted jacket containing an extra 2st 3lb, and is horrified at how it affects his heart rate. 'This is less than I've lost at the obesity clinic and here added together. I can't believe how awful it feels. When it's gradual, you don't notice but this

93

really shows you.' When the jacket is finally lifted off him, the relief is palpable. 'I'm gonna lose it,' he mutters to himself, 'I'm gonna lose it!'

Tony's success at Fat Club Two has made a big difference to his confidence and, despite pressures at work, he now seems more relaxed. 'I'm enjoying it,' he explains. 'I go to the gym two or three times a week and swim a mile at least once a week, usually twice. I love swimming, but I'm not fast. I wonder if it's the best form of exercise to really shed those pounds? I'll have to ask Harvey. Sarah said my calorie count was fine, but she said I wasn't eating enough fruit, not just for weight loss but for health, so I'm trying to make sure I've always got fruit in the car when I'm on the road.'

Fat Club has meant new friendships, and some members are starting to socialise together between weekends. With Tony Curley, Sha and Kelly, Tony goes to Bognor to attend one of Tracy Young's social functions for browsers of her Big Beautiful Women website, but it does not work out the way they hoped. Given the steps they are taking to lose weight, all four feel very put off by the philosophy of fat complacency that underlies it. They are especially taken aback by a hostile greeting from Tracy's very overweight friend Tarnya, who seems to feel that anyone involved in Fat Club is being disloyal to some unspoken brotherhood of fatties. Tracy is unaware of the tension, and for her the evening is a great success. Tony sees it differently: 'We didn't enjoy it at all, none of us. We really felt uncomfortable straight away. We bunked off as soon as we could and the four of us went out to eat together.'

The other social event this month is a far more relaxing trip to Cardiff, this time with Donna, Kelly and Tony Curley, to visit Simon. 'We had a great time,' Tony smiles. 'And we encouraged each other with the healthy eating. We must have looked quite a sight, the four of us out together.' He laughs. 'Quite a sight!'

FAT CLUB THREE

Date: July
Weight at weigh-in: 21st 6lbs (300lbs)

Weight loss since last weigh-in: 12lbs
Total loss: 29lbs
Waist: 54in

> *'I haven't weighed myself since Fat Club Two, but I can feel my clothes are looser.'*

When he arrives at Gorse Hill, Tony is looking relaxed and happy. 'I always look forward to the weekends here, though not to the weigh-in, mind you. I'm very motivated, and I'm feeling pretty fit. I just hope I stay this way.'

His success has even motivated his daughter, who has joined him in changing her diet. 'We take it in turns to go shopping and now she chooses low-fat foods, and lots of fresh fruit and veg too.' As yet he has not got the confidence to prepare fresh food, and is relying too much on ready meals, so his reaction is not surprising. 'I'd say I spend more time on shopping now – reading the labels – and quite a bit more money too. This healthy eating doesn't come cheap. I've been trying something different in the last couple of weeks. I was planning all my meals ahead of time, plotting everything in my diary and working out the calorie counts, but now I'm trying to do it by guesswork. If this is a lifestyle change, and not a temporary fix, I have to rely on my judgement. I haven't weighed myself since Fat Club Two, but I can feel my clothes are looser.'

Sarah is delighted with Tony's progress. 'Unlike many of the other members he is still keeping a careful record of what he eats and the exercise he does, so he can check his calories in and out, and do any fine-tuning based on that information. He has fitted his new eating plan brilliantly around his life. He has acted on the advice to ring hotels in advance and talks to the chef about organising him a healthy meal. Everything is meticulously planned on a spreadsheet and he can follow it exactly – that's the easiest way for him to stick to his new eating regime.'

Where once Tony ate what he could when he could, he now starts the day with a bowl of cereal and fruit, while for lunch he opts for sandwiches and fruit (occasionally a jacket potato). Dinner will almost always be soup, or a tuna steak and salad. His daily calorie intake averages around 1700, but he is trying to add more vegetables and fruit into his eating plan and is dropping ready-made meals for stir-fries. Tony seems to have taken on board Sarah's message that no food is forbidden. 'I still go out with my mates every Thursday night. We go to the pub and I have a few pints. I just work out the calories and cut down a bit elsewhere. That way I don't feel hard done by.'

He is making good use too of the heart-rate monitors distributed during the weighted jacket session at Fat Club Two. 'It gives you the correct heartbeat range you should aim for during exercise to make sure you're burning fat efficiently. When I go to the gym, I enter my age, weight and height and it gives me a readout for the workout. You can check that you're within the range, and at the end of the workout, it even calculates how many calories you've burnt up.'

Tony has been concentrating on cardiovascular work for weight loss. 'I don't want to bulk up, so I do the treadmill, stationary bike, stepper and cross trainer. My heartbeat range is between 112 and 147 bpm [beats per minute]. I'll bet all the members could tell you their heartbeat range off by heart. I'm going to try it out on Saturday when I'm playing drums with the band. That gets your heart going!'

After Tony leaves Gorse Hill, he carries on with his programme of exercise with renewed determination, but his knee is giving him trouble. 'The doctor says it's just wear and tear. He reckons I've got the knee of a man ten years older – whoever he is, I wish he'd swop back! There's nothing I can do about it. but it is very painful sometimes.' To help absorb the impact when he is exercising, he invests in better trainers, and on Harvey's advice changes his gym routine. 'I wasn't doing any weights before, because I didn't want to bulk up, but Harvey has explained that doing light weights won't build up my muscles, just tone them up, so keep me burning calories efficiently. I'm doing a bit of upper body work as well as the cardio stuff. It takes the strain off my knee too.'

Harvey notices the improvement at Tony's fitness assessment. 'I've seen a great improvement in the press-ups. This time he's managed 60, almost triple what he did at Fat Club Two.'

As usual, Tony is upbeat but not complacent. 'To tell you the truth, I haven't found any of this too difficult. But I'm always very busy. Maybe if I was less so, my mind would dwell on food. If I was around the house, like Simon is, I'd find it very difficult, but as it is I'm having no problems with the calorie control. I'd say I'm very happy with the progress I'm making and I get a lot of encouragement from my friends and family. That helps.'

FAT CLUB FOUR

Date: August
Weight at weigh-in: 20st 13lbs (293lbs)
Weight loss since last weigh-in: 7lbs
Total loss: 36lbs
Waist: 51in

> *'I'd advise anyone, fat or thin: learn about what you're eating.'*

Tony, ever upbeat, is the only member to have felt good about a stressful Fat Club Three. 'I do think it was positive, even though Kelly and Jacey did so badly at the weigh-in. I hope it's encouraged them to try harder. I've been speaking to Kelly a lot, and I know she's working hard.'

At the end of the previous weekend the members challenged the production team about the bag searches and it was agreed that these would be discontinued. This minor triumph has cemented team feeling even further. 'It's good to have got things out in the open. I think everyone had underestimated how close the ten of us have become. We can use that to help each other, and we are doing it. We call each other up between Fat Clubs, send e-mails, sometimes get together. It all helps. I'm starting to see a difference in myself now. Since I got the pedometer, last Fat Club, I've been counting up how much exercise I can fit in almost without noticing. When I visit customers, I park a bit further away so I have to walk a bit more. Since the start of Fat Club, I've gone from wearing size 58 to 54 trousers and they're getting too loose for me now. I keep having to hitch them up – I love that!'

The weigh-in is very tense. 'I'm a bit disappointed. We had a group target of 60lb and we were well short of that – we only made 50 lb. When Jacey was weighed and she'd put on 2lb, there was complete silence. We just didn't know what to say. I've lost 7lbs, and I'm quite happy with that, but I've lost 3in off my waist, and that's tremendous. I can't believe it. It must be the toning exercises Harvey gave me. They've made all the difference.'

Once Jacey leaves for good, everyone relaxes a little, and Tony settles in to the weekend. 'The best bits were the endurance session [a gruelling circuit workout], though I didn't think so at the time, and the barbecue. That was fun. We had a bit of a dance, a chance to relax. The food was great too.'

After Fat Club, Tony starts trying to cook more for himself and his daughter, rather than relying on ready meals. Sarah's advice is coming in handy. 'My taste buds are adapting to the way I'm preparing food now. I use one of these aerosol cooking oil sprays to make stir fries. It's supposed to be just 1 calorie each time you spray it, so that can't be bad. Sarah's always saying "Lose the fat", so that's what I'm doing. I'm finding too I can grab the fruit I keep in my car before I get too hungry and get tempted by something fattening. I know all my calories off by heart, too – well, most of them. I'd advise anyone, fat or thin; learn about what you're eating.

'I'm a bit of a planner, me,' says Tony. 'I'm converted to exercise. It's part of my life now going swimming and to the gym. My customers all know about Fat Club and they've all said how much better I'm looking, which is nice really. I think everyone's been very positive this Fat Club.'

Tony is off on a well-earned holiday to Marbella with two of his daughters and a nephew, but is not worried about giving in to temptations. 'I'm really looking forward to it. I feel much more confident, even though I'm still 21st. I feel less self-conscious about my body now, and I feel all right about wearing swimming trunks too. I bought two pairs ages ago, but they were too small at the time so I just threw them in the wardrobe and forgot about them. Well, I tried to, but you know how it is. I got them out before the holiday and they fit comfortably. Things like that keep you going. I know I'm still fat and I've still got a big belly but it's like I'm a real true member of society now. If you think about it, I've lost five stone altogether since I first went to the obesity clinic – about half there and half at Fat Club.'

This new-found confidence has a far-reaching effect on Tony. Over the last few weeks he has been feeling increasingly dissatisfied with his job and the difficulties of being on the road while trying to adopt a healthy lifestyle. He makes a brave decision and just before coming to the next Fat Club, he hands in his notice.

FAT CLUB FIVE

Date: Early September
Weight at weigh-in: 21st 1lb (295lbs)
Weight gain since last weigh-in: 2lbs
Total loss: 34lbs
Waist: 52in

'I just get the feeling that someone's going to have to make up for me this month.'

The holiday may have been relaxing, but Tony is convinced he has put on weight. 'I've stuck with the diet, I reckon, but I had an ear infection so I couldn't swim in the hotel pool and that's how I was aiming to keep up the exercise. My knee's been playing up too. It's bloody painful sometimes and it feels unstable. Anyway, I've played table tennis but that was about it. So I had to be more careful with what I ate. It was a four-star hotel, and the food was fantastic, but I resisted the temptation. A year ago it would have been a different story. I drank water too during the day – last year it would have been beer.'

When he starts to think about the weigh-in, Tony is worried and resorts to extreme measures. 'I've been to the gym twice a day since I came back last week, but even though I've looked forward to each weekend so far, I know I'm going to be disappointed this time.' The hot weather is affecting him as well and he feels worn out. He has a sense of impending doom: 'I just get the feeling that someone's going to have to make up for me this month. I've been losing weight steadily for seven to eight months now, and I think it's got to plateau out.'

In his welcome, Raj points out that the novelty of their new lifestyle is probably wearing off and that weight loss will be harder to sustain. How right he is. The experts have suspected for some time that many of the members make a special effort to lose weight over the last few days before a Fat Club weekend, perhaps even skipping meals on Friday. Weighing them on Sunday, rather than Saturday, may result in a higher but more accurate reading, particularly after the three delicious but calorie-controlled meals a day provided at Fat Club. For members who are not adopting these unhealthy strategies, however, a Sunday weigh-in could actually be better, as it gives them that little bit longer to exercise and maintain the slight calorie deficit that leads to their gradual weight loss.

Tony is right to be concerned. The weigh-in shows that in the intervening four weeks, he has gained 2lb. He is visibly shaken, but puts a brave face on it. 'This month I'm a failure, but I'm quite sure I'll sort it out and lose even more. The holiday was a test to see if I've learnt enough. Obviously, I haven't. I feel such a fool.' He is not the only member to perform badly this time. 'I would have weighed less yesterday,' he admits.

All four experts are concerned by the members' lacklustre performance this month, but Sarah is bitterly and personally disappointed by Tony's poor result. 'I really thought he'd got it. I thought he understood about balancing his calories with his activity, but this shows he hasn't. The whole point is that you should be able to cope with suddenly having to do less exercise. Look at Stuart. He managed to lose weight with a broken arm. I thought Tony was doing so well, but I think he's been relying to much on exercising and not enough on controlling his calories.' It is a mistake that many of them are making: the message is still not getting through that if something stands in the way of exercise, then you must adjust your calorie intake accordingly.

Tony and Sarah argue about this, but neither gives way. Tony denies he overindulged while he was abroad and feels got at considering how well he has done so far. To Sarah the facts speak for themselves. 'If Tony had been controlling his food intake, he would have lost weight even with much less exercise. He's just making excuses.'

Three out of the nine remaining members (Kelly, Tony Upson and Donna) have put on weight this month, and the experts' meeting is a difficult one. Sarah is very upset, Raj despondent, Harvey angry and even Alex, usually so phlegmatic, is shaking his head. 'These three should have been the crème de la crème,' says Raj. 'But they're going the same way as anyone else trying to lose weight. Their failure is drawing down the rest of the members.'

Alex is more hard-hitting. 'They are lying to themselves, and to us. They've internalised the idea of exercise. That's fine. It's something new for them, but they've been fighting with food all their lives. No matter what they say, we've got visible evidence that they haven't taken the message about food on board.'

'I'm sure some of them starve themselves for the few days before they come here,' Sarah adds. 'Some of them have even admitted it to me. They're still dieting. Haven't they got the message that this isn't a diet?' Angry and despondent, the four return to the farewell meeting and remind the members once again of the fundamental message of Fat Club: eat less, do more.

Once the weekend is over, Tony works hard to get back on track, oblivious to the consternation he has caused. Fortunately, in the course of the weekend, his knee seems to have improved, so he can return to the gym with a vengeance. 'I love this now,' he puffs. 'If you'd told me six months ago that I'd be a regular at the gym I'd have laughed at you. One of the reasons I never went before was I didn't think I could physically do it, but every week I'm improving. It's done my confidence a power of good. Once I get under 18st,' he declares, 'I'm going to take up squash again.'

Tony has a new job. Before starting, he pays Tony Curley a visit in Southampton and together they spend the day at the gym, enthusiastically swapping exercise techniques. Tony Curley has done so well in his consistent weight loss that Tony Upson has decided to see what he can learn from him. Side by side on the treadmills, they keep sneaking glances at the speed settings each has chosen. Tony Upson sets his at 8, Tony Curley would usually stick at 6, but soon he has raised it to 9. Tony Upson responds by upping his to 10, and they both end up at 12 – far higher than either would have thought possible. At least they have the good grace to laugh about it – once they get their breath back. 'I know it's a bit childish,' they sheepishly admit, 'but it works for us. It's true, everyone can do more than they think they can.'

FAT CLUB SIX

Date: September
Weight at weigh-in: 20st 9lbs (289lbs)
Weight loss since last weigh-in: 6lbs
Total loss: 40lbs
Waist: 49in

> *'Exercise has been the key for me, and I couldn't have done it without Harvey.'*

Tony is entering a new phase in his life. The new job means more time working from home, which will allow him to fit in an early-morning gym session and be at his desk by 8.30.

He is in a thoughtful mood. 'I'm feeling like we've come to the end of a lot of fun. Hopefully I can get on and lose a lot more weight. I've learned everything I need to know here to do it. It's down to me now, and I know I can do it.'

The weigh-in is more relaxed this time. The members set their own targets – Tony had agreed to 8lbs, but manages only 6lbs. 'Of course I'm a bit disappointed. It would have been nice to go out with a bit of a bang, but I'm in it for the long run.'

Kelly has by now left Fat Club, and once the eight remaining members have been weighed, Raj quickly calculates their total weight loss. 'As a group,' he says, 'you've lost a total of 23st 6lbs. That's Tony Upson's starting weight. You've lost a Tony.'

All eyes are suddenly on Tony. He is still a big man and the group marvel at having shifted more weight than they see sitting before them. It is a feel-good moment and they all laugh. No more Fat Club weigh-ins. The relief is palpable.

The rest of the weekend is more or less fun, with a yoga session in the afternoon and a camp fire session on the

Saturday night, with all the members dressed in their best. Tony relaxes over a few beers, and reviews his experiences at Fat Club. 'I've changed everything in my life,' he says. 'I've got a whole new set of habits, good ones, and they're habits I can stick with. We've had a good laugh all the time, but there have been serious notes and we've all learnt a lot. I remember at the first weekend, when I saw Harvey, I thought he was unreal, but exercise has been the key for me. And I couldn't have done it without Harvey. Now I think he's like a Messiah, and we've seen the light!'

Tony's mellow mood disappears the next morning when he learns what Harvey has in store – a triathlon event including cycling, running and swimming. Tony is quietly determined to give his best, and comes in third, after Stuart and Tony Curley – a pleasing result.

After lunch comes another surprise workshop in the gym with Anita Young, a former soloist with the Royal Ballet. Diminutive but steely, she soon has the group under her control and takes them through a number of postural exercises designed to improve their core stability. She also shows them some quick and effective techniques for looking more confident. She singles out Tony, and asks him to imagine admiring the view from an Italian hillside. Tony visibly straightens up, looking instantly more poised and imposing. At 6ft he is already tall, but Anita helps him to seem commanding rather than apologetic, and everyone marvels at the effect. Naturally Tony's pleased, and decides to work on his posture. 'It's not something I've ever really thought about, but if it can make me look more confident in a work situation, I'll definitely give it a try.' As he leaves the gym, you can already see that he is walking taller.

At the farewell meeting with the experts, Raj has some encouraging words. All remaining members have made significant improvements to their health through losing weight. 'Tony, you have reduced your BMI from 44.7, morbidly obese, down to just under 40, so you're now officially just obese. You're on a journey and you're on the way. Keep going with your rate of weight loss and you'll go on increasing the health benefits.'

Tony nods, taking in Raj's words. 'So many things in my life have changed for the better since I first walked through the doors of Fat Club. I'm going to build on that success.'

From a man who had tried everything and failed to lose weight, he has become an active, confident and well-informed person. He has fitted healthy eating and regular exercise around a demanding, yet fundamentally sedentary career, enlisting his love of order and his systematic, organised nature. And it has worked for him.

Raj: 'I was worried initially, because he'd tried absolutely everything to lose weight and everything had failed, apart from Xenical. I just wasn't sure he had the determination, but he's proved me wrong. I hope he continues to do so.'

Tony' Fitness Assessment

Fat Club 1

Run	Sit-ups	Press-ups
2.39	18	15

Fat Club 6

Run	Sit-ups	Press-ups
1.52	53	100

Chapter 6

Tracy's Story

'If public humiliation doesn't work, nothing will.'

Tracy Young
Age: 34
Lives: Skegness
Occupation: Family flag and banner business
Height: 5ft 6in
Weight at first weigh-in: 20st 2lbs – morbidly obese
Waist at first weigh-in: 50in

Tracy is the biggest of the female Fat Club members. Weight has been an issue since she was a little girl and, because she was adopted at just six weeks, Tracy has struggled to find out whether it is genetic. What she does see is that adoption has had an impact on the way she perceives herself. 'I was always told I was chosen, and introduced as "our adopted daughter". But in rows there has always been reference to me being not quite "family". My sister, Selina, was born 22 months after I was adopted and she has a closer relationship with mum. She's blonde unlike me and a slim size 10. I think I've always been the odd one out, which has had a huge effect. I've always had a sense of "Who am I?" '

As a mother herself, she can now understand what motivated her own mother to give her up for adoption, but as a child she always felt angry towards her. 'I have searched for her extensively. It's weird because I don't want to talk to her. I just want to know what she looks like – I have just one photograph taken just before I was adopted – and find out what medical history runs in the family.'

Tracy is married to Neil, a lean 6ft 1in, and now has a family of her own. It was when she was pregnant with her 11-year-old son Eden that she piled on a massive five stone because, as she admits, she 'really ate for two! I ate like a horse, especially Caramel bars. When I was weighed during a visit to the clinic, I emphatically denied I was 17st. The night before I was induced, I weighed myself again. I was 19st.'

Many women find it hard to shift weight gained during pregnancy, but for Tracy the effect has been dramatic. Her weight has affected her fertility and she has been trying for another baby since she had Eden, but she has not had a period for six and a half years. 'We looked into the possibility of having IVF, and for a short time I took drugs to try and kick-start my menstrual cycle again. Though the clinic we went to could not tell me categorically that my inability to conceive was weight related, they did say they couldn't offer IVF treatment as I was too fat.'

Added to these medical concerns, Tracy developed asthma after Eden's birth, which she now puts down to her quick weight gain, or, she adds wryly, 'perhaps it was too much gas and air during labour'. The result is that for years she has been on frequent courses of steroids, which has not helped in her weight battle, and she says, 'It's rough having to contend with that.'

'I will eat what I've bought until it's gone, whether I am full or not.'

Despite her size, Tracy is adamant that she does not overeat. 'It's a question of the wrong food, not too much of it,' she claims. 'I'm not a drinker, just a bad eater. I miss breakfast and I snack and eat at the wrong times. There is often a couple of rounds of toast mid-morning and though lunch might be a ham or cheese sandwich, I'll have a packet of crisps with it. As a family, we eat far too many take-aways – kebabs, pizza, Chinese – and I will eat what I've bought until it's gone, whether I am full or not.'

Chocolate is not a particular passion, but when she stops at the newsagent to buy cigarettes, she will often sneak in a packet of mints or wine gums, 'something to fill my gob'.

Tracy has tried every diet ever produced and her bookshelves groan under the weight of diet books. Whatever the reasons behind her weight gain – medical, genetic or overeating – and her failure to lose it, it has affected dramatically the way she leads her life. Her personality is refreshingly honest, fun and feisty. It is hard to believe that beneath the wise-cracking façade bubble feelings of self-loathing. 'When you are big you hide behind a sense of humour and I can be gobby and aggressive too.' But this is a foil for her fear of people's fattist attitudes. 'I can be a nasty bitch, especially to my husband, because I feel so unhappy in myself. It has got to the stage that I can't wear my jewellery or even get into a normal bath. I'm so lacking in confidence, I won't hang out my washing on my own, go shopping on my own, eat in public or even cross a zebra crossing. It goes back to a time when I was walking down the street and some lads in a car shouted "You fat cow".'

Tracy readily admits that, despite the tactless remarks of boys, her paranoid feelings may be unfounded: 'I should stop thinking about what people think of me and start thinking for myself. I go from the cocoon of the office into the cocoon of the car, to the cocoon of home. That's why I love the [anonymity of the] Internet so much.'

The Internet has become Tracy's social life. She goes online almost every evening, often until late, chatting with other browsers. 'It's wonderful. No one can see you so they can't judge you.' With her 27st friend Tarnya, she set up a website, Big Beautiful Women, extolling the virtues of being fat, which includes chat rooms and advice, and the pair organise social gatherings for visitors to the site. She admits it is simply another cocoon: 'There's safety in numbers, and it gives a false sense of security.' No women under size 18 are permitted to attend the socials (though, curiously, thin men turn up in droves). Size 18 (around 16st) seems to be Tracy's magic number, and it is this size which she aspires to. 'I'm confident as that. I used to be a kissogram girl when I was size 18 back in 1989, and would be happy to be back at that. I could be that weight and be fitter than people smaller than me. I don't care what the medics say.'

> *'It would have helped to know my weight was the result of a medical condition. It would have been an excuse – something to justify it.'*

If everyone reaches a point when they realise changes have to be made, a broken plastic garden chair incident was the catalyst for Tracy. 'It collapsed under me and that terrified me. When we then went on holiday to Majorca, where all the chairs were plastic, I wouldn't sit down. I finally went to see the nurse at my GP practice, sobbing, and she recommended me to a particular GP, but like all GPs, he knew very little about obesity and it was my asthma consultant who referred me to an obesity clinic in Leeds. There I had four days of tests – a complete MOT. An X-ray showed an enlarged pituitary gland, which may or may not have been a cyst, but it was not the reason for the weight problem. In fact it would have helped to know my weight was the result of a medical condition. It would have been an excuse – something to justify it.' But even the clinic's guidance did not help.

As another string to her bow, Tracy set up a business selling outsize clothes for women at discount prices and, ironically, this was how she heard about Fat Club. She was sent a flyer about the programme by a colleague who runs a website for large men. 'It didn't appeal at first, and in fact my friend Tarnya, who has been featured in a Channel 4 documentary in the past, phoned the number on the flyer hoping it was about putting on weight!' – something that, much to Tracy's amazement, Tarnya is actively trying to do.

For Tracy, joining Fat Club is a last resort. 'If public humiliation doesn't work, nothing will,' she says. 'What Fat Club is offering – the idea of experts on hand – appeals to me. I'm doing it because I can't think of anything worse than having viewers seeing me on those scales at 20st.'

FAT CLUB ONE

> *'In the past breathlessness has always been the precursor to an asthma attack. I have to re-educate myself that being breathless can be good.'*

Tracy's dieting history is a cause for concern for the experts when they first meet. As Raj puts it: 'With a BMI of 47, Tracy has to address a major weight problem. She is a repeated and failed dieter, and has never got beyond losing two stone even when she attended an obesity clinic. We have a real worry that she will fail.'

The reality of Fat Club is like a bucket of cold water for Tracy, who veers between an outgoing persona and the very private and anxious child inside. 'It was awful,' she says after the first weekend. 'I felt desperately lonely even though I shouldn't have. There we were in a group, but we were going through our own struggle alone. Then the horror of the weigh-in! I felt sick. When we had to take our clothes off and stand in our bathing costumes in front of the whole production crew, it was so humiliating.'

If for Simon Payne food obsession is the biggest issue, for Tracy it is lack of exercise and there are lessons to be learnt. It does not help that she arrives at the weekend with a torn ligament in her ankle. 'Harvey really makes us work. I haven't exercised since I left school 17 years ago, and at times I feel as if I am going to die, but exercise seems to be the key. I hadn't understood that being out of breath could be because I was exerting myself. In the past it has always been the precursor to an asthma attack. I have to re-educate myself that being breathless can be good.'

The focus of the weekend is taking the members back to basic principles about eating and food, food groups and fat burning. A one-to-one session with Sarah, who has looked carefully at Tracy's pre-Fat Club food diary, proves that she is not taking in sufficient calories. Sarah suggests 1900 calories per day, and recommends that Tracy substitutes her lunchtime bag of crisps and finds a lower-fat alternative to the frequent take-aways.

For Tracy, who has always been a joker, Alex's advice about the power of laughter and humour in the struggle ahead is just confirmation of her own theory that 'Laughter is good for the soul. I don't think I am learning much from this workshop, but for me a lot of Fat Club is about facing my demons: the perception that I will always be a fat person. The facts are there – you cannot get into aeroplane seats or fixed chairs in restaurants; seat belts don't fit. Alex saying you need to have self-esteem is not going to change things overnight.'

By Sunday breakfast Tracy is exhausted and emotional, and takes herself off for a good cry. 'I had no idea what the exercise routines would entail,' she says. 'But I felt obliged to do it. Here is a 55-year-old woman [Sha] and a man of 28 stone [Simon] doing it, and they aren't complaining. It makes me laugh now to think we complained about the 10 p.m. curfew. By 9.30 I am thinking, 'Hell, there's another half an hour to wait till bedtime!" '

But she leaves Fat Club informed and armed. 'I daren't admit it because the experts are such masochists, but I really enjoy the exercise. Fat Club will work for me. I've done it – I've stood on those scales, and it has given me such confidence.'

Since the weekend, Tracy has become something of a lynch pin of the group, firing off encouraging (and sometimes censorious) e-mails to the other members. With her straight talk and intolerant attitude to fools – and perhaps too because she is the biggest of the women – Tracy has become a kind of spokesperson and 'mother' of the group.

FAT CLUB TWO

Date: June
Weight at weigh-in: 19st 6lbs (272lbs)
Weight loss since last weigh-in: 10lbs
Total loss: 10lbs
Waist: 49in

'I've tried to lose weight for the last 11 years, and am asking myself, how can this be different?'

Since the first onerous weekend, Tracy is really making an effort with exercise. The very next morning, a Bank Holiday, she dons a bathing suit and goes for a swim at the public pool on the sea front at Skegness. 'I think that's incredibly brave! Such a step forward.' With her sister, she has jogged around her dad's field every day, and has joined the local gym. The family too are being made to benefit from her new-found vigour. 'Every night now we go out for walks on the beach together. Something we have never done before because I was always out of breath. Now I'm making us all do it.'

Surprisingly, though, Tracy approaches Fat Club Two with reservations. She is struggling with a chest infection, and is taking steroids and antibiotics again. 'I am terrified,' she admits. 'I left Fat Club One on such a high, and we've been on our own since then. My confidence is low. I've tried to lose weight for the last 11 years, and am asking myself, how can this be different?'

Harvey's bag search on arrival is part of the issue for Tracy and she is not slow to tell him so. 'I really don't think this is necessary. I find it offensive that you think I am going to sneak food in,' she says petulantly. Harvey accuses her of having 'a bad hair day' (one of many favourite phrases – with his shaved head, presumably he never has them) and explains 'rules is rules', but Tracy is still put out. 'I find it hard to accept,' she says afterwards, 'especially as I always pack as though I'm staying for two weeks. It seems petty and unnecessary.' Harvey is surprised how quickly Tracy has revealed a negative attitude – what he calls 'running off her mouth a lot' – but he is impressed by her zeal at the early-morning fitness assessment next day. Her run time goes from 3m 59s at the previous weekend to 2m 58s and she manages almost twice as many sit-ups.

Despite this, Saturday morning's weigh-in is the lowest moment of the weekend for Tracy. 'The thought of standing on the scales makes me feel sick again.' But she weighs in at 19st 6lbs, a loss of 10lbs. 'What do I do? I go and cry – because I thought I'd do better!'

At the weighted jacket session, Tracy carries three extra stone. With this additional load to bear, Tracy's pulse rate shoots up to 168 beats per minute: 'It feels terrible – I think I am going to collapse,' but she is bewildered by the strong impact the session has on Donna. 'Somehow the heart-rate message hasn't sunk in. What I am being told doesn't compute.' She is alarmed.

Tracy has admitted that her failure with diets has had a lot to do with self-monitoring. 'I find it difficult because life is busy,' she says, but the experts are emphatic that self-monitoring is one of the fundamental principles behind Fat Club. Once self-monitoring of activity and food intake falter, then commitment slips. Tracy is certain of her commitment thus far, but there is worry among the experts that she is using the chest infection as yet another excuse.

Between weekends, Tracy invites the two Tonys, Sha and Kelly to a get-together on the south coast of women from the Big Beautiful Women website she edits. 'I want to show them that you don't have to shut yourself away just because you are fat. I want to show them too what I did before Fat Club – that these social events were my only chance to go out without there being people pointing the finger and laughing.' Despite what Tony Upson says, for Tracy the event is a success with her new friends, plenty of laughing and drinking, and a midnight dip in the moon-lit waters of Bognor Regis.

FAT CLUB THREE

Date: July
Weight at weigh-in: 18st 7lbs (259lbs)
Weight loss since last weigh-in: 13lbs
Total loss: 23lbs
Waist: 48in

'Harvey's annoying because he's right.'

Fat Club Three is stressful for everyone. The long gap has not helped and, as Harvey warned, the honeymoon has worn off and there is a negative mood among the group. Friday night's bag search irritates them all, but he has a particular barney with Tracy who is loath to surrender her mobile phone when her brother is ill in hospital with suspected meningitis. 'I expected attitude,' he says. 'These people are not used to discipline, but I wasn't expecting it so quick. That's the thing about leadership, though. You have to adjust it as you go along. I have broken them down with the bag search, and now I have to work out how to build them up tomorrow.' To add to the tension, Jacey has failed to arrive.

She is still not there first thing on Saturday morning, but Harvey keeps to his word, and has plenty of encouragement for Tracy's efforts – another 28 seconds off the timed run. He reminds them all to 'put exercise into your daily lives. It's not a chore, it should be a way of life. Stop making excuses.' Incorporating exercise into her life has not been as hard as she imagined, but Tracy still admits ruefully, 'Harvey's annoying because he's right.'

Despite her claim that she is not bothered by the weigh-in, she is still keyed up about it, and sits with her head down awaiting her turn on the scales. But joy! Tracy triumphs with a 12lb weight loss. The overall results, however, are not good. The members try to stick together by cheering even paltry weight losses from Jacey and Kelly, but despite Tracy's initial whine that Raj is unkind to refer to them as 'just' two pounds, sympathy wears off pretty quickly. On reflection, and in her typical candid style, Tracy has little time for injured egos among the group. 'We are all here for one reason only – ourselves, and there is nothing wrong with saying "You've lost just 2lbs." We have to stop pussy-footing around. I regret not doing this years ago. Especially not playing with my son, Eden, because I hadn't got the energy or it involved going to a public place.'

Throughout Saturday, however, Tracy is irritable and at times aggressive. A dance aerobic session with Maggie Paterson from the Pineapple Dance Studio thrills her, but generally spirits are low and in the evening Harvey invites all the members to write down their feelings in 'love letters' to the experts, in which they can air their views about Fat Club anonymously if they chose to – a technique he uses with new recruits in his platoon. Again and again group members complain about the strictness of the rules – discipline does not come easily to any of them – but all agree with Tracy's sentiment that 'the basic messages of Fat Club are so much better than other diets'.

The complaints are taken on board by the experts and production team, and it is decided to abandon the bag searches. Harvey is relieved as he had not enjoyed them, but stresses that 'patience is a virtue, and all the members need a lot of my patience'.

By the end of the weekend moods have improved, and Tracy enthuses about how much she has loved the workshops with Sarah Schenker, especially the cookery challenge, though she is not so appreciative of the taste and texture workshop, in which the members are blindfolded and asked to guess the foods put into their mouths. They try apple and pear, then rice and cold porridge. Tracy has no problem recognising chicken, but then she is offered a sliver of something else. 'It feels disgusting!' It stays in her mouth for just seconds, and when it is revealed it is frog's legs, Tracy goes off to be sick.

Halfway through the six months of Fat Club Tracy is on the cusp of the two-stone barrier she has found so hard to cross in the past. On paper she is doing all the right things: eating a better diet, exercising and growing in confidence, yet she still admits she needs a proverbial kick up the backside to move her on to the next stage. 'Nothing has shocked me yet,' she says disappointedly. 'Everything that has been said to me has sunk in, but nothing has made me sit bolt upright.'

Once back home in Skegness, Tracy is beginning to relish the changes emerging in her body and her confidence. Plans are afoot to go to Disneyland next year as a family, something she has avoided in the past because she dared not get on to the rides in case she did not fit. 'I remember seeing that happen to a woman,' she says, 'and I'm not going to let that happen to me. As for eating in public, I'm still not coping well, but I'm getting there.'

In an e-mail, her favourite form of communication, she notes: 'It may just seem an incredibly trivial thing, but to me it's huge. My ankles – for as long as I can remember I have always suffered from swollen ankles as soon as the weather starts heating up. But now, nothing! I have normal unswollen ankles and it has kept me amused for the last two days. I can't stop looking at them and prodding them and showing them to people. I am tickled pink.'

Another message follows swiftly: 'Another milestone for me today. I wore shorts! In public! I walked into town in them. Big achievement. I felt so comfortable, and the best feeling was that I was *cool*. In years past, I would have overdressed and sweltered in an effort to cover up my body. Not only did I walk into town, I also walked over *two* pelican crossings – something I would never have done before. My attitude in my head must have changed.'

FAT CLUB FOUR

Date: August
Weight at weigh-in: 18st 3lbs (255lbs)
Weight loss since last weigh-in: 4lbs
Total loss: 27lbs
Waist: 45in

> *'I had hoped that something at Fat Club would slap
> me in the face and that did it.'*

Despite her enthusiasm, Tracy approaches Fat Club Four with caution. 'I don't like expectations,' she says, 'in case I fail. But I can't wait to see everyone again, and I'm looking forward to the exercise because I love the dance we did at Fat Club Three. I will miss it when it's all over. It's so intense, but I'll miss meeting up with people. It would be nice to do a non-Fat Club weekend.'

The whole weekend is dramatically more relaxed than the one before, despite growing tension over the uncertainty of Jacey's continued involvement. The members are not surprised when she finally quits, and although she is liked among the group, there is a feeling of irritation that she has given up. 'Lots of people would have given their right arm to be at Fat Club.'

The weigh-in is disappointing for Tracy, but she was fore-warned. 'I knew this time I hadn't done my weight-loss quota, because the nurse at our GP practice has been keeping a note of my weight loss. I was very upset about it, but the 4lb weight loss was backed up by a 3in loss around the waist. I feel guilty because I have been counselling everyone to hit the target.'

The inch loss has been a revelation to her, and deserved after a conscientious three-times-a-week gym session. 'I have been shopping and bought a size 24 skirt with a fixed waist band. I tried it on at home and could have got it on and off without undoing it.' There are other improvements emerging too: 'I haven't used my asthma inhaler for ten days and can wear jewellery I haven't been able to wear before. I'm finding I'm more comfortable, too, and not folding my arms across my stomach like most fat people do. I can't wait to be able to cross my legs!'

The biggest development for Tracy has been the arrival of her first period in six and a half years. It is proof that the weight loss is beginning to reverse the damage of so many years of obesity, and it raises the possibility of another pregnancy. 'Though I want another baby very much,' she says, 'I'm not ready for it yet physically or mentally. I want to be in control.'

Tracy is still looking for the shock tactic, something to give her a jolt, and at this Fat Club she gets it. During a session with Raj, he shows the members 5lb blocks of artificial fat, as close to the real thing as to be virtually indistinguishable. 'I had hoped that something at Fat Club would slap me in the face and that did it,' she says. 'They couldn't have done anything to shock me more. The visuality of it and the fact that it is in your body!' She holds 30lbs of fat, which represents almost the amount she has lost. 'If I am going to be tempted to binge, I just have to think about this great mound of yellow fat.'

For Raj, concerned about the slowdown in her weight loss, the session has the effect he had hoped for. 'I hope this workshop will have shaken her.'

'In fact,' Tracy laughs, 'I'm already getting fat conscious when it comes to food. I keep looking at people and thinking "Why are they buying that?" I'm so afraid I'm going to be anti-fat. I'll want to say, "No, you don't have to look like that." ' Friends have boosted her confidence, one in particular who has told her they see her as an inspiration. 'One woman I know blanked me out in a shop because she didn't recognise me.' Even Tracy's grossly overweight website friend, Tarnya, has started trying to lose

116

weight. 'I think I've played a part,' says Tracy. 'She's seen the change in me.'

The temptation workshop later in the day is proof that the shock tactic has worked for her. Each member has chosen a food that they cannot resist and, as for Donna, for Tracy it is curry. She has no problem throwing it into the clear plastic bin bag on Alex's instructions. 'I know now I would go for a low-fat curry or something home-made. In fact, all those other take-aways we used to have so often have gone out of our lives. Now I'm cooking more than I ever have, and though I'm not a great cook, I'm becoming dead adventurous.' When Alex asks them to hold chocolate in their mouths, however, neither Tracy nor Simon can do it. 'I kept thinking about the fat workshop and the images of fat around the arteries and there was no way that was going in my mouth.'

The changes are not just physical. 'Fat Club has taught me that I've blamed everyone else, but myself, for the last 11 years. I've made excuses such as "I'm on steroids so I can't lose weight." I've been such a bitch. I even said to the production crew right at the beginning, "If I fail it's your fault." But I feel such an idiot now for saying that. The thought of the programme being broadcast has been such a motivation. I'm growing in confidence, but I seek reassurance all the time. If one person says I'm looking much better I need to ask lots of people.'

The group remains cohesive, but there are definite factions emerging, and Tracy, Stuart and Donna are as thick as thieves. 'We are the smokers,' Tracy admits, 'so we nip out for a fag all the time. But we are close. If one of us is low, the other two will lift the other. We are the three musketeers.' It is a closeness which Tracy relishes, and being strong to support others is a role she seems to like to play.

But Tracy's feisty personality continues to present problems and feelings are not so loving between herself and Tony Curley. Tension has been brewing between them since Fat Club Two. Harvey organises a 'slam man' session, in which the members are encouraged to box with a figure as an exercise vehicle, and to imagine it is someone they dislike as they do it. The look on Tracy's face is enough to tell you she is thinking of someone in particular. Matters come to a head on Sunday. There is a disagreement between Tony Curley, who has changed his mind about not wanting to swim because of an infected insect bite, and Harvey who says if Raj says he should not, then he should not. 'He is too competitive for me,' boils Tracy, 'and when he realises it is a relay race in front of the cameras he wants to swim. Tony has stormed off because Harvey has said he can't swim. I think he is just attention-seeking.'

Tracy admits she is tired, snappy and tearful after a physically exhausting weekend, which included a tough drill session, but she tips off the camera crew as she is about to leave for home that she is going to confront Tony. Tempers flare, Tracy behaves aggressively and Tony eventually walks away saying 'You're not worth talking to.' Tracy's parting shot is a below-the-belt personal jibe about Tony's oral hygiene. The incident certainly leaves a nasty taste in the mouth, and may not have endeared her to other members of the group.

Trouble is brewing at home, too, with husband Neil. Though Tracy perceives that she is now less volatile than she was (Tony Curley may not agree), she still cannot admit she looks good and needs her confidence boosting all the time. 'After Fat Club Four, I was modelling a catalogue for an outsize clothes website and we had our make-up done professionally. Neil looked in and said offhandedly, "I don't know what they've done to you." I felt crushed. I did look good but I needed him to say it, as confirmation after years of being downtrodden by society. The comment from those boys in the car still haunts me.

'It has been hard for me coping with the changes,' she continues, 'and I hadn't taken into consideration the impact on Neil's life. He says I am a different woman, and he is not enjoying it. It is insecurity – jealousy in a nutshell. People are starting to pay more notice to me, and that makes him feel insecure. He thinks I'm going to go off. I used to be so dependent on him. I couldn't even wash the pots and pans without sitting down. Now I'm not so dependent and he has to grow with me.'

Neil admits: 'I've found it very difficult. I've been used to the way she is and has always been. She's looking a lot better, but I find it hard to tell her that. It's like having a new wife.' He does concede that being able to go out socially is a positive thing, but

118

is not certain he is enjoying it yet. 'But it's [a question of] getting used to it. Her attitude has changed. She is less gobby and happier. She can be really quiet and less aggressive. And I am learning to compliment her.'

The wider family, however, are delighted by the changes in her. 'My Dad had tried reverse psychology at the beginning – "bet you'll never manage it" – but even he has mentioned the weight loss. I have a picture of me taken some time ago with Dawn French and even I can see the difference from when it was taken to now. That affirmation means a lot to me. I'm a lot happier in myself and really looking forward to the next weekend, but I'm so tired!'

She will not be deterred now she has come this far. 'Food has been the enemy for so many years and now I'm having to eat it. I'm having to start all over again learning how to cook properly. I've always been a meat-and-roast-potato person and lots of puddings, but now I'm steaming or grilling meat and buying lots of fresh fruit and veg, and eating plenty of pasta but without the creamy sauces. Even roast potatoes I do now with Italian spices and garlic and roast them without fat – I just won't eat anything that's more than 5g of fat per 100g.'

A mid-month 'How ya doin'?' call from Harvey also sends her off on a high. 'It has been a one-to-one which I had craved for – he was human and listening to what I was saying. He had lots of guidance but it was the fact that it was a private call without cameras or being recorded. And he was laughing and I'd never even seen him smile before! I have such a lot of respect for him. I am writing him a thank you letter because he has saved my life.'

Harvey is indeed pleased with her progress. 'Tracy is really doing well,' he says, 'and has a good attitude again. She is starting to look more toned as well and will do fine up until the last Fat Club.' He adds that he has not had 'as much mouth from her as I have had in the past'.

In Alex Gardner's opinion, the advantages of Fat Club for Tracy have been enormous, but he feels she has to grow in confidence. 'She is benefiting hugely,' he says, 'but she has an ambivalence with the relationship thing. She needs to learn that people can see she is attractive, regardless of how she looks. It's back to the question of having a good conceit of oneself, so she mustn't regret compliments about her attractiveness. This may stem from previous encounters with exploitative men – she has felt used and vulnerable. When you talk to Tracy she drops her head. I wonder if she is thinking "Are they after something?" Men see fat women as easy meat, and I wonder if she has been manipulated by men in the past. There is still a sad person under there, and she is suffering from a tension between wanting to lose weight and her responsibilities to her outsize website which is not very productive of her attempts to lose weight.

'She has to lose 34 per cent of her body weight to reach BMI 30 by April 2002. After the initial more rapid loss between Fat Clubs One and Three, her rate of loss has stayed constant.'

He also has strong opinions about her temper: 'Her quick wit I feel is sometimes used as a defence. She has a mercurial temper lying just below the surface and is not afraid to vent her opinion. It is clear that on some Fat Club weekends, she has been exercising some degree of control over events and relationships. Her antipathy towards Tony Curley is clear. He represents an easy target for her and I'm sure she is aware of his social vulnerability. The "slam man" session gave her some opportunity of getting rid of some of her feelings. The contorted face while punching out the dummy spoke worlds about her. I asked her later who she was thinking of and with real anger she told me Tony. The later episode where she and Tony had a "shout out" could well have stemmed not only from the bottling up of feelings but that having vented some of her anger she now felt free to go the whole hog and do her own thing.'

FAT CLUB FIVE

Date: Early September
Weight at weigh-in: 18st 4lbs (256lbs)
Weight gain since last weigh-in: 1lb
Total loss: 26lbs
Waist: 44in

'It has all been down to the exercise. It's all about being bothered to get off your arse and do it.'

Meet Tracy after a few weeks' break and the first thing that strikes you is the ease with which she is breathing. Whereas she would once be out of breath after the smallest activity, suddenly she is laughing, 'Inhaler, what inhaler?!' The changes in her body are tangible, and she is excited to report that for the first time in eight years she can wear her wedding ring, and can at last get into a normal bath without a struggle.

She throws herself into the workshops enthusiastically, but all her confidence comes crashing down at the weigh-in, moved by the production crew to Sunday morning. The results justify all Alex and Sarah's concerns about moving the timing. Tracy has gained 1lb, and is now 18st 4lbs. Tearful, she skips breakfast and dashes back to the safety of her room to lick her wounds. 'I feel shocked, even though I expected to gain weight because I'm a pessimist. That way I won't be disappointed. I have no excuses – I've got my food down to a "T" and have upped my exercise, so now I need to go back and redress. I need to know what's gone wrong. I need to ask Harvey. That's who I feel I have let down. All my confidence in the weight loss has gone.'

Harvey, her hero, comes up with the answers. The gym workouts Tracy has been doing at home have been too focused on muscle tone and not enough on fat burning. From a complete low, Tracy manages to pull herself out and enters the spirit of the trampolining workshop with relish. It is as if she is discovering her inner child. 'You'll have to get me off first if you want a go!' she laughs, while showing surprising ability for a novice.

The evening wind-down session is a controversial one, enticingly entitled 'In bed with Raj', in which he hopes to explore the effect of being overweight on sexual relationships. The majority of the group admit relationships are not easy, but on the whole stay quiet. For Tracy, never backward at coming forward, the session is 'fantastic'. 'This is my level! Yes, there are difficulties for overweight people when they have sex – you can't do it in certain positions – and it can make it almost impossible. But there is more than just the physical side – my sex life has changed from a quick fumble with lights off and nightie on, to lights on, nightie off – you name it! I have so much more energy, and it's all about confidence in my body. Before my stomach would lie on the bed when I lay on my back! I have rediscovered my sexuality.'

Tracy leaves the penultimate Fat Club with mixed feelings – devastated that despite all her hard work she has put on a pound, yet reassured by Harvey that she had been approaching her regime at the gym all wrong. 'It meant so much to me to hear from him that I was doing the wrong thing. Harvey doesn't make excuses so I knew he was right.'

During the break between weekends Tracy has arranged a social event for Big Beautiful Women. 'I was one of the smallest there,' she says afterwards, 'and the PVC outfit I wore, which had been made to measure, was loose! People's reaction was strange. They'd say, "You look great, but don't lose any more." Was that a compliment or jealousy?'

This sisterhood of fatties still has a strong hold over her, and Tracy is not convinced she wants to go below 16st (or around size 18), the weight she is comfortable with. The health issues seem secondary to her. 'I don't care what the medics say. I could be fitter than someone lighter than me. I am out of the morbidly obese bracket now, and it has all been down to the exercise. [She reveals that during Fat Club, having never owned a pair before, she has gone through two pairs of trainers.] It's all about being bothered to get off your arse and do it. It's knowing you can do it and not feeling a tit doing it. There is so much more I can do with my life now. I've been stuck at home for too long.'

With a week to go until the last weekend she has been busting a gut to achieve the best possible weight loss. According to the scales at her local medical centre she has shifted 11lbs, a remarkable achievement but hard won. She has been doing two sessions a day in the gym, five days a week. 'I want to make up for the 1lb weight gain and to prove something to myself,' she says to justify it.

The result, though, is a heavy cold and complete exhaustion. 'I really think I might not go this weekend,' she sniffs. 'I feel so lousy and so tired.' Despite the thick head and sniffles, she realises that her body shape has changed remarkably, and she is suffering the dilemma of not being able to wear clothes which now hang off her – 'My old leggings make me look like Nora Batty!' – and not wanting to buy more now because she will be losing still more weight.

Another amazing fact has dawned on her: six months ago, with a cold like this and with her asthma problem, she would have been on steroids. That she is not is proof enough for Tracy that weight loss can bring dramatic health benefits.

FAT CLUB SIX

Date: September
Weight at weigh-in: 17st 6lbs (244lbs)
Weight loss since last weigh-in: 11lbs
Total loss: 37lbs
Waist: 44in

The enormous (and anticipated) 11lb weight loss this month is confirmation, if she needed it, that Tracy's workout routine had been wrong. For Harvey and Raj it is a cause for regret: 'Think how much more weight she could have lost if we had caught on to it earlier.' But despite all that it has had its benefits. She is thrilled that finally she can run the quarter-mile circuit at the assessments without stopping – her goal for the weekend. It is not a part of the weekends she ever enjoyed, but her exercise regime has meant she can do it.

But Tracy is still full of cold, and her attitude this final weekend is not brilliant. The decision by the crew to cancel breakfast on Saturday morning makes her particularly angry, and she enters the yoga workshop in a belligerent frame of mind. From the start she does not take it seriously and giggles with Stuart throughout, like the naughty girl at the back of the maths class. The spirit of yoga is not really up Tracy's street, and afterwards she pulls no punches. 'Geri Halliwell can keep it. I thought it was bollocks,' she says, 'and it has put me right off trying yoga.'

By the time the workshop exploring hunger comes around, Tracy admits to feeling 'tired and shaky'. But Sarah Schenker's message hits home: though hunger is not a bad feeling, it is better to eat something small (banana, piece of toast) to take the edge off it, than wait for a meal and overeat or eat the wrong things. Sort out your hunger and do not overcompensate for it. It is a small detail in the eating message, but an important one. 'I thought Fat Club was all about diet,' is Tracy's response. 'It's so not.'

Her mood is not improved around the camp fire on Saturday evening, when there is a ceremony of awards for the members with nominations by the members. Tracy is voted the Gobbiest Member, the Media Tart and, to her consternation, the Drama Queen. In view of her opinion of Tony Curley, she is incredulous that this last award does not have his name on it.

Sunday morning there is a triathlon set up by Harvey, which involves four small circuits on a bike, a ten-length swim and a run back up to the main house. As the session starts, the members gleefully reveal their Fat Club T-shirts, customised by Tracy and emblazoned with an image of Harvey and his favourite phrase 'Good to Go'. Harvey is overwhelmed. 'It's awesome,' he smiles, 'I knew there would be a love/hate relationship with them all, but I never expected the warmth. I suppose they like me because I have been a catalyst – in the past they have always made life easy for themselves; they have never had anyone make them do something. Plus I'm hard to please!'

However, any feelings of mutual warmth evaporate when Tracy seeks out Raj and Harvey to say her cold is too bad for her to swim, but she will do the rest. She is met by a brick wall. Both men agree that if she can cycle and run, she can swim in a heated pool. It is just another excuse. It has to be all or nothing. For Tracy it is going to be nothing, and she stomps back to her room in a huff.

Tracy is a confusing woman: part of her is very keen to please and seeks attention and affirmation that she is liked. Yet she has attitude. She can be tough, stubborn and difficult (her car number plate bears the warning 'This Bitch Bites'), and she approaches the posture session with ballet instructor Anita Young in the same 'I'm not going to like this' frame of mind. However, Anita, for all her petite frame and delicate features, is man enough for all the group, and by midway through the session has them all eating out of her hand and making an effort with tough exercises and positions to improve posture. Once Tracy has realised resistance is futile, she rises to the occasion and by the end looks taller, leaner, more poised and confident.

The final meeting of the members and experts is an emotional one for Tracy. She has made some strong friendships, and has been in a challenging but essentially supportive environment. She is more in control of what she eats, and her exercise routine has gone from negligible to regular and effective. 'It has been a unique experience,' she says. 'The best of my life – after having a baby – and I stuck at it. I didn't believe enough in myself to think I would. I now put on clothes in my wardrobe without thinking, and wonder why they don't fit. Then I realise it is because I've lost weight – I've gone down 10 dress sizes. I grin and then I cry.'

But this is only the beginning for her. Though Tracy has lost 2st 9lbs in the six months of Fat Club, she has still only just passed the two-stone sticking point she achieved on other weight-loss regimes, though at a slower and hopefully more sustainable rate. Her affirmation that she would rather be 'fit and fat' is a worrying one. Raj points out to her that she has dropped from a BMI of 45 to 39 – at the top end of the obese section of the chart and only a cat's whisker from morbidly obese. 'You have made huge changes,' he concedes, 'and subsequent gains in health terms, but I sense an end-of-term feeling. You have to leave "school" with lessons you have learnt in your head. You will not reach your target weight at this current weight loss until April 2002. It's up to you to maintain it.'

Thrilled with her new shape, Tracy leaves the last Fat Club and promptly goes off to have her belly button pierced. She then goes shopping and has to try on two shirts sized 22 to make sure she has not made some mistake. To cap it all, she buys herself new knickers, size 18–20. 'Size 18! Can you imagine!' Tracy agrees with Raj's final comments: 'I do have a long way to go but I'm

Chapter 7

Tony Curley's Story

'When I look in the mirror, I don't see me – I just see something totally gross. I hate my body.'

Tony Curley
Age: 40
Lives: Southampton
Occupation: Fork-lift truck driver
Height: 5ft 8in
Weight at first weigh-in: 21st 12lbs – morbidly obese
Waist at first weigh-in: 58in

Tony Curley's weight is ruining his life and threatening his health. At 21st 12lbs he is classified as morbidly obese. But he has not always been this way. Until 1989, only 12 years ago, he was a fit, active man and a slim 11st.

A highly sensitive, emotional person, Tony was brought up by his mother and grandparents. He never knew his father, and soon learnt not to raise the subject with his mother. When he was 24, she died and, with no other ties to his native Scotland, Tony left to go and live in Southampton. With family links gone and friends far away, he started comfort eating, gave up playing football and stopped going out. His body weight slowly doubled.

'There isn't a single area of my life that isn't affected. I can't find clothes to fit me and my confidence is at rock bottom. I can't even bear to go out to the pub any more. I feel that everyone is thinking "Look at that fat bastard." '

In a one-to-one situation Tony is engaging, honest and funny, often making preemptive jokes about his size and his propensity for taking the car to the corner shop, but his acute sensitivity makes larger gatherings painful, and he is very afraid of rejection. 'I'd love to get married and have kids, but I would never approach a woman. Who would be interested in me, looking the way I do?'

Despite this self-hatred, Tony can be an extrovert, but only in situations where he feels in control of the joke. He is a member of the local amateur dramatics society, and does not mind playing 'fat' characters, such as the pantomime dame or the ugly sister, on stage. But recently he has turned down more serious roles. 'I just won't do it. I know I'd look ridiculous as myself on stage next to slim people.'

'I feel trapped in my body. At the moment I'd kill to lose weight.'

Fresh in his mind are a number of unbearably painful situations that have scarred him deeply. 'Once I went out to Kentucky Fried Chicken for a family bucket to share with some mates who were coming over to watch football on the TV. The bloke behind the counter could see I was on my own, but he asked if I was eating in. I couldn't believe it – he must have assumed I was buying it all for myself. I felt totally humiliated. When he looked at me he just saw a fat bloke.'

When challenged, Tony can see that his reaction was probably not justified; people working in fast-food restaurants follow a formula in the questions they ask, but the hurt is real and he maintains that only other people with weight problems would understand how bad it made him feel.

On another occasion he had a job interview that went disastrously wrong. 'One minute I was chatting away, the next I was staring at the ceiling. The chair had given way underneath me.' He shakes his head at the memory, the embarrassment still all too vivid for him. Then the sense of self-irony takes over again, 'I didn't get the job.'

At work, Tony's weight is also causing problems. He has had quite a series of jobs, including fork-lift driving and HGV driving and a period as a security guard, but anything that involves lifting is getting difficult for him and he has to ask for help. His joints have

The experts met to discuss the members at the beginning and end of each Fat Club.

Top: Harvey Walden and Sarah Schenker; *middle* (centre) Professor Alex Gardner and (right) Dr Raj Patel.

In the beginning...
Fat Club, May 2001.
Clockwise from top:
Simon Payne and Jacey
Eze; Jacquie Marsh and
Tony Upson; Tony
Curley; Kelly Mundy;
Donna Norris; Tracy
Young; Stuart Gibbons
and Sha Wylie

Harvey's dreaded fitness assessment... *Top*: the members get to work with their sit-ups. *Bottom*: Tony Upson and Sha take a breather.

Above: Sha, a former marathon runner, would now like to speed-walk the marathon.

Above right and below: Kelly and *centre right* Jacquie work out their aggression on the slam man.

Above left: by Fat Club Six, Tracy had increased her sit-ups by 23.

Right: the boys feel the burn.

Fat Club Six,
September 2001. Over
22 stone has been lost,
and it shows!

Fat Club Six.
Left to right from the back: Stuart Gibbons, Tony Curley, Simon Payne, Tony Upson, Jacquie Marsh, Tracy Young, Sha Wylie and Donna Norris.

begun to ache, and his doctor has made sure he is aware of the many other health risks of obesity.

'I know I should change my lifestyle,' he says. 'I want to, but I feel as if I've hit a wall. I just don't know where to start to make my life better.'

'Life begins at forty, they say – and I want a new life!'

Tony answered an advert about Fat Club for a number of reasons. With his 40th birthday approaching, he wants to arrange a party, but feels he would have to look and feel better about himself before he can. But there is another, deeper reason and one that has been on Tony's mind for around three years. His uncle has bumped into Tony's father and he has been asking after him.

Suddenly, the missing piece from the jigsaw of his life is within reach. 'I really want to make contact with my dad, to go and meet him, but I'm not going to do it until I've lost weight. I want my dad to be proud of me, but I can't go looking the way I do. He's been married and has other children. I could even have a new family waiting for me – but my weight is stopping me from contacting them. It's exciting, yes, but at the same time I'm frightened of being rejected.'

It was Tony's flatmate, Roy, who first heard about Fat Club. 'He was reading the local paper in the next room. Suddenly, the door burst open and he was there, waving the paper. "You've got to apply for this. I think you'd be bloody good." So I phoned up and left a message. I went through the selection process and I was first standby. Someone dropped out at the last minute and I was in. That made me more determined to succeed.'

FAT CLUB ONE

'I deliberately put myself in a situation where failure was not an option.'

For Tony the overwhelming emotion of this first weekend is the happiness he experiences on meeting the other nine members. 'The way we've gelled in such a short period has been the highlight for me,' he gushes. 'I hope we'll be friends for life.' The worst part is the weigh-in.

A difficult moment for everyone, it is particularly tough for Tony. As a long-term psoriasis sufferer, the idea of disrobing in front of a roomful of people and a TV audience is frankly terrifying. 'I was the first to be weighed. I just gritted my teeth. I saw it as something I had to do for other people like me, for psoriasis sufferers. It was very emotional, but the support from the rest of the team was incredible. It just lifted me up.'

The other members break into spontaneous cheers as Tony steps on to the scales, and for Alex Gardner, it is the moment the members bond into a team. He says later, 'I felt the hairs on the back of my neck go up – it was a special moment for me. It welded the group and says a lot about the people selected.'

Harvey's first exercise assessment, involving sit-ups and press-ups on the lawn, is very revealing to this self-confessed couch potato. 'It has hammered home how bad we are when we have to do exercise. I was getting severe stomach cramps and told Harvey so. All he said was, "That sounds like a personal problem – get on with it." I couldn't believe it, but I pushed myself and carried on. I was feeling really angry with Harvey, but then he came up to me afterwards and asked if I was drinking enough water. That's typical of him – he really has our interests at heart.'

As he leaves Fat Club, Tony is buoyed up by the feeling of support between members. 'It's amazing!' he enthuses. 'We've really connected, we can all understand how each other feels. I don't think anyone could unless they've been fat.' Tony throws himself into his new lifestyle with a vengeance. His driving force seems to be a surprisingly competitive nature – something which will later bring him into conflict with some other members of the group – but it has already started working to his advantage.

'I wasn't exercising at all before. I didn't have the will-power or the motivation. What's pushing me on is the thought of Harvey taking us on a quarter-mile run at the assessment. Next time I'm going to beat my time of 2 minutes 31 seconds. I've joined a gym, and sometimes I'm in a little bit of pain, but I make myself go on. Before, if something hurt, I'd stop straight away, and even go to the doctor. To tell you the truth, I was a hypochondriac.

Everything that was wrong with me was weight-related. The medical tests Raj did have all proved that I'm healthy, just fat, so I'm happy to push myself now.'

The competitive streak could easily have landed him in trouble. Ignoring Harvey's advice that he should start with a half-hour gym session three times a week and build on that as fitness improves, Tony cannot resist going one better: 'It doesn't seem worthwhile so I'm going for an hour each time,' he says. Luckily for him he avoids injury.

Tony is not so confident when it comes to changing his eating habits, and he raises an interesting issue: 'They gave us a packed lunch, with a bagel and low-fat cream cheese, to take away with us on Sunday. Well, that was it. That's all I ate for the next week – bagels every day – and I think a few others have done the same too.' He puts his finger on it: 'We're so terrified of food and so unconfident about choosing the right foods. I think it'll take a while before I start to relax.'

Tony does not take long to get into the swing of low-calorie eating and again exceeds his remit. The calorie target given to him by Sarah over the weekend is 2500 a day for the first month, but he soon finds he cannot even get as far as 2000 without feeling uncomfortably full. He phones the experts for advice on this – the first of many calls to them and the production team – but Sarah explains to him that, provided he is not hungry, he should be doing fine. 'I don't think anything serious is worrying him,' she says. 'He just needs a lot of reassurance and a pat on the back.'

It is ironic that he should worry about his calorie intake, because Sarah firmly believes he was faking his pre-Fat Club food diary, his calorie intake was so low.

FAT CLUB TWO

Date: June
Weight at weigh-in: 20st 11lbs (291lbs)
Weigh loss since last weigh-in: 15lbs
Total loss: 15lbs
Waist: 54in

'Like it or lump it, Harvey's the man!'

Tony already seems more confident when he arrives. As before, the weigh-in is difficult for him because of his psoriasis. This time, though, it is definitely worth the stress of taking off his robe. He's lost 15lbs and is clearly delighted. He punches the air, 'Yessss!' But a fly lands in the ointment: Tony Upson beats him by a couple of pounds. Tony is determined it will not happen again. 'About 10 to 15 years ago, I was the weight I want to be now. I'd really like to be the weight Stuart is – just over 17st – by the end of this. That would be great for me at my height. I want it, sure, but I needed medical pressure to make me achieve it.'

The exercise sessions with Harvey are less scary for Tony this time. He shaves around 20 seconds off his running time and almost quadruples the number of press-ups he can manage. 'The first weekend we all bonded and united against Harvey. His attitude was that we are obviously very sad people. But I'm starting to see that exercise is the key to this and, like it or lump it, Harvey's the man. It gave me so much confidence, pushing myself that first time. I did more than I thought I could, and I've been building on that ever since.

'This time, I've managed the quarter-mile run in 2min 10s, so I've really shown Harvey. Give him his due, though, he's made the exercise more fun this time, and he commended us for how much we'd achieved in the four weeks. That's quite something, getting praise out of him, but I still don't think he understands our apprehension.'

After lunch Alex runs a body image workshop for the members, asking them to recall a moment that affected their self-esteem disastrously. Tony squirms with embarrassment. 'Once I went to the fair with my godson, Danny, and some friends. I was having a great time, then on one ride the safety barrier wouldn't fit over my stomach. The other people on the ride noticed and began laughing and humiliating me in front of everyone. The bloke in charge shouted, "Oi! You're too fat for that. Out!" I just wanted to die.'

After the revelations Alex produces a mirror that can be adjusted to show a distorted image, either thinner or fatter than reality. Everyone finds it difficult to look at themselves but, interestingly, all the members imagine they are fatter than they really are, and adjust the mirror to show a larger version of themselves. The fact that they are carrying around a distorted self-image shocks them all.

For all the positive dimensions of Fat Club, there is growing dissension in the ranks and Tony is one of the more vociferous complainers, at worst fuelling others' grievances. The bag search particularly annoys him and he is quick to show it. 'They're treating us like children,' he complains. 'I accept that there have got to be rules, but … no!'

Despite their shared dissatisfaction, by Sunday evening it is clear that the members have split into factions. This is disappointing for Tony who has thrived on the cohesion of the whole group and was eagerly anticipating the reunion. Suddenly everything is no longer as rosy and on reflection he is less enthusiastic about some of his fellow members. 'I'm a bit disappointed this time. I don't know what I was expecting, but it's been a bit of an anti-climax.'

During the next few weeks Tony buries his disillusionment, and his competitive streak fuels him to make a great effort. Tony Upson has become his yardstick and his determination is to beat his weight loss next time; he even admits to being competitive with himself over his calorie intake. Despite being set a target of 2000 calories a day, he still maintains that his highest intake over the last few weeks has been a disturbingly accurate 1667. 'Tracy was shocked because I'd eaten Kentucky Fried Chicken,' he reports, 'but I fitted it into my calorie count. I eat a lot of turkey, chicken, lean ham and venison burgers. What I don't want to see again though is another bagel – not ever! I went through a stage of eating lots of crackers, but I'm experimenting all the time, and I eat heaps of salad.'

His weakness in the past has been biscuits, but even these he has controlled: 'I only eat low-calorie ones now, and I'm delighted that Sarah has told us Jaffa cakes are lower in calories than chocolate digestives! I don't fry anything, I use a steamer, grill, or the microwave. I've also discovered Tesco's less than 3 per cent oven chips. Basically, anything I feel deprived of, I've found something else to replace it.'

FAT CLUB THREE

Date: June
Weight at weigh-in: 19st 6lbs (272 lbs)
Weight loss since last weigh-in: 19lbs

Total loss: 34lbs
Waist: 50in

> *'Determination – it's the new weapon in my armoury.*
> *I've been given the chance of a new life.'*

The seven-week gap between Fat Clubs is a long time for the fledgling group, but Tony's resolve has not wavered. 'I've proved I'm getting fitter,' he reports, pleased as Punch, 'and I'm getting into trousers I haven't worn for four or five years, so I must be doing something right.'

Tony is visibly thinner when he arrives for the weekend, and though he says he has not weighed himself, he hopes he has lost seven pounds at least. He must know it's more. In fact it is a lot more, and when the weigh-in reveals a staggering 19lb loss, he looks as amazed as everyone else. He has turned the tables on Tony Upson, and looks pretty pleased about it.

The change in his lifestyle is really showing results. 'I've taken everything and changed it. I feel like I'm moving into a new phase: my confidence is coming back and I'm feeling much fitter. I'm not finding it hard at all to stick to this. Roy, my flatmate, is shocked at how enthusiastic I am and how much I'm enjoying diet and exercise. I'm getting more confident with my eating, too, cooking more for myself and eating more fish, which is good for my psoriasis. I'm also eating more fruit than I've ever done. I think I've really got the message that none of us is on a diet – we're getting to know food and getting to know ourselves with food. For example, I went out with some friends, and I asked for seafood salad without dressing. It was really good. There's always something you can eat on the menu.'

Tony's new interest in food and cooking stands him in good stead at the Sunday cooking challenge. Sarah divides the members into three groups and gives them a selection of ingredients from which to make a tasty, healthy, low-fat course for a meal. Tony's team concoct a tempting summer pudding, which Sarah declares to be 'just about perfect', knocking spots off filo pastry parcels as a starter and stir-fry main course. It is a fun session and interesting, too, but some members are beginning to be irritated by Tony's evident pleasure at his continuing success. There are some barbed remarks, especially from Tracy's corner, and the atmosphere is tense.

The aerobics session is another high point for Tony. With high-energy music reverberating around the courtyard, the members are put through their paces by Maggie Paterson from Pineapple Dance Studio, and Tony is one of the members who takes to this form of exercise like a duck to water. It comes as no surprise to learn that he does aerobics at home. 'I love dancing and jumping around. To me, this is fun and if it's good for me too, that's even better.'

Despite his success, both in terms of weight loss and in his fitness assessment, which continues to show steady improvement, Tony suddenly claims he is gripped by a fear that he will not be able to sustain his effort, and reacts very emotionally, rushing out of breakfast in tears. This is construed by Tracy as insincerity. She explains: 'I was talking to Kelly and also trying to have two other conversations with the dinner ladies. Tony was trying to talk to me at the same time, and got in a strop because I didn't acknowledge him. He said he was fed up of being ignored, threw his banana skin across the table and stormed out. Then when no one came to talk to him he came back.' She makes no effort to conceal her growing hostility and resentment towards him. An already tense weekend ends on a sour note.

After the weekend Tony is thoughtful, perhaps because he has seen Kelly and Jacey floundering. 'I know I'm going to hit a barrier sooner or later; I hope I'll just tell myself to get on with it.' He carries on his good work with diet and exercise, incorporating long walks as often as he can. 'Determination is a new weapon in my armoury, and it's giving me the chance of a new life. I'm starting to love my body now – that's something totally new for me.'

FAT CLUB FOUR

Date: August
Weight at weigh-in: 18st 10lbs (262lbs)
Weight loss since last weigh-in: 10lbs
Total loss: 44lbs
Waist: 47in

'My confidence in myself has pulled me through. If that had happened in the first week, I wouldn't have gone back.'

Tony is feeling out of sorts at the start of what turns out to be the unhappiest weekend of all. 'I'm feeling uncomfortable in this heat,' he admits, 'and I've got a lump of fatty tissue on my heel that hurts when I exercise.'

The weigh-in is particularly memorable for Jacey's complete failure, but two other members lose only 2lbs and a stiff pep talk from the experts makes everyone feel downhearted.

Tony still fears his resolve may slip, but Raj's artificial fat session helps. 'The fake fat is horrible, quite gross. I feel disgusted. I have to get rid of that from my body, and there's no way I'm going to let it go back on. In a way, it has increased my resolve more than all the things Raj said. I know he's right, but seeing that stuff has had far more of an effect on me.'

That evening, supper is a barbecue and everyone has a good time. The surprise element is the return of a pair of salsa dancers who had led the group in a dance exercise session during the afternoon. Within minutes they have everyone up on the floor dancing, not least Tony who is in his element. 'I enjoy all forms of dancing and I just went for it. Kelly and I both took to it really quickly, but she's got a good sense of rhythm too. People don't realise dancing is so energetic and so good for you. It can certainly be a fat-burning activity.'

The weekend turns nasty, however, when Tony, at first advised by Raj not to swim after complaining about an infected mosquito bite, changes his mind when he sees it involves a relay race. Harvey sticks to his guns that Tony must do as Raj has suggested, and Tony storms off irritated. This behaviour irks Tracy and she is building up a head of steam.

As everyone is leaving for home on Sunday afternoon, suddenly Tony sees Tracy hove into view, accompanied by her posse and a film crew she has summoned. She proceeds to launch into a character assassination with accusations of his over-competitiveness and attention-seeking behaviour and, oh the irony, criticism of how he plays up to the camera. With the bit between her teeth she oversteps the mark, making some spiteful personal remarks, implying (untruthfully) that everyone else in the group agrees with her.

With an outwardly nonchalant 'You're not worth arguing with,' he walks away. But he is devastated, and flees to his room in tears. As if to confirm how far off beam Tracy is, Jacquie is there for him, helping him put the pieces back together again. It is clear that Tracy has opened up some old wounds and Tony reveals the depth of his insecurity: 'I've been fooled so many times before, by people saying they like me then letting me down.'

No wonder Alex is concerned about what might happen as a result of Tony contacting his father. Another rejection, coming on top of Tracy's attack, could be devastating. Alex phones Tony and they talk it through. 'Immediately after the confrontation with Tracy, Tony felt alone, experiencing anger and rejection. I've asked him to consider if these were familiar feelings from the past in relation to his mother dying when he was so young. He agrees that this is possible, and said he felt better when the other members came to his room and reassured him. We talked about this situation as a type of rehearsal for the meeting with his father and how he could control his feelings and stay calm and collected. I explained that the past still had an effect on him and that there was now an opportunity to get rid of some of the baggage he has held for 35 years. Tony wants to rush up to Scotland to set the search for his father more firmly in place. I've advised him to consider if he is really ready for this, both physically and psycho- logically. I hope he waits a bit. In my view, it would be an error for him to do this now.'

After a few days Tony starts to feel better and begins to ration- alise the incident. 'I think Tracy has big problems and she vented them on me, and did it in front of the cameras because she's look- ing for attention. Loads of other people, then and afterwards, told me they thought she was out of order, that I should just ignore her, that she was trying to bait me. I wasn't going to go back at first, but why should I let her spoil it for me? My confidence in myself has pulled me through. If that had happened in the first week, I wouldn't have gone back.'

In the following weeks work, exercise, healthy eating and Tracy dwindle into insignificance compared with the latest development in Tony's life. Even the fact that he has bought his first pair of jeans (size 44) for years cannot compare.

For the first time in his life, he is going to meet his dad. After an exchange of letters with a half-brother, Tony gets a surprise. 'I was out shopping, and got a call on my mobile. When I said, "Who's speaking?" a voice replied, "Tony, I'm your dad." ' Forty years of Tony's life begin to fall into place, as father and son talk for an hour and a half. 'As soon as I spoke to my dad I had a bounce in my step. I felt six feet tall.'

They arrange for Tony to go up for a visit as soon as possible, and the meeting goes better than he had ever dreamed. 'I stayed with him for two entire days. I can't believe how much I look like him – though he's not fat. In fact he's pretty lean and he's got a good head of hair – that was something I'd always wondered about because I have quite a lot myself. I hope he's going to come down to my birthday party, but I'm not getting my hopes up too high. Whether he comes or not, I've had an early birthday present.'

The encounter has had a positive effect all round, and puts the Tracy incident in the shade. 'I'm feeling a lot healthier – even the psoriasis has calmed down, and I'm really looking forward to the next Fat Club. I've taken bits of information from everyone, and I feel much better informed now than before. I'm fitting in exercise everywhere, even deliberately parking as far away from the super-market door as possible.'

FAT CLUB FIVE

Date: Early September
Weight at weigh-in: 18st 3lbs (255lbs)
Weight loss since last weigh-in: 7lbs
Total loss: 51lbs
Waist: 47in

> *'I'm chuffed to bits that I've lost the most so far. I suppose it's a race with myself, to be the best I can be.'*

Tony arrives at Gorse Hill still buoyed up by the excitement of meeting his father. He is encouraged too by the support he received from the other members in the aftermath of Tracy's attack on him, and it has helped him overcome the feelings of rejection and vulnerability that she still seems intent on exploiting. Although he has eaten more than he usually would and certainly had more to drink, as champagne corks were popped and toasts proposed, he has made the effort to control his calories, and feels fairly confident.

Alex's responsibility workshop raises interesting questions. 'What has made you successful?' elicits the answer from Tony, 'I can go to the gym now,' an indication of the importance he and most of the other members attach to exercise. When Alex points out that fat people avoid taking exercise because of what others think, it strikes a chord with Tony. 'I've wanted to go swimming for a long time, but I've always been too inhibited. Now I think, "Why should I not do this when I want to?" I've got so much more confidence. Maybe people glance at me, but it's just as they would at anyone. Nobody is looking at *me*. I don't know if they ever were.' Compared to his pre-Fat Club sensitivity, when imagined slights would hurt him, throwing him off balance for days on end and leading to a cycle of self-disgust and comfort eating, this is major progress.

Tony has one of the few successful weigh-ins this time, although for him losing 7lbs is a poorer result than usual. The irony is that he is the only person to have objected strongly to the production team's decision to delay the weigh-in until Sunday. 'I eat more here than I ever do at home,' he says. 'I know I'd have weighed less if I'd been weighed yesterday.' Even though he achieves the highest weight loss this week, Tony still seems disappointed that he has not been able to do his best. 'I'm pleased for myself,' he says. 'But I feel a hollow for the rest. I'm a little bit embarrassed by my success, to tell you the truth. I know it's not a race, but I'm chuffed to bits that I've lost the most so far. I suppose it's a race with myself, to be the best I can be.'

Tony would probably be even more chuffed if he realised that Sarah is citing him as an example of a success story at the experts' meeting. Discussing the poor performance by the rest of the members at the weigh-in, Sarah says, 'Tony Curley has shown consistency – what's wrong with the rest of them?' She's suspicious about the behaviour of the other members: 'Stuart and Tony are the only ones leading normal lives, and the only ones not living on soup to lose weight before they come here.'

Like several of the other members, Tony seems to rediscover his inner child at the trampolining session in the afternoon. Delighted at the feeling of freedom, he cannot resist trying to do more than the instructor tells him to – and falls over several times. 'I never would have tried this before, but it's fun. I'm finding it hard to co-ordinate, but – what the hell – it's a laugh, isn't it?' It is a feel-good moment for many of the members and most have more than one go, determined to master it if they can. But later in the afternoon things get more difficult.

At the see yourself slim workshop, Tony is horrified by the picture taken at the first weekend. 'I look like Jabba the Hutt,' he says. 'It hurts. I looked really hideous, and I can't believe I was doing that to myself. I was behaving like an idiot.' He does not even want to hold the picture when he is presented with a copy. Alex explains the point of the exercise: 'You might feel anger, disgust, shame and guilt, but you can dismiss that past. Get rid of it, throw it away. Tear it up. If you really want to change, you're going to have to forgive yourselves.' With a flick of a switch, Alex projects the slimmed-down images. Tony's looks great, and he is on his way to achieving the body he sees on the screen. Alex drives the message home. 'It's easy to say you'll change, but from evidence in the past, you've all been failures. You've got to internalise the message, and those who have will have to help those who haven't.'

FAT CLUB SIX

Date: September
Weight at weigh-in: 17st 8lbs (246lbs)
Weight loss since last weigh-in: 9lbs
Total loss: 60lbs
Waist: 46in

'I feel I'm only halfway.'

Tony has turned 40 and, three and a half stone lighter, he has achieved his ambition to weigh less and be healthier by the time of his party. A resounding success by anyone's standards and he even wears a suit he has not been able to get into since 1996. The icing on the cake has been the presence of his dad, the guest of honour among 70 friends who gather to celebrate.

Afterwards there is the inevitable strong sense of anti-climax. It was a big event for him, and now he is tired. 'I'm feeling a bit down at the moment,' he confesses. 'It's been a hell of a month for me. I'm mentally shattered.'

For this last weekend the experts asked the members to set their own targets for weight loss and Tony has agreed to lose 7lb. With vouchers given to him for his birthday, he has bought some clothes and had a detoxifying wrap at a local beautician. 'It was a horrible feeling. They cover you all over in seaweed paste, wrap you in bandages and put you in a big waterproof suit. It's not something I'll be doing again in a hurry!'

At Fat Club, things start as they usually do with a fitness assessment and weigh-in. In the fitness, he excels himself by managing 120 press-ups. At the weigh-in, he exceeds his goal and loses 9lbs, but there's a surprise: Simon has made a gargantuan last-ditch effort and has beaten Tony in the total weight lost during Fat Club by just one pound. Tony has lost 60lbs, Simon 61lbs.

It must be a disappointment for Tony, who has been comfortably in the lead since Fat Club Three. A further unwelcome surprise awaits him. After the morning fitness assessment and weigh-in, breakfast does not appear. Instead, the members are sent down to the gym for a yoga session. Tony is very tense at missing a meal, and it transpires that, in his desperation to meet his target, he has not eaten since four o'clock the previous afternoon, an omission he puts down to being too busy. No wonder he is feeling uncomfortable. 'I just think this is totally unnecessary, missing meals is bad for you,' he fumes, the irony escaping him. 'They're treating us like children. There's no point to this at all.'

But he is wrong. The hunger workshop is intended to remind members of what a primitive and all-consuming imperative hunger is. Sarah warns them against skipping meals for this very reason. 'If you allow yourself to get really hungry, that's when you're going to find yourself in danger of reaching for a high-calorie snack. There's no need to ever get really hungry. If you're eating healthily, balancing calories in against calories out, you should never starve yourselves. Enjoy food. You can't get on with your life if you're not satisfying your hunger.'

Maybe it is low blood sugar, but Tony still does not get the message and continues to complain. He cheers up after lunch, though, thereby neatly proving Sarah's point.

At the camp fire session on Saturday night, the members give out awards to each other, nominated by themselves in secret. Tony is voted Most Dedicated Follower of Fat Club and is pleased, despite some sniping comments from Tracy. He seems content, confident and ready to move on from Fat Club.

He has come such a long way since the first Fat Club weekend and has changed so many things in his life that he is almost unrecognisable. 'I am pleased with what I've achieved but I feel I'm only halfway,' he says. 'The great thing is I do feel in A1 condition. I'm going to keep going with this till my body says enough, and I know I can. I know how to lose weight and keep it off. It's so simple, that's what's frightening, but so many people aren't doing it. I was just the same, but now I've got the exercise habit because I know I'm not going to kill myself by doing it. Something great happened the other day. At the gym I go to they've asked me to be Member of the Month, because I've done so well. I'll have my picture up on the wall and everything.'

Raj: 'Tony is a great Fat Club success. He has shown great commitment to making a lifestyle change. Let's hope he keeps going.'

Tony's Fitness Assessment

Fat Club 1

Run	Sit-ups	Press-ups
2.31	20	10

Fat Club 6

Run	Sit-ups	Press-ups
1.29	55	120

Chapter 8

Sha's Story

'I need to keep working, so I need my health. It's as simple as that.'

Sha Wylie
Age: 55
Lives: Southampton
Occupation: Foster parent
Height: 5ft 2in
Weight at first weigh-in: 14st 21lbs – obese
Waist at first weigh-in: 44½in

Sha is the oldest Fat Club member, and her motivation is somewhat different from that of the others. Following her divorce, her financial state is rocky and she has no pension. As she puts it, 'I need to keep working, so I need my health. It's as simple as that.'

An immensely likeable woman, Sha is warm, direct, sympathetic and funny, with an air of composure and social ease. There are no histrionics with her – indeed, it takes a little persistence to get her to talk about herself at all – and she skilfully deflects questions she does not want to answer. She is modest to a fault and her quiet air of serenity is deceptive. Sha dismisses her considerable academic and professional achievements with an eloquent wave of her hand, and is deeply insecure about her appearance.

'I never had a weight problem until I was 17, when I developed thyrotoxicosis [overactive thyroid]. It's a condition that makes most people lose a lot of weight and become very thin, but

I got fat so it went undiagnosed for a long time. Eventually, I became dreadfully ill with it – my feet and legs used to swell up, I couldn't hold a cup because my hands were shaking so much. I was so exhausted, I had to drag myself upstairs using the banisters. I was finally treated at St Thomas's Hospital where, luckily for me, they were experimenting with non-surgical methods. I took drugs for years to control it.' With an entirely characteristic lack of self-pity, Sha muses, 'I later learned that thyrotoxicosis can be caused by trauma, and there were some problems in my family at that time – I've often wondered if it was connected in some way.'

When Sha was pregnant with her son Damien, her thyroid problems occurred again, but she could not take medication in the latter stages of the pregnancy because of possible side-effects for the baby. 'I'd always been about 8st 2lbs until then and looking back on it now, I didn't get all that big – I went up to about 11st during the pregnancy. Once Damien was born, it cleared up completely.'

'I had a Fat and Forty birthday party and I thought to myself, "That's enough." '

By the time she was in her late 30s, Sha's weight had gradually risen to about 16st. 'It was a very unhappy period in my life, and I wasn't caring for myself – the weight gain was quite deliberate, in a way. I was stuffing myself, looking for food to make up for things in my life that weren't going right. I had a Fat and Forty birthday party and I thought to myself, "That's enough." I got together with a group of women in the area and started running. I had asthma when I started. I'd had it for years – it came on when I was first pregnant – but as I got fitter, it went away completely.' She caught the exercise bug in a big way and started training for the London marathon. 'I ran several half and full marathons in the end, and did it really seriously for about eight years, but then I just lost the urge – I don't really know why.'

Sha's training weight was 11st, and she felt great at that level, but she gave up running around the time her troubled 28-year marriage finally ended. Her weight crept up to about 14st again and, despite having run a successful industrial painting business with her husband for years, she found herself with no pension and very little capital of her own.

Her circumstances changed dramatically. She left the marital home, moved into a small, shared house and had to forge a new career for herself. As the Fat Club psychometric testing revealed, she is a self-starter, and never more so than when she was up against it. 'I've always worked and I've always wanted to. I worked with my husband for about 20 years (although he always thought I played at everything), I've taught English as a foreign language, I was even involved in promoting store cards when they first came out – I was very good at that.'

While she was married, she took a Russian O-level course, followed it with the A-level, then completed a four-year Russian degree at Portsmouth Polytechnic and took an MA in health education. 'I know it seems a bit of a change of direction, and some people couldn't see the logic of what I was doing, but I somehow knew it would work out.' It was to this qualification that she turned for a career.

For several years she worked in the field of health promotion and in helping disaffected young people. Sha has three children of her own, aged 32, 30 and 28, to whom she is very close, and for the last five years she has been using her skills by fostering. 'I felt frustrated when I could do so little to help troubled young people because of the legislative limitations of my job. Fostering is a way to make a real difference.'

She now cares for a 13-year-old, Liam, and will be taking on another foster child in the next few months. 'Teenagers have such a lot of energy, and I need to lose weight so I can give them the attention they deserve. I reckon about 10st would be right for me.'

Sha read about Fat Club in a local free newspaper. 'It was just two tiny lines saying that a TV company was looking for people wanting to lose weight. I felt I needed something radical to get me going, so I phoned up, had a chat, and one thing led to another.'

In the course of the initial Fat Club health check – essential to eliminate any medical reason for the interviewees' weight gain – Raj spotted that Sha's blood pressure was very high, at a level that would require medication were she not about to embark on a weight-loss programme. 'This is a very common risk associated with being overweight,' says Raj. 'Sha is concerned about it and it's an added incentive for her to lose weight. We've agreed to keep a close eye on it, and to see if it improves as the weeks go by. I often find that a specific, weight-related condition is a real motivation for losing weight. If only people could be motivated enough to prevent it happening in the first place!'

FAT CLUB ONE

'I thought I'd die fat.'

Sarah's assessment of Sha is that she is another failed dieter. 'Exercise isn't a part of her life any more and she has plenty of excuses to justify it. I think she's deflecting the blame. She'll have to accept responsibility herself if she wants to succeed.' Raj counters that: 'I'm certain losing weight will improve her high blood pressure. That came as a shock to her, and she is now desperate to lose weight.'

Sha approaches the first Fat Club weekend with her customary intellectual rigour and some brisk pragmatism. 'I feel I know most of what the experts are going to tell us. I suspect most of the other members do too – we've all been trying to lose weight for so long – but having the resources of so many experts is a marvellous opportunity. It will certainly help me to get going. I feel it's like a career move coming to Fat Club.'

With a mischievous twinkle in her eye, she admits, however, 'I've been eating more in the last week before coming here – call it Custer's last stand, if you like!'

Although she enjoys meeting the other members, she is a naturally reserved woman, and is rather quiet at the first weekend. There are no major revelations; she simply gets on with what she has to do, stands back, observes and listens to the experts' advice, especially pointers about diet from Sarah. 'I feel fairly confident about the food side of things. I know what to eat and what not to eat – I'm virtually vegetarian anyway – but it's

146

getting back to the exercise that's the key for me, I think. That's where I'll need help.'

The session with Harvey does not faze Sha at all – her history of marathon running stands her in good stead for the kind of circuit training, involving press-ups, sit-ups and timed running, that is Harvey's speciality, and he holds no fear for her. 'I think he's rather sweet,' she declares, a sentiment which must be unique among the Fat Club members. Although she is undeniably out of condition, Sha gets stuck in without complaining, which wins Harvey's approval straight away. Her running time of 2:33 is the same as Kelly's, and only Stuart and Donna are faster.

Something must have worked, because Sha leaves Gorse Hill motivated enough to sign up at the local gym, and starts off going there regularly, although it is not a form of exercise that she really enjoys. The changes she is putting in place in her life induce a thoughtful mood. 'Coming to Fat Club has made me think about my life and my general situation in a new way. I feel that the balance is wrong in my life. I work, and I care for Liam, my foster son, but I'm not making any space for myself. Spending this weekend doing things for me is such a new experience. It makes me realise how little I do that normally. I've just got out of the habit. I think this regime will force me to pay more attention to myself – right down to what I'm buying in the shops to eat, as well as the exercise I do. I think that will be good for me.'

She is conscientious, too, keeping her food and exercise diaries religiously, but owns up to 'weighing myself, every day, rather than counting calories as such, just to make sure I'm on track. I'm not so concerned about what my weight is in absolute terms – it's more a case of checking that the trend is downwards.'

This, she knows, goes directly against the advice the members have been given. The experts have asked them not to weigh themselves at all between Fat Club weekends, and according to Sarah, it is counter-productive anyway. 'The best time is first thing in the morning once a week, naked and after you've been to the loo,' she explains. 'That way, you'll get an accurate picture of the trend of your weight loss, without the distraction of minor, day-to-day fluctuations.'

Sha finds a good book to help her keep count of her calories. She orders it over the Internet, and e-mails the rest of the members to put them on to it too. This is one of the first of many e-mails that will pass around the group, with advice, encouragement, support and the occasional gripe. Only two members do not have access to e-mail, Jacquie and Simon, but the rest use it with a vengeance, sending gung-ho 'How's it going? Hang in there' messages, sharing low-calorie food finds, and copying each other on everything they send. It is a support network for the 21st century and a terrific way of cementing the relationship between the majority of the Fat Club members, who live miles away from each other.

FAT CLUB TWO

Date: June
Weight at weigh-in: 13st 9lbs (191lbs)
Weight loss since last weigh-in: 7lbs
Total loss: 7lbs
Waist: 44in

'Bagels are my protection against temptation!'

The group meet up at Shepperton Studios for publicity shots. Sha looks stunning in a bright red shirt and flattering black trousers. She may dislike her weight, but with trendy glasses and her hair cropped short, she knows exactly how to make the best of herself.

As before, Sha stands back and observes the excitement and chatter of the other members – she is not one who needs to be the centre of attention – yet her mischievous sense of humour is beginning to emerge. Already she is becoming popular with everyone.

The challenging start to the weekend, with Harvey searching the members' bags one by one, does not faze her a bit. 'He is obviously the "bad cop" of the piece,' Sha smiles. 'But I think he is actually a sweet, although terrifyingly fit, guy. He was apparently looking for "liquor" which I thought quite amusing. All I had to declare was two bagels, which I had taken for our lunch at Shepperton – Tony Curley gave me a lift, and we weren't sure what the arrangements for eating would be. Bagels are my protection against temptation!'

The weigh-in goes well for Sha. She's lost 7lbs and is very pleased, although she was aiming for 10. 'I'm finding the food part easy, it's still the exercise I have a problem with. I feel self-conscious in the gym and I'm finding it difficult to fit it into my schedule.'

This puts Harvey is on the alert. 'I'm a little concerned about her performance at this assessment. I thought she would have improved more based on her efforts at PT, but she hasn't improved at all. In fact her run time is slower and she's managed fewer sit-ups and press-ups. I guess it could be just fatigue or over-training or not eating properly. She has a great attitude, though [he calls her the Wise Lady], and should do really well, but I fear she may never be a big fan of exercise.'

Sha is enjoying the experience of Fat Club again, and throws herself into all the activities. 'I'm finding the whole weekend interesting, and I expect I will go on finding them so, but there have been two profound experiences for me. One involved matching our images as we perceived them in a "magic" mirror, which was adjusted to our directions. Interestingly we all saw ourselves as being bigger than we were – most of us between 30 and 50 per cent bigger. I thought that was only an anorexic's perception, but it shows that we're all carrying round a distorted image of ourselves. I hate looking in mirrors – in fact, I rarely do and some-times I'll be walking along the street feeling, you know, all right and I'll catch sight of my reflection in a shop window. I just feel so crushed. I hope this will help me throw off this negative image I have of myself.'

The second activity, which Sha describes as 'scary and profound', is the weighted jacket workshop. In fact, she is so struck by the relief she feels at removing the weight that she tries it on again. 'It feels awful. It's literally weighing me down, mentally and physically. It's just a burden. It's just brilliant getting rid of that burden. Amazing! It's absolute bliss to take it off. And what it does to your heart – it's just awful. I think if everyone had that opportunity, they would not ever have put weight on in the first place.'

The group dynamics is interesting Sha, and she is concerned that the split into two factions – smokers (Stuart, Tracy and Donna) and non-smokers – could be detrimental overall. She is especially concerned about Kelly. 'She isn't getting enough attention or space to speak. Certain members hog the limelight. I think we're going to have to address that.'

After leaving Gorse Hill, Sha struggles with her exercise regime and attends the gym very infrequently, despite the fact that it is only at the end of her road. She does manage some swimming and a few walks, but she is aware it is not enough. 'The main reason I don't go is that the gym doesn't open until 10 a.m. and I don't have time to go in the morning before work, which would suit me far better. I don't like going in the evening peak time because I still feel intimidated when I go, so I've asked the instructor to break down my workout programme to make it shorter. That way I'll be able to make time in the morning.'

All very plausible, but Sha seems to be falling into the excuses trap and taking, as Harvey would put it, 'the path of least resistance'.

FAT CLUB THREE

Date: July
Weight at weigh-in: 12st 13lbs (181lbs)
Weight loss since last weigh-in: 10lbs
Total loss: 17lbs
Waist: 42in

> *'I do find Harvey inspiring, but I have to work hard to see past his manner.'*

Sha has been finding it difficult to juggle all her commitments, and is so conscientious about her work that she has not been making time for her exercise regime. She has barely been to the gym (as the staff there confirm) and still blames it on the late opening times. She has had a revelation, however.

'A few weeks ago, I discovered a book on the Internet which teaches you a 12-minute workout using weights, telephone directories, furniture and so on. I can do it at home every day, so it should be the answer to my exercise problem. If I can fit three quick cardio workouts in the gym every week alongside that, it should be all I need.'

She is not dreading the weigh-in because, as she says, 'I know I've lost weight, although it's still a nerve-racking experience. It really is very tough. You feel very vulnerable and exposed – well, you're next to naked in front of a room full of people – it's like one of those nightmares, isn't it?'

Sha has lost 10lbs, despite the experts' doubts about her commitment, and is quite satisfied. Already a pattern of slow but steady weight loss is establishing itself. Most members have lost more – apart from Jacey and Kelly who are struggling with a loss of just 2lbs each – but Sha is losing weight at the rate with which her body seems to feel comfortable.

There is good news for her, too, when she has her regular blood pressure check with Raj. This time he is delighted to tell her that it is absolutely normal, and that it is probably entirely due to weight loss. It does drive home the message that even moderate weight loss can make a significant improvement to your health. Sha is delighted. 'It's fantastic. On top of the weight loss, I feel I've really achieved something for my health. I've always been terrified of the idea of having a stroke, so now I've done something positive to fend that off, and it's only taken a few months. It's an extra motivation to do this for a health gain as well as for my appearance.'

With the successful weigh-in safely behind her, Sha comes clean about her problems with exercise. 'I have this Oxfam mentality. I can't resist a bargain, and my local gym was doing cut-price membership if you signed up for two years. So I duly signed up and paid, but I'd forgotten how much I hate gyms. I simply hate to compete. I made a conscious decision at school when I was 12 that I would not be competitive like everyone else, and I've stuck to it, so I find that atmosphere in the gym oppressive. I'm making myself go and use the walking machine and the rower just for cardiovascular work, and I try to do about 30 minutes three times a week, on top of the weight training I do at home, but I absolutely hate it. I don't even use the heart monitor Raj gave us at Fat Club Two. I find it hard to use and I'm just not sure what it's telling me.'

Despite her distaste for them, Sha works hard in Harvey's sessions, and almost doubles her results for sit-ups and press-ups. Perhaps her weight-training is having an effect. 'I do find Harvey inspiring, but I have to work hard to see past his manner. And I just don't respond well to the kind of exercise he teaches. I prefer the idea of this pedometer Raj gave us all this weekend, which calculates how many steps we take each day. I find it simpler to use than the heart monitor and I can actually quantify how much exercise I've taken just going about my normal business. We have been told to aim for 10,000 steps per day – about 10 kilometres – so I'll aim to add little bits of extra activity throughout the day.'

After Fat Club, Sha is a whirlwind of activity and as a consequence is feeling under pressure. She is taking on a new foster child and is involved in all the preparation for his arrival; she is winding up her part-time work on youth projects and has to complete some projects before handing over; she and Liam are going on holiday to the Czech Republic with her sister and, to top it all, she is about to start tackling the very overgrown garden of her house.

'I feel I've overcomplicated my life, in many ways,' she muses. 'Buying and refurbishing the house and committing myself to fostering mean that I'm tied up so much, I have very little time or energy left for myself, but I'd love to meet someone and have a relationship. I feel in many ways that would make my life complete now. It's the only thing that's missing really. That's partly why I'd like to lose weight, I can't believe anyone would desire me, looking the way I do. If I looked all right, I'd be with someone, wouldn't I? My sister's blonde and slim and she gets lots of offers.'

In the busy time of preparation before she leaves on holiday, Sha is uncharacteristically outspoken about some of her fellow members of Fat Club. She sticks up resolutely for Jacey in her confrontation with the experts. 'She didn't threaten to leave. All

she said was she needed time to think about it. I don't understand what all the fuss is about. Tracy is threatening to leave all
the time, and no one pays any attention.' On the subject of the
increasing tension and bad feeling between Tracy and Tony
Curley, she declares, exasperated by their sniping, 'The two of
them are far too alike. That's the problem. They should just go
off and get married.'

FAT CLUB FOUR

Date: August
Weight at weigh-in: 12st 9lbs (177lbs)
Weight loss since last weigh-in: 4lbs
Total loss: 21lbs
Waist: 40in

> *'One thing that has motivated me is the fact that fat
> is stored round your internal organs. It's so scary
> to imagine that you have a fat liver. How could it
> function properly swathed in fat?'*

The holiday in the Czech Republic is a great success. 'We stayed
near a lake, and walked a lot. I drank a bit while we were away.
I was tee total for years and I can take or leave wine, but holi-
days are normally a time for indulgence, aren't they? That's the
great thing about Fat Club, you can allow these little indulgences
as long as they fit into your overall plan. I never feel as if I've
fallen off the wagon, because I'm not on a wagon this time. This
is really the first time ever I've felt confident about the nutrition
and about my weight loss. I know I'm going to have achieved the
weight I want by Christmas.'

Disappointingly, her pedometer packs up while she is there,
but she is so smitten by the information it gives her that she buys
another, and resolves to get one each for her foster sons, just to
make them aware of their activity levels. 'It intrigues me to see
how easily I can slip some extra exercise into my daily routine,
just by walking a little more. It almost becomes a game. I'm still
not really into the cardiovascular exercise, but I'm promising

153

myself that I will get into it when the boys are at school. I loathe going to the gym. It was a really bad investment, and I'm going to see if I can get my money back. I'll find something else to do instead.'

What she cannot explain is her loss of interest in running. 'I've just lost the urge and I used to love it. There's something so spontaneous and joyful about running that reminds me of the kind of freedom one felt as a child. I still like walking, though. It's as effective and much less damaging to the joints. Actually, I'd like to power walk the marathon. I've got the forms already and I'm going to apply.'

Sha has given up her job to become a full-time foster carer, and is not thrilled by the interruption of another Fat Club weekend. 'I take my job very seriously, and I want to give the children the best. If you don't do your best, what's the point of doing it? Normally, I look forward to the weekend at Fat Club, but not this time, perhaps because I have so much going on at home. I'm concerned about the boys, and my new younger boy is going to a new school so, of course, I'm thinking a lot about that.'

It turns out to be an eventful weekend for Sha, particularly the boxing workshop with the 'slam man', a plastic model of a man that the members are encouraged to punch with boxing gloves. 'At first I thought it was going to be great fun. I've often thought about trying one of those boxercise classes to improve my cardiovascular fitness, but my reaction came out of the blue. It totally took me by surprise. Stuart was having little goes at it, and I felt fine and was looking forward to trying myself. But when Tracy went at it so hard I started feeling sick – the look on her face! I could just feel this panic rising inside me. I tried deep breathing, but it didn't work. I went outside but could still hear the whacking noise. I went back in and Harvey started trying to persuade me to hit it. He could see from my face that something was very wrong. If it had been a punch bag I could have done it, but hitting a human shape – I just couldn't.'

It emerges that Sha has some major unresolved issues with violence in her past and this activity has clearly touched a raw nerve. 'They think I'm too controlled here, but I certainly let it all out today. It was like a dam burst. By the time they got Alex along to talk to me about it, I'd calmed down a lot, but it was still helpful. He was actually very sweet and encouraging. I would like to use Alex to move on, but not in front of the nation.'

The fat substitute workshop, with Raj, also makes a big impact on Sha. 'It was totally and utterly gross, seeing the amount of fat we've lost lying there in front of us. We should have had a photograph to take away, just to remind us. I've lost 21lbs altogether and it was really substantial slabs of "fat", it was so heavy! Just to think about the implications was terrifying. I thought, how did I function, carrying all this around with me? Never again! It was one of the things that motivated me to apply for Fat Club in the first place. I had read somewhere that half of the fat you carry is stored round your internal organs. It's so scary to imagine that you have a fat liver, for example. How could it function properly swathed in fat?'

The members are ready to go home, and Tracy has her run-in with Tony Curley. As someone who hates confrontation, Sha is upset by it: 'In many ways Tracy and Tony are very alike – they're both drama queens. But he's very vulnerable – what she said was quite unacceptable. We are baring our souls to each other here and we've done it without having negotiated any boundaries. OK, he drives her up the wall, but I drove back with him and he was desperately upset. He should just leave her alone, but he tries to talk to her and to improve their relationship all the time, and that really irritates her.

'He has no idea about space. I said to him, "You don't have anything in common with Tracy. You don't have to avoid her – just keep your distance." The nice thing about being adult is you don't have to spend time with people who make you feel awful, but there are some very interesting, good people here, and they were very shocked by Tracy's behaviour.'

FAT CLUB FIVE

Date: Early September
Weight at weigh-in: 12st 6lbs (174lbs)

155

Weight loss since last weigh-in: 3lbs
Total loss: 24lbs
Waist: 40in

Perhaps the biggest surprise for Sha has been how little she has internalised health messages in the past, even though she worked in the field of health education for so many years. 'Suddenly, I'm so aware now of the health aspects of obesity. It just didn't get through to me before. I was at lunch with some people the other day, and I was chatting to a woman the same age as me who had just been diagnosed as having diabetes. And I thought "My God, that could have been me." I'm getting very censorious now. When I see fat children around, I feel like glaring at their parents – because it's the parents' fault. They are storing up problems for the children when they're older. We all know a lot of information and we've been given a lot more here. But it's not about knowing, is it? It's about doing. That's the difference, and my blood pressure reading has proved it.'

Sha has certainly been getting on with 'doing' since the last Fat Club. She is enjoying her daily workout and is really beginning to see a difference in her body. 'I do the weights every day, and I haven't yet lost two stone, but the difference to my body is amazing, particularly my shoulders and the tops of my legs. My clothes are hanging off me. I was wearing size 18 at the start of summer, but I tried on a 14 the other day, and it was pretty close to fitting.'

She is also starting to make her peace with cardiovascular exercise, thanks to the pedometer. 'I've been doing some calculations with it. I do an average of 6000 steps a day running round after the boys, but I wanted to work out how much more I would have to do to make a real difference. Sarah told me that a deficit of 500 calories a day would give a loss of 1lb per week, so I'm fine-tuning my calories and my exercise to make sure my weight loss is steady at 1–2lb. I'm aiming for 10,000 steps a day, with some power walking too.'

One of the first activities of the weekend is an 'iron member' contest, a test of strength and endurance. The members stand round in a circle in the courtyard, and as Harvey prowls, encouraging and cajoling, they start with an activity where they are expected to hold bags of sugar at shoulder level with arms fully extended, for as long as possible. It has many of the members giving up with groans of exhaustion, and they drop out of the activities one by one. Finally, only Sha and Stuart remain, and Stuart lasts only seconds longer than she does. Sha is amazed by her own success, and puts it down to good toning exercises on her previously weak upper body. She may not like to admit it, but her determination to see the competition through to the end does indeed come from a competitive spirit – the difference is, Sha is competing against herself. Harvey is right to put it down to mental strength: 'that carries her through'.

At Alex's see yourself slim slide presentation, Sha gasps when she sees the picture of herself taken at Fat Club One and the digitally altered image of how she could look. 'I don't like that first picture – it looks awful, embarrassing. It's only in the last week or so that I've been able to look at myself in the mirror and sometimes I like what I see. But I don't like the slimmed-down image either. That body looks blobby to me and that's not how I want to look now. I'm getting very picky. I want to have a really great body, and I'm liking my body so much better now. I can really see the difference; it makes me want to look better and better.'

Alex is still intrigued by Sha's slight reserve. 'I have often wondered why Sha became a member of Fat Club. She presents such an air of a contained self-sufficiency and seems to guard her personal life with great care. Why she is happy to have her life presented to the viewing public is still something of a mystery.' Nonetheless he is happy with her progress. 'She has slowly and successfully been losing weight and seems to have her schedules well worked out. At the current rate she will be expected to reach a BMI of 30 by October 2001, and to get to a healthy BMI of 24 in March 2002, having lost one-third of her body weight. Her rate of loss is fairly constant so it appears that she has things under control.'

After so many years of neglecting her body, Sha now feels empowered but gets slightly frustrated with this slow though steady progress. 'I would like to move forward more quickly. I'm keeping active but I've got big plans for exercise for when the boys go back to school. I'll make sure I go for an early-morning swim, before I blitz the house. I'm much more active and so much more energetic now than I used to be. I thought I'd achieve my goal weight of 9st 13lbs by Christmas, but at my current rate of weight loss – 1–2lbs per week – I know I won't.' The experts are emphatic however: weight lost slower is weight that is more likely to stay off.

FAT CLUB SIX

Date: September
Weight: 12st 2lbs (170lbs)
Weight loss since last weigh-in: 4lbs
Total Loss: 28lbs
Waist: 38in

> *'Sha's a slow winner.' – Sarah*
>
> *'When you find a form of exercise that you enjoy, it's like a door opening.'*

The last weekend is looming, but Sha is still feeling impatient about her rate of weight loss. Against her better judgement, she is keen to go out with a bang at this last weigh-in. 'If it weren't for Fat Club, I could go on at 1lb a week effortless weight loss quite happily, but I feel I have to make an extra effort for this weekend. I've been doing weights for four months now and my legs are so toned, they don't match my tummy any more, so I know they work brilliantly.

'I e-mailed the author of the weights book I've been using, *12-Minute Total Body Workout* by Joyce L. Vedral, and to my amazement she e-mailed me right back. She's told me about another book of hers, *The Fat Burning Workout*, that combines the resistance exercises with fat burning, so I've ordered that and I'm going to have a real go at losing weight before the next week-end. I've lost two stone now, but I've seen such a change in my body. It's different from when I was running. I was skinny then, but not particularly toned. I've become so body aware. I went to

Tony's 40th birthday party and I was laughing at myself – I've become so judgmental of fat people.'

She is not alone in wanting to impress on this last weekend. The members all feel under pressure to perform well for the weigh-in, and some are suspected of resorting to desperate measures against all the advice they have learnt. At least Sha comes clean: 'This new book has what it calls the "Insanity Programme" and that's what I'm following to make the last weigh-in better.'

Sensible or not – and it is certainly not a route the experts would recommend – Sha's late effort pays dividends. She looks marvellous when she arrives at Fat Club and at the weigh-in has indeed achieved a total weight loss of two stone, and has even shifted two inches from her waist in the last month. 'I love the way I can sculpt my body with this programme. I've been this weight before, but I've never been this shape before.'

She is in a sartorial dilemma. 'I can't shop at Evans any more,' she says. 'The clothes are all too big for me! But I don't really know what suits me any more. I'm so used to dressing to hide my tummy, so now I don't know what to choose when I no longer have to wear loose tops. I've been wearing sleeveless T-shirts in the past few weeks, because I love the way the tops of my arms have developed a lovely toned shape, but it's getting a bit cold for that now.'

She is less fussed about the food she is eating, and has her daily routine down to a fine art. 'I'm never hungry. A typical day would be: two Weetabix and banana or porridge for breakfast with skimmed milk, and I love blueberry Nutrigrain bars. I'll have a bagel with low-fat cream cheese or soup for lunch, and perhaps tinned spaghetti on wholemeal toast with no butter for supper. For snacks I'll plump for fruit.' Cutting out fat has been the easiest part: 'I don't eat butter or any spread at all, and I dry fry almost everything.

'I've changed the way I see food,' she realises. 'I always had expectations of it as a comfort, and dieting always seemed like a penance. Now I never feel deprived. I find myself getting fed up with people who go into work with their special little Tupperware boxes with a few slices of cucumber in it. No wonder they fall off the wagon. The way we all eat here, no one even suspects us of being on a diet. Everyone's asking me, "How did you do it?" '

Around the camp fire on Saturday night, the mood, for the most part, is mellow. Sha reflects on Harvey's role in her weight loss, and her relationship with exercise. 'We're all talking about our sessions with Harvey as if it was some spiritual revelation, but that's what it feels like. You have to find your own salvation – and it really is salvation. We've been saving our own lives. I'm the oldest here by quite a few years, but Harvey has made no concession at all. He's expected me to give my best and I've always tried to do that. It's done my ego a lot of good.'

To reminders from the experts that they have all done well but are still fat, Sha retorts, 'We've done well *and* we're still fat. No buts about it. Don't take anything away from our achievement. We know we've got to keep going.'

Raj: I'm delighted about her blood pressure. Sha's got a potentially life-threatening condition under control, simply by losing weight. And she's looking terrific. That's got to be an inspiration.'

Sha's Fitness Assessment

Fat Club 1

Run	Sit-ups	Press-ups
2.33	17	35

Fat Club 6

Run	Sit-ups	Press-ups
2.15	50	80

Chapter 9

Kelly's Story

'I hate to be seen eating in public. I think every-one's looking at me.'

Kelly Mundy
Age: 20
Lives: Oxford
Occupation: Student
Height: 5ft 3in
Weight at first weigh-in: 17st 7lbs – morbidly obese
Waist at first weigh-in: 48in

The youngest member of the group, Kelly seems to have every-thing going for her. She is ravishingly pretty with a bob of shiny brown hair, big blue eyes and a lovely skin. She is very bright and focused, articulate and sensitive. What she lacks is self-confidence.

Kelly appears completely unaware of how attractive she is – in fact she loathes the way she looks – and has a vulnerability and slight wariness that suggests she is used to having her feelings hurt. Her weight is marring her happiness and she knows she has to tackle it, yet she seems overwhelmed by the situation, as if she is powerless to change.

The reason she gives for joining Fat Club says it all. 'I want to lose weight to be accepted, to fit in with other people my age without feeling I have to apologise for myself all the time, and I want to be able to buy clothes in high street shops. At the moment, if I go shopping with my mates, we have to split up and I go to the outsize shops alone.'

Kelly grew up in Cornwall, and hit puberty at the tender age of eight. By the time she was nine or ten, she started to be 'a little bit tubby' and became aware that she was not a skinny little girl any more. Her parents' marriage broke up and her mother took the very unusual step of leaving her with her grandparents at the age of 12, to start a relationship with another man. Though Kelly does not say so now, this experience must have been devastating at such a vulnerable age. 'At school I thought I was fat, but looking back at the photos, I wasn't really. When I was doing A-levels, I was about a size 16, but it wasn't until I went to university that the weight piled on.'

Unlike many of the Fat Club members, Kelly has always been good at sport and being not long out of school, was active until quite recently. 'At secondary school I was always in school teams, but I let it tail off when I was doing my A-levels, because I was studying all the time. Now I've just got out of the habit completely, and it's difficult to get started again, particularly now I've put on so much weight.'

'I can start all over again.'

She began her degree course in biology at Oxford Brookes University, but finding herself unhappy there, she has decided to start again with a radiography course at Bristol. 'My new course starts in October 2001 and I want to be a different person when I go there. I can start all over again and, with any luck, I'll have lost quite a bit of weight. I'd like it if the new people I meet like me for the way I look, rather than just for my personality.'

This overwhelming insecurity makes Kelly very anxious about people's reactions to her. Her character is an intriguing mix of confidence, flirtation and a little-girl-lost manner that may explain to some extent the problems she has had with boyfriends in the past. She has either been badly treated or let down but, according to Kelly, most of the men attracted to her 'turn out to be gay or the ones I don't fancy'.

162

'I just binge on chocolate or biscuits in my room.'

Like Stuart, Kelly blames the student lifestyle for her recent weight gain. She shares a flat with a number of other girls, but as none of them has a weight problem, she feels that they really do not understand how she feels. 'I used to go out all the time, drinking and clubbing with mates, but I've stopped lately. I feel too self-conscious about the way I look. Sometimes I just binge on chocolate or biscuits in my room, but then I feel ashamed, and I have to hide the packets so my flatmates don't know about it.'

Another powerful motivation for Kelly are the side-effects of her weight. She is beginning to find that her part-time job as a carer, acting as a home help for the elderly or disabled, is becoming difficult because of the amount of exertion the work involves. She has to get them out of bed, wash, dress and feed them, sit with them and take them out for walks, do their shopping and clean for them. For Kelly it is exhausting. More serious, however, is the fact that both her dad and her half-sister are diabetic. Because she is morbidly obese, Kelly's risk of developing diabetes is hugely increased.

An item on the radio first alerted Kelly to Fat Club. She scribbled down the phone number, screwed up her courage (egged on by her flatmates) and called, describing herself as a 'Dawn French type, bubbly and big'. After a number of interviews, a medical and a screen test, she was on the programme. She has many powerful reasons to want to lose weight and change her life.

FAT CLUB ONE

'If I could run away, I would.'

The experts are fairly positive about Kelly and her involvement in the Club, and seem to be blind to the depth of her self-loathing, at least partly because of the way Kelly presents herself, well groomed and smartly dressed, with a ready and infectious giggle. Get her looking good, they think, and she will be fine. 'I think she'll do well,' says Sarah. 'It should be easy for her to lose weight because she's so young. She doesn't have the long history of failed dieting that so many of the other members do, and she's never managed to stick to a diet for more than a month. Well, that's all right, because this isn't a diet.' Raj seconds that: 'Kelly seems very well motivated, and I'm optimistic because of her youth. She takes no exercise currently and her poor eating habits are connected to her social life, so we can see things that could be put right straight away.'

Kelly is terrified by the first meeting at Gorse Hill. Just before the first session, she is almost in a panic. 'I can't believe I'm doing this to myself. I keep thinking, "What have I let myself in for?" If I could run away here and now, I would.'

Intensely unsure of herself, she contributes little to the first sessions, preferring to look and listen. Far younger than any of the other members, apart from Stuart, who exudes a level of self-assurance unusual for his age, she seems overawed by their confidence and readiness to talk on camera.

Always quick to blame herself, she feels she is failing straight away. 'I'm surprised at myself, the way I am reacting at Fat Club. Among my mates, I'm very confident and I've always got something to say. I'm quite mouthy, I suppose. Here, I just feel so much less interesting than the other members. I'm beginning to wonder why I was chosen for the programme at all.'

Her tension is soon relieved, largely by Tony Upson's warm and friendly manner towards her, which breaks the ice immediately. Much to the surprise of the experts, the group has bonded by the time the weigh-in is over, and Kelly's endearing manner, obvious insecurity and youth appeal to everyone's protective instincts.

Like the conscientious student she is, she pays close attention to everything that is discussed and earns the approval of the experts for appearing to take Fat Club seriously. It looks as if her attitude will ensure that she is a winner.

'When it came to the end of the weekend, I didn't want to go home. It was so good being with all the others, I felt really emotional. We were all saying goodbye, and I wanted to hug Harvey. Well, the look on his face! "I don't do hugging," he growled. I felt a bit upset about it at the time, but it was quite funny really.'

On the way home, she is disappointed to find her packed lunch, supplied by the Gorse Hill kitchens, is nothing more than a bagel and cream cheese. 'I hate bagels,' she says. 'I tried a cinnamon one once and that was it. I certainly won't be eating any of those, even if they are low in fat.'

Her hopes are high for the next weekend already. 'It was great meeting everyone. It was so relaxing to be with people who understand, for a change. One thing I don't like is the way the group is splitting. Tracy, Donna and Stuart keep giggling together and going off in a huddle. Also, I didn't like Jacey so much. I thought she was too opinionated.'

Back at college, Kelly dutifully joins a gym and starts going regularly, even jogging around the streets of Oxford. It looks as if she is sticking to the programme, but her self-esteem is still rock bottom. She even refuses an invitation to the university May Ball because she feels self-conscious about her appearance.

The close connections she has made with her fellow members Tony Curley, Tony Upson, Sha, Jacquie and Simon are continuing with regular, encouraging phone calls, text messages and e-mails. She is part of a new community now, and she seems to be thriving on it.

FAT CLUB TWO

Date: June
Weight at weigh-in: 16st 13lbs (237lbs)
Weight loss since last weigh-in: 8lbs
Total loss: 8lbs
Waist: 45in

> *'It's great to be back with everyone again. I've been looking forward to coming here.'*

Kelly's hard work on her new lifestyle over the four weeks between clubs is beginning to pay dividends, and she is enthusiastic about the changes she has made. Sarah has set her a calorie target of 1400 per day, and Kelly is working hard to resist student fare. Breakfast, a meal she would often previously skip, is now two slices of toast with honey or a bowl of cereal; lunch is quick and usually a ham and salad sandwich and some fruit; dinner is typically spaghetti bolognese and salad (although she has eaten so much salad in her life that she does not enjoy it much). With time at a premium, Kelly mixes ready-made low-fat supermarket foods with home-made, but she is keeping an eye on the fat content of everything she eats. Already she is looking slimmer.

At the weigh-in she is keyed up and nervous. It seems unnecessary in view of her very successful result: she has lost 8lbs and has whittled 3in off her waist, but she is tearful and clings to Tony Curley and Tony Upson for support. This is clearly an emotional and difficult experience. 'I just feel so exposed at the weigh-in. When I know it's coming I start to feel sick with nerves and I know I tremble. Waiting for Raj to read out my weight seems to take for ever.'

Nonetheless, there are things about Fat Club that Kelly looks forward to. 'It's great to be back with everyone again. I've been looking forward to coming here. I get such a sense of security from the other members during the weekend.' Tony Upson is a key figure for her, and she has relied on his support in the weeks between clubs. Coincidentally, he has a daughter of much the same age as Kelly and with the same name. He is becoming something of a father figure – Kelly jokingly calls him 'Dad' – and his warmth and stability obviously provide a much-needed anchor for her. (Alex sees Tony's role from the psychologist's point of view, and wonders if the break-up of her family has left her needy of an important male character in her life. He even goes so far as to suggest privately that she may have missed sitting on her daddy's lap as a child, and still has that unfulfilled need.)

Kelly remains unenthusiastic about some of the other members: 'Tracy, Stuart and Donna have really cut off from the rest of the group and they make a lot of sarcastic remarks. I find them intimidating so I just stay clear.'

Once again, Kelly is quiet but attentive throughout the workshops and demonstrations and tries hard in Harvey's PT sessions, although the number of press-ups she manages actually decreases since the first assessment.

For the first week after the weekend away, Kelly swims every day and goes to the gym three times, but boyfriend and money problems contrive to make all her good intentions fall apart. She gives up on exercise altogether, stops keeping her exercise diary, stops counting calories and starts comfort eating again. The prospect of a long interval until the next Fat Club (a gap of seven weeks) should give enough time to make some real changes. It does not. She is not galvanised into action and things go from bad to worse. 'It's not the same at home without the experts and the other nine members,' she moans. 'I just can't keep my enthusiasm going on my own. My boyfriend's been messing me around, and I'm in debt so I'm going to have to take on more work. That won't leave me any time to exercise.'

The excuses come thick and fast, and Kelly is on a downward spiral, seemingly unable to control her behaviour. Her salvation comes a couple of weeks later when she sorts out her financial situation and becomes involved with a supportive new boyfriend, Ben. 'I'm feeling much happier now than I was a couple of weeks ago,' she claims, and hauls herself back on her exercise regime, going to the gym twice a week for a one-hour workout and swimming twice a week for an hour.

'My exercise has definitely improved since a few weeks ago, but I could still do a lot, lot more. I don't really seem to enjoy the exercise, especially jogging, as much as I thought I would. I have to force myself to go to the gym and, well, sometimes I don't. My diet is more or less back on track, but working more now, I do sometimes skip meals, then I'm really hungry. Also, I have been out drinking sometimes and I know that's not really good. I've given up on keeping my food and exercise diaries. It's a bit boring writing it all down and I just haven't got the time. I know I've done really badly in the last few weeks, but I didn't give up. That's something.'

It sounds as if Kelly is trying to console herself for her own inadequate performance by moving her personal goal posts, but the Fat Club scales will not be fooled. Kelly seems to be motivated only by her desire to please other people, or at least to avoid being told off – something which is looking increasingly likely as the weekend approaches. As problems arise, she is treating them as insurmountable obstacles, and is making excuses for not dealing with them.

FAT CLUB THREE

Date: July
Weight at weigh-in: 16st 11lbs (235lbs)
Weight loss since last weigh-in: 2lbs
Total loss: 10 pounds
Waist: 45in

> *'The others are being really nice about it, but I feel I've spoilt it for them.'*

Kelly is revelling in those exciting early days of a new relation-ship. Things are going well – Ben is kind and seems to have her best interests at heart – but as Fat Club approaches, she becomes increasingly apprehensive. She still cannot find the motivation needed for meaningful weight loss. 'I'm really worried about the weigh-in. I know I haven't lost any weight since Fat Club Two and I'm worried about getting shouted at when I go to Fat Club Three.'

As the moment arrives, she looks frankly terrified. She has prepared the way by telling all the other members that she has not lost anything, and by telling herself that, providing she has not actually put on any weight, everything will be fine, but her words sound hollow. Waiting for her turn, she is visibly trembling, and when Raj says she has *'only* lost 2lbs', she bursts into tears. Afterwards, she is only just holding the tears back. 'I'm devas-tated. The others are being really nice about it, but I feel I've spoilt it for them.'

Raj's deliberate choice of words to describe the paltry weight loss by Kelly and Jacey initially causes outrage among the members. Because of the few poor performances, they have failed to reach their group target loss, and Raj gives the whole team a stiff talking to. In private the experts vent their anger:

'Two pounds in seven weeks?' splutters Harvey. 'She could have taken a crap and lost 2lbs!'

Afterwards, in the members' lounge, they huddle together in mutual support, complain about Raj's attitude and manage to concoct a theory that, provided they do not put on weight, any loss is good progress and should be celebrated as such. The logic is weak and the argument unconvincing. Surprisingly, Kelly herself is far less defensive than the other members. 'I deserve to get told off. Two pounds in seven weeks is hopeless, I'm just sorry that the rest of you got told off as well.'

She works diligently at the rest of the tasks and activities, improving on her assessment on Sunday and throwing herself into the dance aerobics session. Her efforts do not go unnoticed, and she manages to regain Harvey's good opinion, at least. Usually Kelly is the quiet member of the group, but her problems have contrived to make her the centre of attention, and the experts devote a large chunk of their private meeting to her.

Raj feels her very emotional response may mark a turning point. 'She was very upset, despite her claims of being happy not to have gained weight. She clearly feels very guilty and that she has let herself and the group down. She did thank me for being honest with her at the weigh-in. I just hope I got through to her.'

Sarah is less optimistic. 'She didn't do that well at Fat Club Two, but it went unnoticed beside Jacey and Jacquie, who did even worse. I think we were too soft on her then. Remember she has youth on her side. It should be easy for her to lose weight, but she also leads a student lifestyle, where peer pressure can be very powerful. I wonder, is she strong enough to withstand it? She doesn't demand attention like many of the others, so we will have to make sure we focus on her more. I will be surprised if she hasn't done well by next Fat Club, but if she hasn't then there is a reason we are missing completely.'

On Sunday morning, before the swim, Harvey has a pep talk with Kelly about her poor performance, and his uncharacteristically gentle manner almost reduces her to tears. Her reaction encourages him to give her the benefit of the doubt, and he defends her to the other experts, who are wondering if she is a candidate for an official warning. 'I must say, I'm a little worried about her. I honestly feel that in previous Fat Clubs she has not gotten half the attention she probably deserves, but I feel like she will come around after the talk I had with her. I am really willing to believe that she will give a commitment totally now. If not then I will take the bad call on judgement this time. Don't we owe her a chance? We have given Jacey a thousand, why not one for Kelly? She has not been a quarter of the pain Jacey has. Kelly could be a beautiful woman if she toned up and lost weight. She's my Sunday Project. You see, I can give compassion where I'm needed to.'

After a wobbly start, Kelly's impression of the weekend is favourable overall. 'It's been really up and down, but despite a weird atmosphere with Jacey's failure to arrive on Friday, I have enjoyed it. After all that stuff with the weigh-in, I've come out of myself and I haven't been so quiet or overwhelmed. I've even felt more confident with Stuart, Donna and Tracy.'

Back in Oxford, Kelly starts to make an effort with her food. 'I'm cooking more instead of buying food ready-made, but I do love Tesco's healthy-eating pizzas. Other than that, I have reduced-fat sausages and rindless bacon, and I don't buy anything that's over 5 per cent fat. I'm not that mad on veggies – I have to have my meat, so I choose chicken, turkey or ham.'

She is philosophical about the trauma of the weekend. 'I need to be nagged and motivated or I lose interest. I let my work slip at university because I wasn't checked up on, and it's the same thing again. Raj saying "only 2lbs" made me think "I'm gonna show you." We have to lose 60lb between us for next time, so I'm going to go out and buy some scales. There's no way I'm going to be humiliated again. I'm determined to get back on track.'

FAT CLUB FOUR

Date: August
Weight at weigh-in: 16st 5lbs (229lbs)
Weight loss since last weigh-in: 6lbs
Total loss: 16lbs
Waist: 44in

'It does work – when I remember to do it.'

The resolve may well be working in theory, but not always in practice. Like a lazy schoolgirl, Kelly seems to be doing the bare minimum, just enough to placate her teachers, missing the point entirely that she needs to do it for herself.

'I've had fewer lapses with food,' she reports, 'just some chocolate, a Chinese take-away and a pizza. I don't really bother counting calories any more but, for example, if I'm going to drink wine, I eat less. I'm still not doing my diaries – I just don't have time – but I should be eating about 1300 calories a day. I've given up on jogging, but I've been swimming and I go to the gym for some cardio work alternating with strengthening exercises. In the pool, I do breast stroke with crawl and back stroke, and I probably swim for about an hour altogether. I'm so determined not to be in the same position as last time. I've been feeling really good for the last three weeks, but I still haven't really recovered from Fat Club Three. I just felt so ashamed of myself.'

In place of self-monitoring, she has been keeping a beady eye on her new scales, which show she has lost 6lbs for her efforts. 'I don't know if it'll say the same on the Fat Club ones.' Her confidence may not have increased about the weigh-in but she feels more comfortable now with the rest of the members, and is really looking forward to seeing everyone: 'They've just been so supportive, particularly Tony Upson – he's my best mate.'

There is much to enjoy at the weekend, and it turns out to be a good one for Kelly. At the weigh-in she has lost 6lbs and, although the atmosphere is very tense because Jacey leaves the programme, Kelly's success delights her and Raj. 'This is clearly a great achievement and I think we should build on it. She's still not a great fan of exercise, though.'

Kelly disputes this. 'I do enjoy the exercise with Harvey. We all work much harder than we usually would, and it's nice to exercise with other people.' Her favourite expert is Alex, but her reasons for this may highlight the whole issue of her struggle to maintain the Fat Club ethos, if indeed she has grasped it at all. 'He's not always on about diet,' she says. 'He's just like normal. I've had sessions with him, trying to find the underlying reasons for why I eat. I don't really understand it myself, and I can't explain why I do it, but he has given me a little affirmation to say to myself every day. When I'm tempted by food, I just say, "I have a small appetite." It does work – when I remember to do it.'

The salsa session during Saturday afternoon is a great hit with Kelly. She is naturally graceful with an excellent sense of rhythm and this is the kind of exercise, disguised as fun, that appeals to her. At the barbecue in the evening, she lets her hair down, swaying to the music, a look of pure pleasure on her face. Being with the other members seems to make her happy, and she laughs, flirts and jokes the evening away on the moonlit terrace.

No wonder it is hard for her to leave on Sunday. The support, attention and encouragement she gets here nourish her far more than her rather mundane student-on-holiday lifestyle back in Oxford. Encouraged by her success, she decides to take it easy for a while, and does no exercise at all for a week. In the second week she loses control of her eating, but intends to make up for it in the fortnight before the next Fat Club. 'Despite what Raj thinks, I don't have a bad feeling about sport,' she says, 'but it's just getting round to it and making time. The other night I was going to go to the gym but first I met Ben and some friends in the pub. My friends started saying, "Why are you going? Stay and have something to eat." We argued about it for almost an hour and a half and in the end I went, and Ben said later, "I'm really proud of you, babe." '

An hour and a half just to deflect the well-intentioned invitation of her friends? With friends like these . . .

Tony Upson has been a good friend to Kelly this month, calling her frequently to encourage her and offer emotional support when she has felt down. She depends on him, and on the other members she has become close to. But without this external encouragement she is still failing to absorb the Fat Club message about the need to change her lifestyle – her efforts have been mere gestures – and external pressures are still more important to her than her inner needs. Kelly's personal motivation seems so weak that the least obstacle or distraction drives her disastrously off course.

It is summer holiday time, and many of the other carers at the agency where she works are away, so Kelly is being asked to take on more work at short notice, though she can ill afford the time. When faced with a choice of going to the gym or going to help an elderly or disabled person and earn some money into the bargain, Kelly's choice is clear. She's found a guilt-free way of excusing herself from getting fit, but she knows deep down that she could and should be saying "no" more often and caring for herself as well as others.

With little time to spare, Kelly has let her regime fall apart and her relationship with Ben seems to revolve around going out to the pub or eating in together. 'I'm going to make a huge effort for the last few days,' she protests, but she's put on 7lbs altogether. And Fat Club Five is on the horizon.

FAT CLUB FIVE

Date: September
Weight at weigh-in: 16st 7lbs (231lbs)
Weight gain since last weigh-in: 2lbs
Total loss: 14lbs
Waist: 44½in

> *'I gave her 110 per cent. She gave me nothing.'*
> *– Harvey*

> *'Everyone went on and on ... it really did my head in.'*

The weigh-in is to be delayed until Sunday and the news brings consternation to most of the group. Not to Kelly, however, for whom putting off the inevitable is a relief. She knows what is coming even if the experts do not.

Sarah has been phoning her regularly, and Kelly has reported good progress, healthy eating and regular exercise in the hope of escaping detection. Sarah, like the other experts, is fooled, but they are tipped off that she is being economical with the truth.

They call a meeting and agree that Kelly is motivated but only externally. Alex offers to have a session with her to try to help. He even suggests that she might be afraid of achieving normal weight, because of feelings of self-blame and guilt. 'It's a worry that she doesn't seem to be able to take responsibility for herself. She still needs a parent figure to tell her what she can and can't do.'

Kelly and Alex meet and she does confess that she has given way to temptation. This time Alex, despite his gentle, coaxing manner, lets her get away with nothing. 'You felt you deserved a treat because of your weight loss at Fat Club Four, so you treated yourself by stuffing your face. Was that a good or bad choice?'

He goes on to explain that she has to change her belief systems and tries once again to give her affirmations to recite to herself: 'I believe this chocolate bar is not good for me', 'I believe I am in control of my life', 'I believe I am a person of value'. He knows about Kelly's talent for playing the piano, and uses it as an analogy. 'You will have to practise these new attitudes if you want them to become second nature, just as you would practise a new piano piece. Start feeling good about helping Kelly, believe that you can.'

Once again Kelly gives the impression that these messages have affected her deeply, and even Alex believes they will hit home. She has played this game before and got away with it. Luckily for her, a 2lb weight gain (she has managed to lose 5 of the 7lbs she put on between weekends) is less glaringly obvious next to glitches for other members at the weigh-in. Her friend, Tony Upson, has put weight on for the first time, and Tracy has gained a pound too. Weight losses for the whole month are down on what was expected for everyone, but in the general gloom, the successful members of the group begin to confront the failures on what has gone wrong, and sympathy for Kelly turns to anger. Donna especially goes for her jugular: 'If you don't do something positive about your weight, you're going to be a fat, dead Kelly,' she shouts. Well meant this may be, but Donna has misjudged Kelly, who flinches under the repeated accusations, turning her face away. Now she has another justification for her self-loathing.

The experts have one of their most difficult meetings yet. Harvey, who had taken a special interest in Kelly, is furious. 'She should pack up as of today. We should tell her she's a bunch of trash. Self-discipline is what she lacks. If we'd imposed more discipline, it would have been second nature by now. There's no way we can let her stay. D-day is right round the corner.'

Sarah is annoyed at Kelly for lying to her. 'I think she wants to go, but doesn't have the guts to do it herself. She wants to be a victim so she can cry and get more attention. She doesn't want fairness.'

Raj agrees that to ask her to leave would be relieving her of the responsibility. His approach is gentler: 'Can we keep her in and give her a warning, check her progress before next Fat Club and, if she fails, not let her come back?'

Sarah has had enough. 'I don't care if she stays or goes any more. I'm fed up with her. She'll only go on some ridiculous diet. She's here for all the wrong reasons.'

Alex, as usual, finds the way ahead. 'Let's not fail her now by taking a negative attitude. I want to phone her every week now. This is a real downtime. Let's confront her about her lack of monitoring. I'd like to see if the new approach I've given her works.'

The experts finally agree that Kelly must restart her diaries and be weighed again in two weeks. If she has not attained a weight loss of 4bs, she will have to leave the Club. She tearfully agrees to their conditions.

The rest of the weekend passes in something of a blur for Kelly. Her logic is awry: in her mind, she has managed to lose 5lbs in the space of about a week, and feels quite pleased with herself because of it. Pressure from the group seems to have had no effect: 'I just feel really mentally tired. Everyone went on and on at me during the weigh-in, especially Donna. It really did my head in, and I just don't want it.'

As Kelly leaves Gorse Hill, she must know there is a possibility that she will not be coming back.

Alex calls Kelly to see how she is progressing, and he feels encouraged. 'She was delighted to hear from me and said that she was OK after the bruising she got at Fat Club Five. She said she was trying the statements I had suggested to her and she felt confident that they were working. I reminded her that constant vigilance was required and that even small things had to be looked at carefully to see if they were the start of another slippery path.'

Another expert appeased – but Kelly is getting wise to what she knows people want to hear.

In the week after the warning, she claims to be doing as much as she can, but is clearly resenting the regime as being something externally imposed. 'I've been to Cornwall and I haven't done any exercise, but I'm trying to control my calories to compensate.' Her 21st birthday celebrations start there, continue in Oxford, then finish with a family party back in Cornwall. 'I didn't push the boat out, and I kept my alcohol intake low too. I really wanted to enjoy myself, but I felt under pressure because of the weigh-in. The fact that I had to lose 4lb in two weeks was on my mind the whole time.'

But clearly not enough. She meets Harvey alone at Gorse Hill, without other members there to support her. 'I knew I'd only lost 2lbs. Harvey said that my commitment level was zero, and really went off on one. I was a blubbering wreck. Actually, I was relieved when he said I was out. He threw my food and exercise diaries on the floor in front of me and walked out. It was a weight off my shoulders.' An unfortunate choice of words for a girl with so much weight to lose.

Kelly appears to recover quickly from the trauma. 'I'm relieved I'm not doing it,' she says now. 'I'm sad because I'm not seeing everybody, but I've hardly thought about it. I've had too much to think about. I'm now at Bristol, and I've just done Freshers' week, so I haven't been watching my diet or doing any exercise. I'm just going to get settled in, then I'll look into going to the gym and swimming, and incorporating it into my new Bristol lifestyle, that's what Fat Club has taught me.'

Brave words, but the experts have heard it from Kelly too many times. Most alarming for them is Kelly's careless attitude towards her health. Morbidly obese already, she dismisses the well-documented risks. 'I know that if I put more weight on, my health risks are going to go up. But I've had medicals and I am healthy. I can run as fast as Stuart can. I'm only 21, I don't really see the health thing as an issue for me. At Fat Club, I lost just over a stone, and it was a start for me. I don't see myself as a failure.' Once again her concern is for what others think: 'I just wish Harvey could see that I really did try those two weeks. He just doesn't believe me. I'm so worried that people who care will think that I didn't try.'

She is right to worry. 'I really thought that we had got through to her this time and that she would take on board all the messages she was sent,' says Alex, who has taken the trouble to follow up her departure with a phone call. 'I gave her a telling off. I asked her if she'd like sticking needles into herself. She said, "No", so I told her to think about developing diabetes and having to do just that for the rest of her life.'

Raj, too, is concerned about the health issues: 'I'm very disappointed that Kelly hasn't taken responsibility for her health. She's running serious risks, and she must know it deep down.'

But Sarah and Harvey are simply disappointed and feel fooled: 'This was a once-in-a-lifetime opportunity,' says Sarah, 'and she wasted it. She deceived us but, more importantly, she deceived herself.' Harvey is mad as hell: 'I now expect the worst from Kelly, that way I won't be disappointed. I gave her 110 per cent. She gave me nothing.'

For someone who cares so much about others' opinion of her, Kelly will be most pained by the response of the rest of the group to her failure. Simon Payne sums it up: 'She's thrown away the chance she could have had. At her age, the weight would have fallen off and she could have shifted her 4lb target no trouble. Viewers of the programme will see her as a bit of a loser and I don't think she has thought about that. They could have been there instead of her.'

Kelly's failure has proved that weight loss is not simple. As Alex warned from the start, it is about finding the right mindset and motivation to succeed. For all her early efforts and the support of the groups and the professionals, Kelly was lacking in the resolve and self-belief to overcome the temptations and difficulties of everyday life. At Fat Club she thrived on the discipline imposed by the experts. What she failed to do was carry through the lessons into real life.

Kelly's Fitness Assessment

Fat Club One

Run	Sit-ups	Press-ups
2.33	17	35

Fat Club 5

Run	Sit-ups	Press-ups
2.00	29	69

Chapter 10

Jacquie's Story

'I could make clothes to fit me in the styles and fabrics I want, but that's not the point, is it?'

Jacquie Marsh
Age: 37
Occupation: Art director
Lives: London
Height: 5ft 5in
Weight at first weigh-in: 15st 7lbs – obese
Waist at first weigh-in: 40½in

Jacquie's main reason for wanting to lose weight is, she says, her love of fashion. She has always been fascinated by clothes, even as a child, and studied fashion at college. One of her major frustrations is not being able to buy clothes on the high street to fit. 'I could make clothes to fit me in the styles and fabrics I want,' she says ruefully. 'But that's not the point, is it?'

Jacquie has been big for as long as she can remember, and puts this down, at least in part, to the attitudes to food she learnt as a child: she was a fussy eater and her parents would reward her with something nice (usually sweets) if she ate things she did not like. Despite the years that have passed, her mother still displays the same contradictory approach. 'She'll comment that I've gained weight, then when I'm just picking myself up off the floor, she'll say something like, "Eat up the last potato," or "You have to have the dessert because I made your favourite." It drives me mad!'

'When it comes down to just me and the mirror, I loathe my body.'

Jacquie is an attractive woman, with striking black hair and pale skin, and it seems amazing that her love life has been difficult (she is a lesbian), but she firmly believes that her weight has played a part. She is afflicted with a deep lack of confidence. 'I've always felt that I have to try harder. People have to get to know me before I have any chance with them. The gay world is more critical than people think, and appearance counts for a lot.'

She is currently in a satisfying and ongoing relationship, although her partner, Al, lives in Brighton and they only see each other at weekends. They had known each other as friends for years, but gradually lost touch. A chance meeting at the Gay Pride Mardi Gras led to their current relationship.

Jacquie's understanding of fashion makes it easy for her to dress in flattering styles that conceal her size. 'Most people are surprised when they find out how big I am. I can fool most people; sometimes I can even fool myself; but when it comes down to just me and the mirror, I loathe my body.'

However, work is one area where Jacquie feels totally confident. Her keen eye and artistic skill have stood her in good stead and she loves what she does. She has a successful, but very demanding career, as a design studio manager in Brixton and runs a creative team designing live events, corporate images and pop promos.

Despite the style-conscious environment, she finds that here she is not judged by her weight. 'It's never held me back, because people know me for the quality of my work.' Jacquie has the most demanding work schedule of all the Fat Club members, and this brings it own pressures and problems.

Jacquie is a gregarious woman and when her job allows, she loves to cook and entertain. In short she loves good food such as Thai and Mediterranean, even if she tries to be careful with what she eats. Though she never mentions her father's death from diabetes at 65, she is clearly well-informed of the importance of good health and nutrition. She does not drink, but among her group of friends she is usually the one who invites everyone round to dinner. With unpredictable schedules and tight deadlines to meet, she often has to work long hours and frequently skips meals. The temptation to call out for food with the rest of her colleagues at the end of a long photo shoot can be irresistible and, despite her best intentions, the demands of her job make take-aways the obvious option.

Yet Jacquie clings to the belief that her diet is basically a good one. 'I really don't know why I'm big, although I must admit, I'm not very active.' This is something of an understatement. She is a classic example of someone whose life is out of balance.

'My gym teacher, Pratt by name and Pratt by nature, made my life an absolute misery.'

Jacquie would be the first to admit that she loathes exercise, particularly anything regimented, such as circuit training. 'For me, exercise does not equal fun. I put it down to PE lessons at school. My teacher, Pratt by name and Pratt by nature, made my life an absolute misery. We used to go out running round the streets near my school in our gym knickers. Can you think of anything worse? I was pretty well developed and I was always one of the last. Having to puff round the streets behind everyone else was the ultimate humiliation, and then there were the lorry drivers, yelling the most disgusting things at me. It was like a violation. It still brings me out in a cold sweat to think of it now.'

The only kind of exercise Jacquie now enjoys is dancing, something she does whenever she gets the chance. 'I'd like to go more really, but I don't go to clubs much these days. I just don't have time any more.'

Her increasing size has worried her for years, and its harsh reality came home to her when she had a laparoscopy (an investigative operation involving keyhole surgery) ten years ago. When she came round from the anaesthetic, she was told that the doctor had been unable to get through the fat on her stomach. 'I was horrified. I mean, what an image! I was so embarrassed. Then one of the nurses asked me if I had an eating disorder. I was completely shocked. I felt like a freak, and that was obviously how they saw me.

181

'I tried so many times to lose weight and finally, in desperation, I tried some hypnotherapy sessions, to see if it could change my relationship with food. I lost a stone but, at £45 per session, it was too expensive to go on. I saw an ad for Fat Club in Hot Tickets, the *Evening Standard* supplement. It said they were looking for overweight people with large personalities, so I left a message on the answering machine saying I had Vanessa Feltz envy and wanted to lose weight.'

FAT CLUB ONE

'If I'd known that was what was planned, I don't think I'd have even applied.'

'I think Jacquie is probably the brightest of all the members at Fat Club,' writes Sarah in her early notes, 'but I'm not sure that will work in her favour. For a start I'll have to dispel a lot of dieting myths before she'll accept what I'm doing. She has to trust the fact that she doesn't have to be on a diet.'

When she arrives at Gorse Hill, Jacquie is not sure what to expect. 'Just before I came, the production team sent me a questionnaire asking if I had any objection to military-style exercise. Well, that's my worst nightmare and if I'd known that was what was planned, I don't think I'd have even applied.'

Despite her qualms, her first impressions are positive, even the inevitably awkward moment when the members first meet and introduce themselves. 'Meeting the other members that first time has been a big thing for me. I feel I bonded with the rest of the other people quite quickly. We all had to say why we are here, and I said that I've battled with my weight for 14 years, which is true. And everyone in that room understood what I meant. There isn't anyone there who has judged me because of it. It is a liberating feeling. But when Harvey introduced himself, it was a nightmare come true. I just felt panic-stricken when I saw him.'

Her panic is well-founded. 'The exercise sessions are, if anything, worse than I'd ever imagined. I didn't know what to expect, but Harvey is just so scary. He shouts at us, it seems, all the time. When I was doing the running, I had this sharp pain under my tongue. When I told Raj, he examined me thoroughly and that reassured me. He and Alex thought it was probably all in my mind, and it did go away.'

Despite her strong feelings, Jacquie manages to pull the wool over Harvey's eyes. He has no idea of her aversion to his form of exercise and is impressed by her efforts. 'She seems very determined and has a good attitude. She looks like she takes her exercise very seriously and should do well.'

After the weekend is over, Jacquie reflects on what has happened. 'It has been horrendous in parts and it isn't necessary for it to be so. It reminds me of why I don't exercise. I can honestly say I've hated every minute of that part. I wish I could be more open-minded about different ways to be fit, but there are some things I just can't bear to do. I know the exercise is going to be my stumbling block. I'll have to try and make myself do it. I'll have to join a gym – I'm dreading all that.'

Her meeting with Sarah is more positive because this is one area Jacquie feels she knows about. Sarah's concern is that she may be hoping to rely too much on food for her weight loss. 'I know she leads a hectic, unstructured lifestyle, where it will be extremely hard to stay in control of her eating and what food is available to her all the time. If she lapses too much she won't be successful. Is her love of clothes and fashion powerful enough to keep her going? Probably not. Ultimately you have to do these things for the right reasons.'

FAT CLUB TWO

Date: June
Weight at weigh-in: 15st 5lbs (215lbs)
Weight loss since last weigh-in: 2lbs
Total loss: 2lbs
Waist: 40in

'I hate bloody food!'

Jacquie has been on holiday to Spain since Fat Club One and has tried to be as good as she could with her eating while she was away. But it has been a difficult time, not the relaxing break she had hoped for. Her loyalties have been split between her girl-friend, Al, and her friends who, she is now coming to realise, are very unsupportive of her.

Not one asks her how her diet or the programme is going. Perhaps as a consequence of her ambivalent feelings, she has done nowhere near as much exercise as she was intending to during the holiday. The whole experience really upsets her and she feels that she gives, gives, gives and never takes.

'I really don't like exercising, but Al encourages me to go running in the park near where I live. It just brings it back to me, though, how much I hated exercise at school and it put me off the whole thing. I feel as if I should be able to get over this, but it's such a strong feeling. I've also found it hard to follow my eating plan because of my job. I don't always know when I'll be working late, and there is literally no time to go out and get some-thing sensible to eat. Before you know it, it's too late to get to a shop and someone's ordered out for a curry. By then I'm starving and I just have to eat it.'

When Jacquie arrives on Friday night after the photo shoot at Shepperton, she is feeling pretty down, only to be faced by Harvey's bag search. 'It is like adding insult to injury. I am really pissed off about it and I just feel like leaving.'

It seems that Sarah's concerns about diet are well founded. At the Saturday-morning weigh-in, Jacquie awaits the results with eyes closed. 'I've really been trying hard, but I haven't noticed my clothes feeling any looser, so I know I can't have lost much at all.' She has shed only 2lbs, the lowest of any member. After a moment's pause, the other members start cheering and congratulating, but Jacquie is not consoled. 'It's so depressing. I know it's not enough really.' Devastated and tearful, she sobs silently, and Jacey, close behind with a 4lb loss, offers a supportive arm and comfort at what is a terrible moment for Jacquie.

At breakfast Jacquie breaks down again. 'I'm fed up of feeling guilty every time I fucking eat anything!' Clearly this is a crisis moment, and Sarah is quickly by her side. 'I'm obsessed by food.

It's like there's two voices in my head, one saying "Eat it", the other saying "You fat bitch". I hate bloody food!'

Sarah is worried that Jacquie cannot (or will not) eat anything at all after the weigh-in and the alarm bells start to ring. That evening Jacquie reveals more. 'I'm not a crying sort of person, but I was gutted after the weigh-in. I still don't understand what's wrong. I meant what I said. I do feel guilty when I eat anything and I'm beginning to think that I could be on the edge of bulimia – that really scares me. My friends and colleagues are giving me no support at all. I've had enough!'

It has been a terrible weekend so far for Jacquie, but she tries hard to perk up after a confidence and morale-boosting chat with girlfriend Al, and joins in all the activities as best she can.

Alex's self-image workshop brings up a painful memory. 'I went out with some friends in Newcastle, we were going out clubbing and we all got dressed up. I spent ages getting ready and this guy, this friend of mine said, "You look amazing, you look gorgeous." Then he leaned close and whispered, "If I was your girlfriend, I'd starve you." I just felt worthless.'

This memory confirms for Jacquie that her friends' comments and attitude are hurting and damaging her, something she has been thinking for some time. It is clearly not helping her self-worth. As she leaves she makes a telling comment. 'If I only lost 2lbs next time, I'd have to evaluate if it's worth everyone's while my being here.'

Whether it is worth *her* while does not even seem to be part of the equation. While worrying about everyone else, Jacquie is not attaching enough importance to her own needs, but at least now she is starting to realise it.

Over the next few days Jacquie makes some decisions. She thinks about quitting her job and having showdown talks with her friends. This is a crisis point for her: 'After the weekend, I couldn't stop crying, and I couldn't tell anyone what was the matter. I felt like the whole of life was closing around me, and everyone wanted a last bit out of me. I went to see my GP, and he signed me off work with stress. I've never, ever had anything like this before, and I was really shocked when he told me. He suggested I could pull out of the programme, but although I'm sure Fat Club is adding to my stress, it's not causing it. I've got to re-evaluate everything. I'm working late hours and it's really getting to me. Fat Club is the first thing that I've done for myself. I just don't make time for me usually. I've dedicated just about all my life to my career, and this is where it's got me.'

FAT CLUB THREE

Date: July
Weight at weigh-in: 14st 7lb (203lbs)
Weight loss since last weigh-in: 12lbs
Total loss: 14lbs
Waist: 38in

> *'I'm really starting to feel the difference. I don't feel out of breath any more.'*

Jacquie is anxious about the approaching weekend. 'Last month's weigh-in was a disaster,' she says. 'If I haven't lost weight this time, I'll need some more advice. I had lots of problems straight after Fat Club Two. I was working away and I just found it impossible to keep to the eating plan, but in the last three weeks I've been going to the gym and I've exercised a lot, trying different exercise classes: aerobics, step and yoga and I'm managing to go about three times a week. I just can't fit any more in.

'Between Fat Club One and Two, I tried to emulate the kind of exercise that Harvey was showing us, but I just hated it. It's not what I enjoy and I knew I wouldn't be able to keep it up. The amazing thing is now that I'm actually enjoying the classes I do, particularly dance aerobics.'

The experts are not as optimistic about Jacquie's progress. Sarah believes 'Jacquie thought she would lose weight through diet change alone, and skip the exercise ... the truth is now setting in. But she isn't even keeping up her food diary, so I have no way of knowing what she eats.'

Harvey is annoyed and suspicious that she has also stopped filling in her exercise diary. Even Alex, usually so optimistic, is disquieted by the fact that Jacquie comforts herself with such phrases as: 'I'm not going to get completely stressed out over exercise … it's not worth it,' and Raj actually phones her in the interval, accusing her of being negative, in an effort to shake her into action.

If she does not show an improvement at the weigh-in, the experts are planning to give her a warning. Jacquie, however, feels she has turned the corner and, when she arrives, is looking more relaxed and noticeably slimmer. 'I was shocked after the last weigh-in, but this time I feel more confident. I reckon I've lost around 9lbs and I'm really starting to feel the difference. I don't feel out of breath any more.'

In fact, she has lost 12lbs and looks quietly content. The other members are delighted at Jacquie's progress – she is a very popular member and they were willing her to do better. She says modestly, 'I feel pretty good about it.' Inside she must be over the moon.

The experts have the good grace to admit they were wrong about her, and Sarah is amazed by Jacquie's progress. 'I don't know what spurred her into action, but I really thought that if she hadn't been able to achieve it by the second weekend, she would never do well. It must have been a combination of the holiday and the humiliation of the second weigh-in when she realised everyone else had done really well. She must have been dying inside. I am hopeful her success this time will motivate her further to carry on doing well.'

Jacquie now finds herself in the novel position of being held up as an example to the less successful members, Kelly and Jacey. She further shows her commitment to Fat Club by dashing home, late on Saturday evening, to be with Al who has brought her seriously ill dog to London for treatment, then returning early Sunday morning after two hours' sleep to continue with the activities. She is delighted with the dance aerobics session on Sunday, and joins in enthusiastically. Harvey watches po-faced from a safe distance. 'I don't do dancing!' he grunts.

Jacquie certainly does, and in his assessment of her performance for the weekend, Harvey notes how hard she works at it and that her results for run time, press-ups and sit-ups at the fitness assessment have all improved.

At home again, Jacquie talks about the classes she attends at her gym. 'OK, so I'm still the largest person at the exercise class and that was quite a barrier at first, but I can out-step and out-dance lots of thinner people. I like the exercise regime I've got now. I don't want to be competitive, I just want to enjoy it. I don't dislike Harvey at all, in fact I quite like him, but I dislike the regime. If I'd wanted to join the Marines, I'd have joined. You know, if I'd realised it was going to be this kind of exercise, I wouldn't have joined in the first place.'

FAT CLUB FOUR

Date: August
Weight at weigh-in: 14st 5lbs (201lbs)
Weight loss since last weigh-in: 2lbs
Total loss: 16lbs
Waist: 37in

'Everything seems to be a hurdle at the moment.'

Despite her resolve last month, Jacquie finds herself too busy even to think about a job change, and chickens out of handing in her notice.

She admits to finding it hard to 'fit Fat Club stuff in'. She is missing the point. This is not about adding to your life, it is about changing it. 'It's ruining my social life,' she goes on. 'I haven't seen some of my friends for almost three months, and even the closest ones I haven't managed to see for the last two or three weeks. Al lives in Dover, so I only get to be with her at weekends. I'm doing aerobics two to three times a week, and I'm just not prepared to do things I don't like.'

But her efforts are in the right direction: 'Since I've started yoga every Tuesday, I've felt a lot calmer too. I'm trying to eat loads of fruit and veg, and I'm buying less processed food. I suppose I've become even more aware of healthy eating, and I'm adapting recipes using low-fat ingredients. For example, I make fajitas with chicken cooked on a griddle with peppers and onions, and I made my own guacamole. I'm even reading packets in the supermarket, looking out for low-fat foods and calorie counting, but I have given up keeping my food diary. Raj has been on at me about that, but it's just so obsessive!'

Maybe Raj was right to nag. Jacquie arrives late for the week-end because she has been working on location. She gets home at 2.45 a.m. on Saturday and gets up in time to reach Gorse Hill at 7.30 a.m. 'I was sooo tired,' she sighs. When she arrives the other members are all doing their warm-ups. Harvey notices she is late, and that her results have not really improved, and gives her a hard time. Jacquie stays behind to speak to him about a problem she is having with her foot and to explain why she was late, but he brushes her explanations aside and will not listen. As far as he is concerned, this is just another example of her making excuses, and Jacquie's frustration at not being able to get through to him is palpable.

Things only get worse when the weigh-in reveals a paltry 2lbs loss – again. 'It's been a terrible weigh-in anyway,' says Jacquie afterwards. 'Jacey has now left after actually putting on 2lbs, so you can imagine how we're all feeling.' Disaster follows disaster, and in the circuit training Harvey criticises the group because they have not achieved their weight-loss target. Jacquie gets up and walks off, giving Harvey a mouthful on the way. Afterwards, she is slightly shamefaced about it. 'It's not really like me to do that, but I'd just had it. I got up and walked off in the middle of the session. I was so angry. I said something like, "You can fuck off. I've had a bellyful, and I've been up half the night." '

Meanwhile, the experts discuss the merits of her case, and vote, narrowly, to give her a warning. She is very upset, and feels unfairly treated in that her total loss is the same as Kelly's, who escapes a warning. Raj defends the experts' decision on the grounds that her rate of loss has deteriorated, but Jacquie feels that they are not taking her circumstances into account.

For Jacquie, this is the dark night of the soul. 'Everything seems to be a hurdle at the moment. The gym I go to is being refurbished and they've halved the number of classes they're doing, I'm working really hard, and I've got this foot problem. I'm not making excuses – it's really painful.'

Raj tells Jacquie she is suffering from plantar fasciitis, a condi-tion of the foot which manifests itself as a sharp stabbing pain whenever the heel is brought in contact with the floor. There is no real cure, although weight loss and stretching are both thought to help. He advises her to take Ibuprofen in the first instance, and to see her own GP if the problem persists.

Jacquie realises she needs help and asks to see Alex in the afternoon. 'I'm so tired, I don't even know if I'm making sense, but Harvey is just my worst nightmare. He fills me with fear, just his persona. It's really beyond anything rational. It's just this really awful feeling I get. I feel like "Oh my God, I can't bear this," and part of me thinks "Why am I here when I have a choice? Why am I putting myself through this?" I think it's a masculine thing. I don't like being bossed around by men. When I'm at the classes I enjoy, even when my heel is hurting, I do give it all my commitment. I'm sick of people questioning me all the time, telling me I'm negative or I'm making excuses. They're not excuses – they are real obstacles and problems.'

Alex's remedy is based on the information he gave to the members during the laughter workshop in Fat Club One. 'When you feel like that, just smile and laugh. Fake it 'til you make it. If you do that, it reframes your experience.'

Jacquie does not think she can manage to do this. 'I just don't think it's funny, though. I can't make myself laugh about it, I can't even pretend to laugh. Harvey's the ultimate symbol of male domination to me. His uniform terrifies me and it's even worse when he's wearing that hat. In his tracksuit, he doesn't scare me nearly as much.'

Alex does get through to Jacquie later on in the day at the temptations workshop. He gets together all the food the members admit to loving and gets them to throw it away into a clear plastic bag. He goes on to talk about the nature of temptation, the role of food in the members' lives and the fat content of the food in the bag. While he is talking, the bag is passed round for the members to look at. By the time it gets to Jacquie (whose choice was chocolate), some of the food is beginning to melt and it looks disgusting. 'That's done it for me. No one could have been tempted by it. I'd normally look on that kind of food as a treat, but now I'm thinking about what it's doing to my body long-term. It's not a treat at all.'

Sarah finds time to spend with Jacquie again during this Fat

Club, trying to come up with ways of helping her to reduce her calorie intake. 'I've always thought that Jacquie is one of the most intelligent members of Fat Club, but it's not necessarily an asset in terms of understanding the information given. She may find it too simple, not enough to stimulate her and get her teeth into. Everyone has received the same info to date. But I wonder if she would benefit from more in-depth explanations that would give her a better understanding?' Unfortunately, there is no time for Sarah to have a one-to-one with Jacquie, though it might have been just what she needed at this stage.

Fat Club Four is over and for Jacquie everything seems a problem. 'I didn't really enjoy it to tell you the truth,' she rants. 'I never realised how stressful it was being filmed. Normally I'd have loved the salsa dancing and the barbecue on Saturday night, but my foot was hurting whenever I danced. I couldn't even bring myself to enjoy the food because I'd only lost 2lbs. Al's gone ballistic because she hasn't seen me for three weeks. I haven't seen my other friends since the end of July. The only good thing on the horizon is that the dog's starting to get better.

'Here I am getting told off and shouted at when I know I'm not going to lapse back into my old eating habits, I'm more knowledgeable about how much I'm taking in and putting out. Sarah is so helpful – really genuine.' The biggest step forward for Jacquie is the conviction that she is going to keep up with the exercise. 'That's been the biggest revelation, but I still maintain you have to do something that you enjoy.'

FAT CLUB FIVE

Date: Early September
Weight at weigh-in: 14st 3lbs (199lbs)
Weight loss since last weigh-in: 2lbs
Total loss: 18lbs
Waist: 36½in

'People are asking what I've done, they say I'm looking great. What more motivation could you ask for?'

'Work's all right, a bit hectic as usual,' Jacquie reports, 'but I've been to Corfu with my brother and my seven-year-old niece, so I was very active. Every time I'd get settled on a lounger, she'd come along and want me to swim with her. It wasn't restful, but it was good fun. I'm not looking forward to Fat Club. I got shouted at last time, because I hadn't lost enough weight, and I'm dreading a repeat performance.'

The experts meet and Jacquie is a major topic of conversation. Harvey is adamant. 'If she puts on weight, she has to go.' But Alex is kinder, believing her to be more self-motivated now. 'She's been getting good feedback from her friends,' he says. 'And that's very important to her.'

Jacquie is looking different too. She seems younger and her complexion is firmer and fresher. She concedes that she has realised some important facts about her relationship with food. 'All or nothing – that was how I dieted. When I was fat, I just got fatter, and whenever I strayed off my diet, and I always did, I felt so miserable I'd just give up. I feel so much better now, more in control. In the last three weeks I've had so much positive feedback from everyone I've met. People are asking what I've done, they say I'm looking great. What more motivation could you ask for?'

Come the delayed Sunday-morning weigh-in, Jacquie has lost only 2lbs again and is bitterly disappointed. 'I've tried really hard. Sarah thinks it's down to my eating, but I think it's because I've hardly done any aerobic exercise. My foot's just so painful, but I'll just have to bite the bullet and take a painkiller. Maybe I'll have a look in my local gym to see if they do trampolining – I could probably manage that. I did it when I was a kid and I really enjoyed it.' Jacquie does not know it, but a trampolining session has been scheduled for that very afternoon.

When the members go outside into the grounds, there are gasps of amazement as they see the trampoline waiting for them, and Jacquie's face lights up with genuine delight for the first time at Fat Club. She is the first to have a go, and after a few moments to get used to the feeling once again, she is soon having the time of her life. 'I haven't done this for – oh – 21 years. I really feel happy. I'd love to take it up again.'

It has taken five weekends to stimulate Jacquie into an exercise she can really enjoy – and the trampolining has the same effect on everyone after a stressful 24 hours. Even the members who are hopelessly uncoordinated end up laughing and relaxed.

It helps them cope with the challenging see yourself slim presentation which follows. The image of herself as she was five months ago fascinates Jacquie, and she looks at it almost dispassionately, as if it were another person. 'I don't think I do look like that any more,' she says, a new realisation dawning that she has left that shape behind. 'I don't want to go back there.'

She can now see that her reality lies somewhere between the size she was initially and the size she could be if her weight loss continues. Jacquie is travelling forward at last towards a slim future, and looking back is uncomfortable for her now. Her 'after' image is elegant and feminine and that appeals to her and her love of fashion. When it appears on the screen, there are gasps of amazement from the other members at the way she could look. Jacquie nods in quiet determination.

When she looks back at photographs of herself taken in the past, she regrets the time she has wasted worrying about her weight. 'The sad thing is when I look back at pictures of myself even when I was quite thin, at the time I thought I was fat. In fact the only time I thought I was thin was when I was about 16. What I'd really like is a bum like Jennifer Lopez. I think she's just so sexy and womanly. That's my dream anyway.'

After this positive reinforcement, Jacquie finally grasps the exercise nettle – the missing part of the jigsaw for her. She has a meeting with Harvey, and at last he becomes an ally for her. 'He reckons I'm not doing enough cardiovascular. Also I haven't been keeping my diary up and he had a go at me about that. I'll just have to find some low-impact work that won't hurt my foot. I can't even do step at the moment, because coming down off the step really jolts my foot.'

FAT CLUB SIX

Date: September
Weight at weigh-in: 13st 13lbs (195lbs)
Weight loss since last weigh-in: 4lbs

Total loss: 22lbs
Waist: 35½in

> *'Harvey is right. Exercise does work, and I'm the
> living proof.'*

It's the last Fat Club and Jacquie looks like the cat that's got the
(reduced-fat) cream when she arrives at Gorse Hill. It doesn't
take long to find out why. For the first time in years, she has
bought a pair of off-the-peg jeans in a high street store. 'I just
went into River Island and took a pair of size 16 jeans off the
rack. I was really nervous in the changing room. I was thinking,
"What if I can't even get them up over my thighs?", but they
slipped on really beautifully, and I could do the zip up without
even tugging. I didn't have anyone with me to tell, so I said something to the bloke outside the changing rooms. He looked at me
as if I was mad, but I didn't care. I felt like dancing.'

'I've been doing more low-impact work, and exercise is less of
a problem now. I never thought I'd hear myself say this, but I'm
addicted to aerobics. It's a real buzz, and the teachers at the gym
I go to are great. They spark something in me to make me motivate myself. I use my pedometer a lot too, and I aim for 10,000
paces plus each day. Provided it's not high impact, I can manage
it.'

The most ironic news of all is that, as she has progressed with
her exercise, her foot problem has started to clear up. Although
it is known to be a condition that flares up intermittently, Raj
congratulates her because weight loss could be part of the reason
why it has ceased to bother her.

What a moment for Jacquie! Her whole reason for coming to
Fat Club was to be able to buy clothes in the high street, and now
she has managed it. Even the weigh-in holds no fear now. She's
lost 4lbs and over an inch from her waist in a month, but the real
difference is how she feels, and it shows. There is an end-of-term
feeling about the members today, and Jacquie is definitely sharing in it.

A yoga session in the gym contributes to Jacquie's feeling of
relaxation and competence. This is an exercise she clearly enjoys

and she looks very comfortable with the positions and breathing techniques, unlike many of the other members.

At the camp fire awards ceremony in the evening, she is voted Best Shaker and Mover, a fitting tribute to a woman who has at last found the right type of exercise – one that she enjoys and will keep up with. Jacquie remembers her feelings at the first weigh-in. 'When I saw Harvey I was panic-stricken. He was my nightmare come true, and it got worse before it got better. But Harvey's right. Exercise does work, and I'm the living proof.'

Sunday morning brings a gruelling triathlon, with cycling, running and swimming. Jacquie comes in a triumphant fourth, behind Stuart, Tony Curley and Tony Upson, and looks surprised at herself. Considering this is the kind of exercise she hates, she is showing some fine form.

Raj: 'Her father, a diabetic, died of a heart attack in his 60s, and I think that has been a powerful spur to her. By reducing her weight, she has greatly reduced the risks of developing it herself.'

Jacquie's Fitness Assessment

Fat Club 1

Run	Sit-ups	Press-ups
2.43	15	25

Fat Club 6

Run	Sit-ups	Press-ups
2.05	35	60

Chapter 11

Stuart's Story

'Instead of going into a shop and saying "I like that", I have to ask if they have anything to fit me.'

Stuart Gibbons
Age: 22
Lives: Chichester and Ashford, Kent
Occupation: Postgraduate student at Kent University
Height: 6ft 3in
Weight at first weigh-in: 17st 1lb – obese
Waist at first weigh-in: 45in

It is Stuart's intelligence that strikes you first. It comes as no surprise to learn that this highly articulate man has a degree in law, and a master's degree in medical law and is hoping to teach the subject. 'It's my first love,' he says, 'and that's what I want to do.'

At a lofty 6ft 3in, he does not appear to be very overweight. He is just a big, good-looking man, with an incongruous slightly camp demeanour and a habit of poking fun at himself. His face is open and friendly and a ready laugh is never far away.

Stuart comes from a broken home, his parents divorcing when he was six and his mum subsequently separating from her second husband, but for all that he had a privileged upbringing in Chichester, went to private school and has always had a close relationship with his father. 'The curious thing is, my parents are now the best of friends. If my mum is going up to London, she always stays with my dad, who has never remarried. I think they talk to each other on the phone more often than I do to them.'

Size has always been an issue for Stuart. 'I went on my first diet when I was seven,' he admits. 'My mum is big too – about a size 22 or 24 – and we used to diet together and have weigh-ins on a Saturday morning.' Luckily for him, he had a close year group at secondary school of just 15, so teasing and bullying were not a problem. 'When I was a teenager I went around in a shell suit and briefcase for heaven's sake – I knew nothing! It was worse though when I was five or six. Other kids would shout, "Don't go near him, you'll catch fat!" I was never exactly sporty,' he says with irony, 'and my PE teacher and I had an under-standing. I used to have a "please can Stuart be excused games" letter in reserve just in case.

The problem for Stuart has always been food – the wrong food. 'I'll eat anything that isn't nailed down and take little exercise. As a student I've had very little structure to my day, so if a lecture finishes at noon, and I don't have another until 3 p.m., I go with friends to the student bar and have cheap student food, burgers, chips or pizza. I won't think twice about buying chocolate. The GP at my first-term medical asked me to get on the scales and after I saw the result, I was motivated to lose weight ... for the first day!'

Because he is a happy-go-lucky man, popular among his fellow students, no one has nagged or pushed him into losing weight, but he is sensitive to derogatory comments. 'Getting uptight about jibes about my weight is my own fault really. I am the first to take the mickey out of myself, so others follow my lead, and then on some days realise that I'm not too happy about it. It is the superficial things that get to me. I want to look good, but instead of going into a shop and saying "I like that", I have to ask if they have anything to fit me. Nothing fits me in any high street shop except Marks & Spencer, and even if a shop does do trousers with a 44in waist, the leg is invariably 29in. Clothes manufacturers can't believe you can be tall and big.'

Unlike the other members, Stuart did not apply to join Fat Club directly, but came in via another TV programme. 'I applied to go on *Richard and Judy* for the bikini dieters show for a laugh

– I rather fancied a tiger-print-two piece.' Series producer Denise Seneviratne needed another participant. 'They showed her my letter and she thought I fitted the bill.' Out of the blue he received a phone call from her, and liked the sound of the programme. But his attitude was different to what it had been for the *Richard and Judy Show*. 'I am deadly serious about this,' he says.

FAT CLUB ONE

'I can't pile on the weight again before the programme is aired.'

Stuart's grandmother has died a week before the first Fat Club, which has left him no time to become nervous about the programme. 'From the start, I feel self-motivated, but support for each other in the group is the greatest help. At first I was intimidated that there weren't more younger people, but after a few hours we are getting on so well. It is great meeting new people, and the type of people I probably would never have met before. Had I seen some of the bigger members of the group before I would have thought "Poor buggers", now I think what courage they have to do the Club at all.'

Fat Club has made him think more deeply than he ever has before. 'At first I just wanted to look good, but it has made me question the health angle. My ECG [electrocardiogram which measures electrical pulses of the heart] at the initial medical examination was perfect and I thought "Well, I haven't done any damage ... yet. I've got a chance to do something about it." '

The early-morning start for fitness training nearly cripples Stuart – he is a student after all and 7 a.m. does not exist in his world – but the novelty of the Club is enough to get him going. 'I've done well in the jogging, because it has been less time since I did exercise than for most of the others. It isn't such a shock. I had been warned that I would be smaller than some of the others, and I was worried that they might think "What's he doing here?" In fact one member commented after the jog, "You're not fat anyway." '

In this disparate group, Stuart clicks with Tracy and Donna – 'perhaps because we're the three smokers and keep nipping out for a fag', he reckons. 'When there are ten, you are bound to be closer with one or two from the group, but I don't not get on with anyone.' He is unfazed too by the continual presence of the cameras. 'In fact as time goes on I've forgotten about them even being there, but they are a motivation. I can't pile on the weight again before the programme is aired.'

His only concern is hearing his own voice on TV, which he hates, but he is comfortable with the idea of baring his weight problem on air. 'Hopefully it will motivate people. They will think "If those people can put up with humiliation, I can do it too." '

Stuart's first meeting with Harvey is head on. Stuart refuses to swim in the freezing cold pool. Harvey sees it as an excuse and is resolute: 'Get in the goddamn pool, Stuart!' he bellows. Harvey wins out but afterwards Stuart says, 'He has been rude to me, and I'll answer back if someone is rude to me,' and the episode makes him sceptical about Harvey's involvement in Fat Club. 'I was expecting someone more like Mr Motivator – lots of spandex! I think Harvey was brought in just for the entertainment value. We don't really need a US Marine to teach us. If I achieve what I should, I think the programme makers want it to be like the film *An Officer and a Gentleman*, and have me say, "Oh yes, Harvey was right all along." ' But Harvey is more than a match for Stuart's attitude. This is not the gym teacher from schooldays who could be fooled by an off-games letter. He is merciless in his assessment of Stuart: 'He's a loser – always making excuses, making goddamn excuses. He's really pissing me off.'

The meeting with Alex is even more strained. 'It's only the first day, the TV cameras are there, and we have to try and be natural.' He recounts what happened afterwards: 'There was Alex saying "We are going to investigate you." At one point he asked me what I thought about psychologists. I said I thought they were great, but that I was bound to leave here with a "problem". "Anything I say will incriminate me. If I'm too loud you'll say I'm covering something up, if I'm quiet you'll say I have a communication problem." At one point I was flustered and got food and Freud muddled up. Alex was quick to pick it up!' He mimics

Alex's Glaswegian accent: ' "I notice you had a problem there, Stuart." Oh God! I don't know what he thinks of me, but for some people in the group who have had emotional problems in the past, he will be very useful.'

Stuart may have initial suspicions about the experts, but the reaction is mutual. Raj sums it up: 'I worry that Stuart is a clown and just here to have a laugh. He is more interested in being on TV and I think he will fail.' But Stuart leaves Fat Club in high spirits. 'I feel motivated. It has been exciting,' he says in the following days. 'I went home in my Fat Club T-shirt and went straight to the pub. Everyone was asking me all about it, and the motivation didn't wear off. I know that after three months weight loss will plateau, and the novelty will wear off, but at the moment this new way of life they are teaching us is not part of our lifestyles yet. When it is, that's going to make us all fed up. The hardest part will be to get through that.'

FAT CLUB TWO

Date: June
Weight at weigh-in: 16st 1lb (225lbs)
Weight loss since last weigh-in: 14lbs
Total loss: 14lbs
Waist: 41½in

> *'If one diet worked, you wouldn't be here.' – Sarah Schenker*

> *'Your friends can help up to a point, but they can't sympathise with the temptation you have from a chocolate digestive.'*

When the group meet up for the photo shoot, they fall on each other like long-lost friends. 'We have been in touch on the phone and via e-mail in the interim,' Stuart explains, 'but it is great to see people again. I don't know how we'd feel if we were together all the time, but over the month we have become very close. The thing I like best about Fat Club is seeing the group again. Everyone is interested in everyone else and their failures and achievements. Your friends can help up to a point, but they can't sympathise with the temptation you have from a chocolate digestive.'

Stuart has been a strong influence in persuading Donna to come back for the second weekend. 'She had been ill between sessions and was worried she hadn't lost weight. Tracy and I persuaded her that, even if she hasn't, she has been eating better and exercising, so she has been being healthy. She got so fed up of us phoning she's finally given in.'

Once at Gorse Hill, the clowning around does not stop. 'We've gone past the ice-breaking stage with everyone,' says Stuart, 'and at the weigh-in we have all lost weight which was great. But the bag search by Harvey when we arrived was bloody silly. We'd had a month to eat what on earth we liked, so what was so important about that weekend? I had been staying with friends before I arrived, so I made sure my dirty underwear and snack wrappers where on the top of my suitcase. You can get annoyed or you can laugh. I took it as a laugh.'

However, he would be surprised at Harvey's positive reaction to the whole group's motivation. 'They shattered the assessment scores they turned up with for Fat Club One, and this has totally blown me away, because it came so soon. Maybe they are serious about losing weight and being fitter.'

The food session with Sarah is an eye-opener for Stuart. She gathers the group around the table groaning under the weight of pizza and burgers. 'This is amazing,' says Stuart. 'This is all stuff I like.' No surprise then to discover it is an exact replica of the four days' worth of food Stuart catalogued in his pre-Fat Club food diary. 'She even has it down to the right quantities,' he says wonderingly, as the group roar with laughter. Sarah may have chosen Stuart's diary as a good example of bad food; more likely she knew this self-deprecating man would be able to shoulder the criticism. For all the laughter, it is a serious lesson. Sarah draws attention to the pizza, pies, chocolate and beer. 'Stuart's balance of nutrients is all wrong,' she explains, 'and for successful weight loss you must aim for five portions of fruit and veg each day.' 'So what is the theory behind fad diets like cabbage soup, then?' Stuart enquires. 'They are incredibly low calorie and you are unlikely to overeat, so weight loss will be quick,' explains Sarah, 'but you will simply pile on the pounds again once you are "off" the diet. If one diet worked, you wouldn't be here.'

The food diary was pre-Fat Club, and in the intervening weeks Stuart has made headway with his eating habits. His biggest challenge and temptation has been chocolate, but Sarah's messages have been received. 'The great thing about what we have been taught is that you don't have to give anything up. Just eat it in moderation. If I'm with friends and we get a take-away pizza they say, "Hey, you're on a diet." But I've learnt I can eat it, just not every day. It's a case of a whole life change.'

The weight session with Raj, in which the group explore the effect extra body weight has on the heart, brings Stuart up short. His body slumps and his leg muscles strain under the weight of a jacket packed with an extra 8st (designed to imitate something nearing the extra weight load carried by Simon), and his heart rate jumps from 75 to 135 beats per minute without taking a step. The actual weight difference between Stuart and Simon is nearly 10 stone, and Raj's message is blunt: 'If you don't lose weight, Stuart, in another 20 years when you are Simon's age, you could be carrying that extra 8st.' It is a sobering thought for Stuart, who realises he has enough time to put things right.

FAT CLUB THREE

Date: July
Weight at weigh-in: 15st (210lbs)
Weight loss since last weigh-in: 15lbs
Total loss: 29lbs
Waist: 38½in

> *'I perceive that I am "pigging out" – actually all I am eating is apples and Tracker bars.'*

Bitten by the exercise bug, Stuart has been enthusiastically rollerblading, and has fallen over and broken his arm at the elbow. The plaster has been on for only two and a half weeks, but exercise has been difficult because of the danger that he might fall on it again. 'I can walk briskly,' he says, 'but I can't drive to get to Canterbury to use an exercise bike.' He has even struggled to prepare food for himself, and battles one-handed with a sharp knife and an uncooperative bag of low-fat oven chips. 'Aaaah!' he yells with frustration. 'I can't even eat bad food!'

Stuart's fears about a drop in enthusiasm among the members has proved accurate and he has been in touch with Tracy, who is suffering from what Harvey calls the 'New Year blues'. He can sympathise. 'It's hard to get motivation and everything is a chore. I was worried that with my arm stopping me exercising and getting out, I had started to eat badly again, but when I actually look at the contents of my cupboards, nothing is more than 5 per cent fat. I perceive that I am "pigging out" – actually all I am eating is apples and Tracker bars.' The weigh-in proves it. Stuart has lost a remarkable 15lbs.

During the weekend, and despite the fact that it is out of plaster, Stuart's arm is still giving him trouble. 'I have the attitude that I have done my best with a broken arm and I have still lost weight, but Harvey just shouts at me because I'm not jogging. I am annoyed as I have been told by the surgeon I should not jog … or at least I was annoyed for about three minutes then it all went over my head. He's never happy, is he? I just don't listen when he talks, because I know a load of crap is going to come out.'

Harvey is more forgiving in private. 'I knew I would have to tighten him up right off the bat,' he says, 'to let him know that I won't tolerate his smart attitude. Every now and then he will test me and do just enough to get by. But he should do well. He's young and wants to be accepted by his peers.'

Like everyone else, Stuart is affected by the stress of the weekend, caused in the main by Jacey's failure to turn up on the Friday evening. 'I am pissed off – it isn't anyone's fault, but I just don't have much tolerance or patience at the moment and my arm was hurting. Add to that getting shouted at for not being committed when I have made a good weight loss.'

Despite all this, the eating messages continue to hit home in the cookery competition. With Donna and Tony Upson, Stuart is in the 'starters' team and cooks pasta with a Mediterranean sauce. 'I am so proud of the filo pastry parcels we have made with sun-dried tomatoes and low-fat cheese because they were my idea, but we have rather overdone the oil. Sarah has suggested using milk to stick the pastry together.'

The dance aerobics is a hit too. 'When you get drunk in a nightclub you fancy yourself doing dance routines, but I had never done this kind of thing as exercise. It just shows you don't always have to stick with the sweaty gym. You can do different things and get out and meet new people. I get bored easily and it's good to do different things.'

FAT CLUB FOUR

Date: August
Weight at weigh-in: 14st 9lbs (205lbs)
Weight loss since last weigh-in: 5lbs
Total loss: 34lbs
Waist: 36½in

> *'I could go into any high street shop now and buy something off the peg – if I had the money!'*

Stuart has spent the weeks between Fat Clubs poring over the first draft of his dissertation for his degree, which has to be handed in shortly. Not only has this meant lots of sedentary work but he has also spent the time house-sitting for a friend, who has conveniently left his cupboards full of crisps and chocolate biscuits, what Stuart calls 'bad food'.

Despite the temptations, he has resisted – most of the time. 'It's late at night when I have the problem,' he says. 'The other night, I sat through all the episodes of *Buffy the Vampire Slayer* with a friend, and by nine I was famished! But compared to four months ago I ate like a stick insect.' The last night of *Big Brother* is almost his undoing, however, and in the face of the tension he eats pizza, washed down with beer and wine, and finishes off with Ben and Jerry's ice-cream – 'But I'm working it off!' he is quick to assure.

Stuart is nervous for the first time about the weigh-in, but his weight loss is 5lbs and he has gone from obese on the BMI scale to bordering on 'healthy'. The great difference, however, is in inches. The day before he is due at Gorse Hill, Stuart treats himself to a pair of jeans with a 36in waist. Before he was wearing 44in. 'I just had to buy them and loved walking up to the counter saying loudly, "Can I have these SIZE 36 jeans please?" Things have changed tangibly. I could go into any high street shop now and buy something off the peg – if I had the money!'

The salsa dancing is a hit too. 'I'd never done it before but, as the rollerblade incident showed, I am not very coordinated and the dancing is not very pretty.' He is also affected strongly by Raj's demonstration with the artificial fat. 'He explained how it is hard to do surgery because of the difficulties of cutting through fat and how 50 per cent of your fat is around your liver and heart. It is shock tactics and it has worked. Raj has given us the facts and he hasn't pussy-footed around.

'I suppose I came to Fat Club wanting to wear Gap clothes, but this really showed me that health is an issue too. I'm young and I hadn't really thought about my health – who the hell does at 20? – but heart trouble does run in our family.'

Stuart is now teased that he does not really belong at Fat Club any more, but he is still adamant about the important message of the regime: that it is about changing your life for a healthier lifestyle, even if you have only a stone to lose. 'It's about lowering life risks.'

For Raj, it has been a question of eating humble pie. He was wrong about Stuart and is keen to praise him now: 'Stuart is a shining example that you can have an injury, but still remain active in ways other than exercise.' The health news is good too: 'His BMI is just over 25, so he is no longer obese and on the cusp of not being overweight either. He is looking great.'

In Alex's opinion, Stuart is an intelligent man and has all the right information he needs to be able to reach a target weight loss and keep the weight down. 'He has benefited from negative role models: he has seen bigger people and realised he doesn't want to be like that, but now he has to move on to the second stage of the programme. He needs to tone up now he has lost all this weight. I have noticed how gawky he is, as if he has grown out of his body. His posture is still not good and I wonder if the Alexander Technique would be a good idea. He needs to think "Walk tall" and exercise with a positive feeling, translating that into his physical posture.'

Harvey agrees: 'Stuart is still nursing his injury, but is looking well as far as weight loss is concerned. He definitely should start building some muscle.'

FAT CLUB FIVE

Date: Early September
Weight at weigh-in: 14st 4lbs (200lbs)
Weight loss since the last weigh-in: 5lbs
Total loss: 39lbs
Waist: 34½in

> '*The stranger in the street who walks past you just sees a fat person – they don't give a toss about your health or your life.*'

The message has got through to Stuart, but for all the members this weekend is crunch time. 'They've had the shock tactics,' says series producer Denise. 'It's at this stage that the psychology comes in.'

When the group explore how they will cope once the crutch of Fat Club has gone, Stuart is philosophical. 'It's like a moving staircase. Before I would have had a McDonald's and fallen right back down to the bottom. Now there is so much support behind me and because of all the work I have put in, I will only fall back a couple of steps.'

To mark his success, Stuart comes through with flying colours in the 'iron member' contest. The group has to undergo a series of endurance exercises – holding sugar bags in front of them with arms outstretched, star jumps and press-ups – until all but two are eliminated. The final head-to-head is with Donna on the exercise bikes. Stuart, panting and exhausted wins by just 10 points, and for his pains receives a set of dumb bells as a prize. They seem the perfect gift to put the finishing touch on his weight-loss achievement. 'That's great,' he enthuses. 'I was going to buy some myself anyway.'

The chance to work on his muscle tone comes sooner than he thinks, as Harvey whisks him off to the Fitness Centre to teach him the techniques of good exercise. 'I see people in gyms going through the motions, but they are doing more harm than good,' says Harvey. 'Learning the right technique is important.' While demonstrating press-ups and stretches, with the perfect precision one has come to expect from Harvey, he tells Stuart he wants him to do this series of super sets every day, 'first thing every morning. Feel those muscles working.' For the first time Stuart sees sympathy and understanding from Harvey – it has been a hard-won respect – and in response Stuart works hard, his body trembling under the effort of diamond press-ups and crunches.

Back home, with his university dissertation now handed in, Stuart waits for the results and to hear if his application to do a PhD has been accepted. So, like all impoverished students with overdrafts to pay off, he moves back home to Chichester to live with his mum and to take up a temporary job in the local housing department. Stuart's mum has had a lifetime battle with her weight and has resorted to diet pills, and the arrival of her new-look son has quite an impact on her. 'She is so impressed. I've joined a local gym which has a discount for people who work for the council and mum's joined too. She's been twice in the first week. My experience really seems to have rubbed off on her.' The latest recruit is having an impact in the council department too. 'I'm working in a room full of women and each day when I come in they take a look at my lunch box, ask me how many calories so and so has, and copy it the next day.'

The last few weeks have not been without their temptations, however. 'Everyday someone brings a plate of cakes into the office and they sit there on the desk all day. I suppose I've had about one a day, but last Christmas I would have scoffed the lot.'

The impact of Fat Club on Stuart's life has been remarkable. 'I'm starting to talk as if I was some kind of gym freak. The main thing is that I am thinking about the gym in a different way. It wasn't a financial thing in the past (as college membership was only £30 per year), it's a mental thing. I used to try and find excuses not to go, now I see it as my private time. I get on the running machine and put on my Walkman and no one can call me on the phone or interrupt me.'

Stuart did not have as much weight to lose as the other men on Fat Club, but unless he tackled his weight problem while he is young he was storing up trouble for later, and he now realises his limitations. 'I couldn't have done it without Fat Club. It has helped me to change my attitude. I can't isolate any one of the experts who has been most effective. They have all made a contribution: Harvey and the exercise and Sarah and diet are tangible, but Raj's and Alex's messages have been more subtle. At the beginning I think we all arrived reckoning we had tried all the diets going before, and we sat back expecting to be spoonfed by the experts. But by Fat Club Two, we realised that we were the only ones who could do something about ourselves. The stranger in the street who walks past you just sees a fat person – they don't give a toss about your health or your life.'

It is this self-motivation, so strongly emphasised in Alex's guidance, which has struck a chord with Stuart. He knows where it missed the mark. 'That is where Kelly went wrong. She couldn't have changed her attitude no matter how long Fat Club had gone on. She thought "I'm coming along" and that coming along was good enough. You can't just go to the gym and try and absorb the exercise atmosphere by osmosis. You have to sweat or you aren't doing anything.'

So what does he think of the new Stuart? 'It's a double-edged sword,' he reckons. 'When I was 17 or 18st there was no point in worrying about how I looked. I was just huge. Now I'm more critical. I think to myself, that love handle looks too big. That arm is more muscly than the other.' At the see yourself slim workshop with Alex, when each member is shown a digitally mastered picture of how they were and what they could become, his reaction is almost guilty when he sees the changed image. It looks much like Stuart looks now. 'I feel embarrassed in front of the group, because I know that if I look in the mirror I would see that today.'

He is still not confident of the impression he is now making on other people. 'I saw some friends the other day that I hadn't seen for months. They said, "Wow, where have you gone?" That makes me feel great. But I still am not sure whether people are looking at me – in a nightclub, for example – because I'm attractive or wondering how on earth I could wear a shirt or trousers like that.'

He approaches the last Fat Club with mixed feelings. 'I shall miss it – it is something completely different to do every month and I shall miss the people – Tracy, Donna, Jacquie and Sha especially – she's so interesting – but I know that now the rest of our lives is up to us.'

FAT CLUB SIX

Date: September
Weight at weigh-in: 13st 10lbs (192lbs)
Weigh loss since last weigh-in: 8lbs
Total loss: 47lbs
Waist: 34in

> *'I get frustrated with friends who are on fad diets now. I want to scream "You don't do it like that!" '*

With his slim face and new physique, Stuart now looks like an interloper at Fat Club. His trousers are too big and gathered under his belt, and at the weekend's baggy clothes parade, he has to hold up the jeans he wore at Fat Club One. He explains with delight how he tried on a medium T-shirt in the last few days and was staggered to discover it fitted. The weigh-in confirms it: at under 14st, he has now a BMI of 25 and is in the bracket of acceptable body fat. The group is congratulatory and wonderfully supportive – the members nominate him in their own award ceremony as having the most Impressive Weight Loss and being Body Beautiful – and their affirmation is having an impact on Stuart's demeanour. Gone is the apologetic little boy lost, and here stands the man.

The posture workshop could have been designed for him – he admits his posture is not good: Anita Young, the engaging instructor from the Royal Ballet School, makes a bee line for him during the session and explains how ballet training is the finest for muscle toning and posture, and how, by standing the right way, one immediately looks thinner and taller. She drives him through tough and challenging exercises, and teases him, with a slap on the bum: 'You are young and good-looking. You should have a good physique.'

This is confirmation of a successful weekend for Stuart. He wins the triathlon and the Fat Club quiz and becomes the hero of Fat Club. When he looks at the food mountain piled up in front of the group during the session, he is teased that it looks like student fare. He admits readily: 'I can't see anything there that I haven't eaten in the last six months, and just because I'm not eating much of this kind of food any more doesn't mean I don't still quite like it. But I have learnt that I can eat it, in the right proportions. In fact I get frustrated with friends who are on fad diets now. I want to scream "You don't do it like that!" '

Stuart does ask for Alex's support during the weekend, however, because he is finding temptation hard to resist, particularly that plate of biscuits left out all day at work or the seconds of the Indian take-away with friends. For Alex the very fact that Stuart has come to him shows he is aware it is a bad situation. He encourages him to have a chat with himself when faced with temptation: is this cake important to me? What would I advise someone else if they were in the same situation? 'When a belief in something is deep-seated, that's when you start to make changes. You have to believe in the message yourself.'

At the final session of the whole programme, Alex is quick to reinforce this message to the group: 'We the experts are not here any more to help you. You have to ask the questions for yourself, get the stabilisers off your bike. Make sure the people around you know you are different. Self-honesty and self-monitoring are the only way to succeed.' Raj is quick to congratulate Stuart, but equally swift to remind him he has a task to maintain his weight loss. 'Don't use the pounds lost to measure your success, think about the lifestyle changes.'

Stuart is sad to leave Fat Club. He has made close friends and even though the amount of weight he has lost is on a par with the other men, the physical change is most dramatic in him. 'I do feel pretty pleased with myself, and I'm amazed people thought I wouldn't stick at it. Thanks for the confidence!'

He leaves aware that he has work to do, but on reflection reckons, 'I don't know how I'd feel if I was Simon who has still only knocked the tip off the iceberg – but then again, he is working to lose weight and get results. I've got to work to stay the same.'

Raj admits he misread Stuart from the start: 'How wrong I was! Stuart is focused, intelligent and highly motivated. He has done very well indeed.' All the experts have their own opinions of who will stick on the path of weight loss, but Stuart appears on everyone's list.

Stuart's Fitness Assessment

Fat Club 1

Run	Sit-ups	Press-ups
1.57	28	9

Fat Club 6

Run	Sit-ups	Press-ups
1.20	54	82

Chapter 12

Fat Club and You

Final weigh-in results:

Simon Payne: 23st 4lbs (total loss: 64lbs)
Donna Norris: 13st 5lbs (total loss: 25lbs)
Tony Upson: 20st 4lbs (total loss: 45lbs)
Tracy Young: 17st 9lbs (total loss: 35lbs)
Tony Curley: 17st 7lbs (total loss: 61lbs)
Sha Wylie: 11st 13lbs (total loss: 31lbs)
Jacquie Marsh: 13st 11bs (total loss: 24lbs)
Stuart Gibbons: 13st 12lbs (total loss: 45lbs)

The group met up one last time for a final weigh-in in November. Weight losses were not as dramatic but were still heading in the right direction. The Fat Club members have lost 23st 6lbs between them. That is more than the starting weight of Tony Upson, and over 15 per cent of the whole group's combined starting weight. A remarkable achievement, but for the eight remaining members of Fat Club, the end of the programme is just the beginning. They were encouraged, cajoled, even at times bullied, through six exhausting months of exercises and workshops and have come out the other side inspired and resolved to change their lives for the better.

As for Jacey Eze and Kelly Mundy who failed – well, nobody said it was going to be easy, and anyone who started the Fat Club regime hoping for a magic wand was bound to be disappointed.

There were indications early on that they were not truly committed. The experts and other team members gave them all the support they could, and finally felt desperately let down by their continued refusal to take responsibility for their lifestyle.

There are no excuses for willingly putting your life at risk, and make no mistake about it, the risks Jacey and Kelly face are grave. Both were still morbidly obese when they left Fat Club and neither had made any meaningful changes to their lives. Even they, however, have received information and been taught techniques that will make it easier for them to take charge of their health when they are ready to make a genuine effort.

But it is the success stories that are important here, and there is much to celebrate. Stuart now has a BMI of below 25, which puts his weight in a healthy zone; Donna is no longer morbidly obese; Simon has shifted over four stone and is heading in the right direction, and according to Alex's projections, if each of the eight members carries on with their current rate of weight loss, they will hit their target weights this year. Some will have managed it already.

Fat Club has succeeded without a diet, diet pills, special foods, concoctions or drinks. This shows that, with determination and an understanding of food and the importance of exercise, even people with serious, long-term weight problems can change their lives. Many of the members were people who had failed at keeping to a diet or exercise programme in the past. This time they are well on the way to success.

But what has it done for you? Have you been inspired by the stories behind Fat Club and the members' battles with long-term weight problems?

One thing all the members have learnt is that success comes from within. Losing weight to please someone else or to conform to some outside view of how you feel you should be is doomed to failure. The successes of Fat Club belong to those who were prepared to examine their lives honestly and to make fundamental changes. Their stories show that taking responsibility for lifestyle changes was actually a liberating and enjoyable experience. Instead of relying for their weight loss on a diet imposed by someone else (usually a skinny expert), they relied on themselves and their understanding of the balance between their intake of food and their energy expenditure.

Despite their dependence on the Fat Club team of experts in the initial stages of the series, they have all gone on to become their own self-motivated experts, devising eating and activity routines and attitudes that fitted comfortably with their lives and their aims. They have developed better body awareness than ever before and gained pyschological insights into their relationships with food and exercise. They have learnt to fine-tune the food they eat and their activity, and in the process have come to enjoy both more than ever before.

Using the guidance of Fat Club's experts, you too can make these changes.

You and Your Health

Dr Raj Patel

'The prime aim of Fat Club is not just weight loss. It's helping people to change their lifestyles, with weight loss as a bonus.'

IMPORTANT: As we saw in the first chapter of the book, being overweight in most cases is a result of overeating foods that are too high in fat and sugar, combined with lack of exercise. There are certain medical conditions, however, which cause obesity, or make weight loss very hard. These include thyroid dysfunction, pituitary disease and polycystic ovaries, and we advise that you consult your doctor to check you do not suffer from any of these conditions. Being overweight can also cause high blood pressure, and we encourage you to ask your doctor to check this for you and to suggest safe exercise levels to start off with.

Because of the many different factors involved in obesity, anyone serious about losing weight and embracing a healthy lifestyle has to take a holistic approach, one that tackles all areas of their lives. As the successful Fat Club members found, this can have far-reaching effects. All have acquired confidence, learnt new skills and fulfilled long-held dreams. And all because they have started to regard themselves as winners, as being in control.

The three-pronged attack – mindset, diet and exercise – against weight and bad eating habits has resulted in the kind of healthy weight loss that Raj and any other GP would be delighted to witness in their overweight patients. As Raj told the members, even a 10 per cent reduction in their weight will immediately reduce their risks of death from diabetes by 30 per cent.

CALCULATING YOUR BMI

BMI stands for Body Mass Index and is a term that health experts use to describe the amount of body fat a person has. You can work it out through a mathematical equation that takes into account your height and weight, and is far more accurate than any previous height and weight charts. BMI can be used as a healthy weight indicator by anyone who is 18 or more years old, except for competitive athletes, body builders, pregnant or nursing women, or elderly people who are not active and therefore may have lost muscle mass.

BMI is worked out by the formula: weight in kilograms ÷ height in metres squared. (1st = 6.3kg)

For example, take an adult woman weighing 60kg who is 1.6m tall: $60 ÷ (1.6 \times 1.6) = $ **23.4.** With a BMI rating of 23.4, she is a healthy weight.

You can rate your BMI using this chart:

Below 20	Underweight
20–25	Acceptable
25–30	Overweight
30–40	Obese
Over 40	Morbidly obese

The ideal BMI figure is between 20 and 25. This is considered to be a healthy level. People with BMIs between 25 and 30 are at increased risk for illnesses such as heart disease, diabetes, high blood pressure, gall bladder disease, osteoarthritis and some cancers. Body shape matters too. Women with a waist measurement greater than 35 inches and men with a waist measurement greater than 40 inches are also at greater risk. People with BMIs over 30 are at extreme risk for these diseases, especially if they have the waist measurements mentioned above.

Your and Your Life

Professor Alex Gardner

Are you ready for the challenge?

Congratulations! You have reached the point when you know you have to take action about your body and your health. That is the first and most important step forward. Being overweight is a complex issue. Each member of the club had a reason why they were heavy: they could not say 'no' to food, they ate for comfort and to make themselves feel better, they were frightened of exercise, or thought they were too worthless to bother looking good. These are emotional reasons that transcend the food or the exercise itself, but until the emotional issues are faced, losing weight will always be a battle.

Once you have been honest with yourself, you need to maintain that honesty. It has been clear throughout Fat Club that overweight people are experts at making excuses: 'I was on holiday', 'I hurt my arm', 'Someone close to me died', 'I've been too busy' are just some that emerged. There should be no excuses – you are only fooling yourself – and the reason that Jacey Eze and Kelly Mundy did not succeed in their life change is because there was always a reason for letting go of control. Before any life-change plan can be effective, you need to make a commitment. A commitment to taking control of your life and to achieving your goals. To check you are on target, self-monitoring is the most important factor. Once self-monitoring stops, commitment slips.

Ask yourself:

Can I really do this?

The answer is yes if you come to believe in yourself. Ask yourself how important it is for *you* to lose weight, and have a good clear reason why you want to get the weight off. Find a realistic goal that you feel you can reach. Do not do it because of pressure from anyone else. Weight loss is personal and you should reward yourself when you are successful, but with something in keeping with your long-term aims. Forgive yourself for your past life as an overweight person, and look to the positive future.

How can I get help myself?

The important thing is to make an open commitment to losing weight, so tell everyone that you are working to do it. Weight loss clubs are a great source of personal support, so try to find one near you that you can join. You could even ask people to sponsor you for charity. Tactics like these can all be part of your personal motivation.

How difficult is it to get my weight down quickly?

The ethos of Fat Club is that there is no magic wand that can be waved to achieve successful weight loss quickly. You need to think longer term and have a long-term plan in mind, but take each day a step at a time, with a simple daily routine.

Do:

- keep a record of what you have eaten, your exercise times, your weight loss and inch loss.
- take a picture of yourself as you are now without tucking in your tummy or disguising fat with baggy clothes, and stick in on the fridge or the biscuit cupboard.
- constantly monitor yourself. Write yourself an exercise log and diet sheet (including the amount of calories you have allowed yourself each day) and keep checking it.
- have a goal that is attainable and then pat yourself on your head (or your diminishing bottom!) when you reach it.

218

- set a new goal and go for that. Success will breed success.
- have a 'mantra' you can repeat to yourself: e.g. 'I have a very small appetite', 'I must not eat this. I will only harm myself', 'I value myself too much to do damage to myself by being overweight', 'I don't want to have to stick needles into myself, but I may develop diabetes if I don't slim down', 'I want to wear a smaller size'.

Don't:

- weigh yourself every day. Do it once a week or once a fortnight, on the same set of scales. Aim for a 1–2lb weight loss per week.
- be too ambitious. You will only be disappointed by failure to achieve unreasonable goals.

Danger moments: I have broken my diet, so I'll just splurge out today

This is part of a slip in your commitment, but it is not a disaster. Everyone gets tempted, in all sorts of ways. Do not see a slip-up as a failure, just a temporary hitch in your plans. The secret is not to slip up regularly. Once you are on the weight loss slope, a moment's indulgence can take a few days' hard work to recover from. Ask yourself: was that cream bun/bar of chocolate/bag of chips worth it?

You and Exercise

Harvey Walden

'I used to try and find excuses not to go to the gym, now I see it as my private time. I get on the running machine and put on my Walkman and no one can call me on the phone or interrupt me.' – Stuart Gibbons

Diet and exercise work hand in hand as the most effective way to lose weight. Once you have your mindset right and have begun to look at your eating habits, it is time to incorporate exercise into your life.

There are many benefits to exercise, which go far beyond weight control. For example, exercise can reduce depression, anxiety and stress; it can enhance mood and self-esteem; and it can improve sleep quality. As we said in Chapter 1, there is an alarming and growing trend in inactivity in the UK, especially in children, and this is a problem that needs to be tackled if the increase in obesity is to be reversed.

From the word go, and at the beginning of each weekend, Fat Club members were assessed by Harvey to see how they were improving their exercise times. These sessions involved a timed quarter-mile run, press-ups and sit-ups, and they were an effective indication of how each member was progressing with fitness and stamina. As with the food diaries, members were also encouraged to keep an exercise diary of their activity between each Fat Club. This is an excellent means of self-monitoring (try it yourself – you will soon notice when you are slipping in your regime), and a great way of disciplining yourself to take some form of exercise. In a short time, you will find you know your body well enough that you can dispense with the diary completely and still be motivated.

RECOMMENDATIONS ON ACTIVITY FOR OBESE PEOPLE:

- The amount of time spent in sedentary activities should be reduced.
- Vigorous activity should be avoided.
- Bouts of longer periods of moderate and sustained exercise would be more beneficial.
- More weight-bearing movement should be encouraged.

BEFORE YOU START TAKING EXERCISE

Harvey recommends that, if you are overweight and/or have not exercised for a while, you should see your GP, who can assess your general health and ensure you have no medical problems before you begin. He stresses, too, that there are two types of pain to be aware of:

- The first is the pain of discovering muscles that you never knew you had! This is the weakness leaving your body and is the start of really productive exercise.
- The second is the pain you feel when you have overdone the exercise. Overweight people may also suffer from joint problems. It is a chicken and egg situation: the less you exercise, the larger you become. The larger you become, the greater the strain on the muscles and joints and the harder it is to exercise. Overdoing exercise can result in injuries (such as happened to Simon Payne) and, at worst, can lay you up for weeks and jeopardise all the good work that you have done.

ANY EXERCISE IS GOOD EXERCISE

No one is expecting you to train for the Olympics. The Fat Club ethos is that any activity is good activity, and there is little point in driving to the gym once a week for a half-hearted 30-minute workout. It would be better to do your gym sessions enthusiastically, or take a brisk 30-minute walk three or four times a week. Look at ways to incorporate more physical activity into every area of your life:

- Forget working lunches. Get up from your desk during the lunch hour and walk for 30 minutes, or use your bike to go to the local shop or to post a letter.
- Better still, bike to work if you can.
- If you live in a town with an underground, walk up the escalators, or get off your bus a stop early and walk the rest of the way.
- Ban yourself from using the lift in department stores.

VARY YOUR EXERCISE TO STOP BOREDOM

Increasing your activity levels can happen in many ways, but routine can become tedious and demotivating. There is no shortage of books and videos of good exercise techniques and you can find them in bookshops and at your local library. Effective exercise does not have to be expensive either and involve a gym and up-to-the-minute running machines. Exercise can be free and if done often enough can really burn up the calories:

- gardening (digging – 480 calories per hour)
- brisk walking with the dog (360 calories per hour)
- playing football with the kids, or tennis (420 calories per hour)
- gentle running (280 to 400 calories per hour depending on speed)
- dancing (410 calories per hour)
- cycling (from 250 to 600 calories per hour depending on speed and terrain)
- shopping (240 calories per hour)
- swimming (between 510 and 600 calories per hour depending on how fast you pound up and down the pool)

FIND THE RIGHT EXERCISE WHICH SUITS YOU AND YOUR BODY

Ask yourself:

- Are you a morning or an evening person?
- Could you incorporate a swim on the way home from work?
- Are you an early riser who could use the time before the family wake up?
- Do you prefer to exercise alone or in a group situation?
- Are you competitive? Could you join in a team sport?
- Do you hate being sweaty? If so, would swimming be more comfortable?

Whatever you do and whenever you can, do it!

THE FAT BURNING ZONE

The most effective way to burn fat is to increase your heart rate (aerobic exercise). When you begin your exercise programme, exercise at least three times a week for a period of at least 20 to 30 minutes. The 'fat burning zone', as it is called, is the optimum heart rate for burning fat and is calculated by subtracting your age from a 220 beats per minute heart rate. Between 65 per cent and 80 per cent of that final figure is your fat burning zone, i.e. if you are 35 years old, your fat burning zone is around 165 beats per minute. Doctors and health officials recommend that when you start exercising for the first time you focus on staying towards the bottom level of your fat burning zone. Once you have become fit (it may take around six months), you can push it up to 85 per cent.

If you are very overweight, brisk walking may be all it takes to raise your heart rate sufficiently. Now gradually increase the intensity of your workout to get your heart rate up to the right fat-burning level. If your heart rate is too fast, you will exhaust yourself, be out of breath and will not even be burning any fat (anaerobic exercise). Leave that to super-fit athletes.

Important: Always stop if you injure yourself, become dizzy or get very tired, and make sure you don't become dehydrated.

GET WARMED-UP

Do not start violent exercise straight away. Warming-up is a must, as is stretching lightly for a count of 10 to 15 before you begin any exercise. This warm up should last at least five to ten minutes. After you have finished your workout, cool down and stretch. This time the stretch should be held longer, for a 25 or 30 count.

You and Food

Dr Sarah Schenker

'Every one thinks they know about food. I thought I did, I didn't but I do now.' – Tony Upson

'I'm an expert on dieting. I've done them all!' – Tracy Young

There are no 'wonder' diets or foods that can cause weight loss. If you take in more calories than you burn off, you will gain weight. Take in less than you burn off and you will lose weight. It is as simple as that.

WHY YO-YO DIETING IS BAD FOR YOU

Are you like Tracy and Donna used to be, trapped in a cycle of yo-yo dieting? Trying one after the other, and throwing yourself into an impossibly strict regime that makes you feel constantly hard-done by, hungry and miserable?

Here is why it can never work. When you follow a very low-calorie diet, you certainly start by losing weight quickly, though the loss is mostly water trapped in fat cells, but your basic metabolic rate (BMR), the rate at which you burn up calories, reduces too. BMR depends on the amount of lean tissue in your body, so if you lose weight rapidly through restricting your calories and without exercise to back it up, your BMR drops because, in addition to fat, you also lose some muscle – more so on a very low-calorie diet.

This makes it more and more difficult to lose weight. And when you start eating more again, as you must to survive, you put on weight rapidly because a normal calorie intake exceeds your body's reduced need. Some faddy diets (no-carbohydrate regimes especially) are particularly detrimental, because they can rob your body of essential vitamins and nutrients.

There is nothing more depressing than seeing the needle on those scales creep up again. It is so disheartening to regain lost weight and end up right where you started. Yo-yo dieting can cause personal upset and in many cases can even result in poor body image and a negative attitude towards food.

This is what keeps the diet industry afloat, of course, but Fat Club has shown it does not have to be that way. A calorie intake of about 1500 kcals a day for women, 2000 for men, combined with an increase in physical activity, leads to healthy, sustained weight loss and a toned healthy body.

'I don't feel as if I've fallen off the wagon – because this time I'm not on a wagon.' – Sha Wylie

The benefits of the Fat Club's weight-loss approach are:

- It is not damaging to health. A very low-calorie diet (consuming less than 600 kcals a day) can be dangerous as the body loses too much lean tissue (as well as body fat). This type of diet can also be low in certain nutrients.
- It is easier to stick to because you need never be hungry.
- It helps you to improve your eating habits and your health.
- It does not rely on special diet foods so it will not collapse if you go on holiday or out for a meal.
- You can follow it even if your circumstances change.
- It teaches you how to shop for healthy, low-fat foods.
- You learn to balance calories taken in with energy expended.

CALORIE COUNTING – IT'S GOT TO BE DONE!

All the Fat Club members were encouraged to keep a food diary before they started Fat Club and during the programme, and were asked to be really truthful about what they ate. Try doing the same thing, but be honest with yourself. Sarah Schenker suspected that some of the members lied about what they ate because they knew the experts were reading their diaries, but you can keep yours private.

Work out how many calories you are *eating now* in a day (you can buy good calorie calculating books, like Thorson's *Calorie Counter* (£3.99), in most bookshops) then take an average for the week. Don't forget those odd biscuits and drinks too. The daily calorie intake recommended on the labels of food packaging is 2500 per day for men and 2000 for women. These are guidelines for the 'average man' at 11st and the 'average woman' at 9½st – but there are precious few of them about!

Here's how to calculate the amount you need to eat each day to maintain your weight:

- **Males 18–29 years** (15.1 x weight in kg) + 692 × 1.4 gives total calorie requirement for one day
- **Males 30–59 years** (11.5 x weight in kg) + 873 × 1.4
- **Females 18–29 years** (14.8 x weight in kg) + 487 × 1.4
- **Females 30–59 years** (8.3 x weight in kg) + 846 × 1.4

Reduce the final figure by around 500 to 800 calories per day, or as many as you feel you can realistically sustain, and you will soon start to lose weight. Combine this calorie reduction with exercise and changes in your diet and the type of foods you eat, and you will begin to see a very real difference.

A sensible rate of weight loss is about 2lbs (approximately 1kg) a week. For many people this will mean reducing their energy intake by about 500 calories a day, but this will depend on how much weight you need to lose and how active you are.

A woman aged between 30 and 59 weighing 80kg (12½st) needs 2114 kcal per day to stay at that weight, but she would start to lose weight with a drop of just 300 kcal (that is two Mr Kipling Caramel Shortcakes!).

When he came to Fat Club, Simon needed 4088 kcal per day to sustain him at the weight he was. ($11.5 \times 178 + 873 \times 1.4 = 4088$ kcals). He would start to lose weight just by dropping to 3000 kcal a day, though Sarah recommended 2500 with exercise and better food choices.

LEARNING ABOUT FOOD

Food should be a pleasure, and you can still enjoy it while eating healthily. Become label aware: it takes only slightly longer in the supermarket to learn which foods have low or high sugar content or are low or high in fat. Fat is the most concentrated source of energy, and though saturated fats are the ones to be avoided, all fats have the same number of calories – 9 kcal per gram. By lowering your fat intake, you can reduce your calorie intake often without even noticing. Food manufacturers have finally become fat-aware and are falling over themselves to produce low-fat/healthy alternatives. To really see a difference, look for products which boast less than 5 per cent fat content per 100g. But you are not necessarily confined to 'diet' bars. A very satisfying fun-size Mars Bar delivers fewer calories (92) and less fat than some 'low-fat' brands. OK, so that is more calories than an apple, but sometimes nothing else will do!

Caramel biscuits

How to read a label: the important information for weight loss is highlighted in bold.

For example:

Typical values per 100g

Energy	**488 kcal**	2036 kJ
Protein	5.0g	
Carbohydrate	**72.0g**	
Of which sugars	39.0g	
Starch	32.0g	
Fat	**20.0g**	
Of which saturates	**7.0g**	
Monounsaturates	**9.0g**	
Polyunsaturates	**4.0g**	
Fibre	0.8g	
Sodium	0.4g	

- How do you stop yourself feeling hungry? Fill up on fruit and vegetables. It does not matter if they are fresh, frozen or tinned (but avoid fruits preserved in syrup).
- Starchy foods too – e.g. bread, rice, pasta – especially wholemeal or brown varieties will also help you feel 'full' and keep your energy levels up.
- There is no such food as bad food, nor is any food banned. Browse through most diet books, and you are faced with a list of foods you must not touch ever. Is life worth living without chocolate or mayonnaise? It is all a question of balance. Tell yourself that cheese and crisps are forbidden and you will find yourself thinking of little else! Do not deprive yourself of anything, just be sensible about how much you have. Once you start calculating your daily calories, you will soon realise how much of these foods you can incorporate.
- Sugar versus fat. Sugar has the least calorie-dense nutrients and some people argue that the sweetness of sugar satisfies

your hunger craving quicker, but too much is still a bad idea. The worst combination is fat and sugar together. But either way too much sugar will add to calories.

- You will be doing yourself no favours by skipping a meal. Hunger can lead to tiredness and headaches, and you may find you end up eating more because you are ravenous.
- Do not let yourself get too hungry. Look out for the signs and keep some fruit (bananas are ideal) or a low-fat biscuit close at hand wherever you are. Eating it will take the edge off your hunger and stop you eating twice as many calories at the next meal.

TEN SWEET TREATS FOR UNDER 150 CALORIES

Chocolate treats

Even if you are trying to watch your calorie intake, chocolate is not off the menu altogether. These chocolate treats will satisfy a craving for less than 150 calories.

1 Twix finger	134 kcal
1 Cadbury's Flake cake	115 kcal
1 Jacob's Chocolate Club	121 kcal
1 McVitie's Penguin	131 kcal
1 two-finger Kit Kat	110 kcal

Tea time

Are you the sort of person who just has to have something to go with their cup of tea? Then choose from any of the following to fill the gap.

2 fig rolls	124 kcal
3 Jaffa cakes	144 kcal
3 Garibaldi biscuits	123 kcal
1 Kellogg's Nutrigrain bar	113 kcal
1 French Fancy	99 kcal

25 WAYS TO CUT FAT

Fat is an energy-dense food, and 10g of food stored as fat may show up as 50 to 60g of extra body weight because fat cells are 80 per cent water. Fats provide 9 kcal per gram, so cutting fat will reduce your calorie intake considerably.

Breakfast

Poached *vs* scrambled eggs

Two poached eggs on two slices of wholemeal toast with low-fat spread contain 11g of fat compared to the 25g of fat found in two scrambled eggs with milk and butter on buttered toast.

Nuts can push up the fat content in breakfast cereals, although it is the healthy monounsaturated type. A bowl of Kellogg's Crunchy Nut Cornflakes with semi-skimmed milk contains just 4g of fat, compared to more than double in a bowl of Nut Clusters, especially if served with full fat milk.

A croissant will give you 13g of fat; butter it and you get an extra 5g. Alternatively, replace it with two Scotch pancakes drizzled with a little maple syrup and save yourself 13g of fat.

Choose jam, marmalade or Marmite for toast toppings – they are fat-free – as opposed to peanut butter which is 54 per cent fat.

A grilled rasher of lean bacon is only 19 per cent fat (3.5g of fat per rasher), a fried rasher of streaky bacon is 45 per cent fat (9g of fat per rasher).

Lunches

Fill a large baked potato with baked beans instead of cheese and cut out 30g of fat.

Replace the cream cheese in a smoked salmon bagel with Philadelphia Light and reduce the fat content by 33 per cent.

A prawn sandwich made with low-fat mayonnaise will provide 7g of fat, far less than the 22g of fat found in half a tub of taramasalata.

A slice of pizza topped with vegetables instead of cheese will cut out 19g of fat.

Twiglets have half the fat content of low-fat crisps.

Dinners

A portion of potato-topped cottage pie has 15g less fat than a pastry-topped meat pie.

Lean roast beef is a much lower fat meat than lean roast lamb.

Substitute penne arrabbiata for tagliatelle carbonara next time you visit the local Italian restaurant and cut out 10g of fat per portion – but go easy on the Parmesan cheese!

Per 100g, white chicken or turkey meat has 3g less fat than the dark meat.

An average portion of lasagne provides 6g of fat whereas the same portion of moussaka contains 10g of fat.

Dried egg noodles give you 6g of fat per 100g; a packet of Super Noodles gives you 20g.

Cooking

Frying with spray oils rather than pouring will save you 4g of fat.

Replace Mascarpone cheese (40 per cent fat) with the virtually fat-free Quark when making a sauce or topping.

Puddings

Top with custard not cream to save 10g of fat.

Jelly is fat-free compared to mousse which contains 7g of fat per 100g.

Replace rice pudding with crème caramel to save 4g of fat.

Take-aways

A McDonald's Fillet-o-Fish or a McChicken Sandwich contains 17g of fat, 10g less that a Big Mac.

A portion of pilau rice gives you 10g of fat compared to 1g in a portion of boiled rice.

Swap chicken korma (40g of fat) for chicken biryani (20g of fat) and cut out 20g of fat per portion.

At a Chinese restaurant, go for a spring roll starter (9g of fat each) instead of the prawn crackers (27g of fat per bowl).

DISPELLING DIETING MYTHS

Most people who are trying to lose weight will tell you that they have tried every diet ever devised to shed the pounds. As Fat Club has proved, many of these faddy diets just left us back where we started – overweight. This is because trendy diets are often devised to provide a quick fix, not slower, sustainable weight loss, so we are being fed half-truths and bogus science. Here are a few popular myths.

Diet myth no. 1 – All dietary fat is bad

If you are trying to lose weight, it is a good idea to reduce the fat in your diet because fat provides more calories than either carbohydrate or protein (fat provides 9, protein 4 and carbohydrate 3.75 kcals per gram). In fact even if you do not need to lose weight, reducing your fat intake to less than 35 per cent of your total calorie intake is recommended for good health. However, some fat is still necessary in the diet as it provides us with essential fatty acids and fat soluble vitamins such as vitamins D (essential for bone health) and E (an important antioxidant that can help prevent heart disease). High amounts of saturated fats (animal fats) in the diet can increase blood cholesterol levels, increasing risk of heart disease, whereas monounsaturates, polyunsaturates and fats from oily fish can help reduce risk of heart disease. Therefore, choose lean cuts of meat and low-fat dairy products to lower saturates, introduce healthy fats by cooking with small amounts of olive oil and eat nuts and fish such as salmon and trout.

Diet myth no. 2 – Fat can be lost rapidly

Very often when people start to diet they find that they can lose vast amounts of weight in the first week and then the weight loss slows down. This is when they start to feel demoralised and often give up, only to repeat the cycle a few weeks later when the next 'miracle' diet hits the magazines. Fat we store in our bodies cannot be lost rapidly. During the first week people usually lose carbohydrate stored in water. It is this which produces a dramatic effect on the scales. Once this is lost, fat loss will start, but, being much more energy-dense than carbohydrate, fat requires a greater calorie deficit to be used up. A simple fact of life and slimming is that, to lose weight, we need to take in fewer calories than we use up throughout the day. Even a daily deficit of 50 calories will make a difference. Be prepared for slow steady weight loss, increase your activity and make a few small changes to your diet that you can live with long term.

Diet myth no. 3 – There is a special female fat called cellulite caused by toxins

Cellulite, as ugly and horrid as it might appear, is not a unique type of fat that requires special treatment and it is not caused by toxins. It is simply a build-up of fat in areas where we are genetically predisposed to lay down fat. For women this tends to be the hips, thighs and bottom. It may seem unfair that when you diet you sometimes lose weight from all the places you do not want to lose it from, but unfortunately you cannot change your genetic make-up. With regular exercise and healthy balanced eating, you will eventually be able to lose weight everywhere, but you may still be left with a few unsightly wobbly bits. Toning exercises using resistance (like swimming) or light weights are the best remedy.

Diet myth no. 4 – You should regularly detoxify your system

You cannot 'detox' your system through diet nor can you cleanse or flush out toxins. This is the job of your liver should do efficiently, and, if you suffer from gallstones or any other symptoms of poor liver function, you should seek medical help as soon as possible. Enjoying all foods in moderation, eating plenty of fruit and vegetables and keeping well hydrated is the best way to improve your health and sense of well-being.

Diet myth no. 5 – You can spot-reduce fat, particularly on the hips and thighs

As unfair as it may seem, there is not much we can do about the sites from which we gain and lose weight. Some diet-writers advocate extremely low-fat, low-calorie diets to target these so-called 'problem' areas. Very low-calorie diets have been criticised by the Department of Health as being potentially dangerous. It is recommended that a person should not go below 800 calories per day. Many 'celebrity' diets are close to this level or even below it, but these diets are very difficult to stick to and most people would find that they are continually hungry and tired. It is much better to eat a healthy, balanced diet and take up some form of enjoyable exercise that you can do regularly. You can then target areas which need particular attention, like the tummy or thighs, with muscle-toning exercises.

Diet myth no. 6 – Particular foods or combinations of foods can boost metabolism and speed up weight loss

As amazing as it might sound, overweight people do not have slow metabolisms, in fact quite the opposite. The bigger you are, the harder your body has to work, for instance to pump blood around the body and carry your large frame when you move, so the higher your metabolism. This means that, if you are very large, you do not have to drop to an impossible 1000 calories per day to lose weight; you could easily lose weight on 1500–1800 calories per day. As you become smaller your calorie requirement will drop, but you can compensate by increasing your exercise level to maintain the deficit. The weight loss will be slower but the weight will stay off.

There are no special combinations of foods that will affect your metabolism one way or the other. All foods provide energy (calories) – that is why we eat them. Some, such as fruit and vegetables, are lower in calories than others such as cream and butter. By getting the balance right, you can enjoy your food and still lose weight.

Diet myth no. 7 – Poor digestion of foods or 'allergy' to foods can cause weight gain

People suffering from food allergies or food intolerances do not gain weight by eating the culprit foods, in fact quite the reverse.

Food intolerances usually cause sickness and diarrhoea. Food allergies (for example, an allergy to nuts) can have very serious consequences, the most serious being anaphylactic shock; milder reactions include asthma and eczema, none of which is responsible for weight gain.

Diet myth no. 8 – You should not mix protein foods and carbohydrate foods at the same meal

Dr William Hay invented 'food combining' at the beginning of the last century. He believed that disease resulted from the accumulation of toxins and acid waste in our bodies. The way to cure disease, he reckoned, was to avoid eating 'foods that fight'. By this he meant that you should not mix proteins and carbohydrates in the same meal, and you should eat foods which restore the body's natural balance between acids and alkalis. There is no scientific evidence whatsoever to support this theory. The rules are rather complicated to observe and inherently contradictory, and the whole idea of food combining is nutritional nonsense.

It is possible to lose weight following the Hay regime, but this is because it greatly increases the intake of fruit and vegetables at the expense of more calorific foods. But, while it is not harmful, do not be fooled into thinking that food combining offers any great nutritional benefit.

Diet myth no. 9 – Carbohydrates are fattening

Carbohydrates have suddenly become the villains of the nutrition world, as Hollywood celebrities banish them from their diets in favour of more protein and fat. Diets that are high in protein and very low in carbohydrate encourage you to eat all the meat, fish, eggs and cheese you want, but at the price of cutting out potatoes, bread, pasta and fruit. Even the slimmer's favourite energy snack, the banana, is banned. The theory behind this is that it is sugar and not fat that makes us fat. Sugar is rapidly absorbed into the bloodstream causing glucose levels to rise.

Insulin is then required to lower blood glucose levels back to normal. Insulin also happens to be the hormone responsible for promoting fat deposition. This is true, but it is irrelevant to dieters. If you are taking in fewer calories than you are using up, you will be using your fat stores as a source of energy. Not only does the no-carbohydrate diet go against all current healthy eating advice, which is to increase carbohydrates and lower fat intake, but it can be dangerous. You may well be missing out on essential vitamins and nutrients, and anyone trying to exercise while following this diet will feel tired, lethargic and irritable.

Diet myth no. 10 – Your blood group dictates which foods you should and shouldn't eat

Diets based on the idea that your blood group can dictate which foods are likely to cause weight gain have no scientific basis. In these diets foods are split into groups which are 'highly beneficial', 'neutral' and 'to be avoided'. For instance, people with blood group O are told to avoid sweetcorn as this will cause weight gain, whereas it is acceptable for those with a different blood type. Sweetcorn is low in fat and high in fibre, so it is difficult to understand why this should be the case. You may well lose weight on this diet because it is so restrictive, but because of this it is also likely to be unbalanced. Daily consumption of fruit and vegetables of all types should be encouraged to help prevent heart disease and cancer.

Diet myth no. 11 – Healthy eating costs more

Several of the Fat Club members complained initially that their shopping bills had increased. It transpired that, unconfident about food and fat contents, they were buying proprietary brands or supermarket own-brand cook-chilled calorie-counted products. Once they grew in confidence and understanding, they realised they could buy fresh ingredients cheaper and prepare meals from scratch at home with the help of low-fat cookbooks and common sense. They were also comparing their new shopping bills to

Chapter 13

Fat Club Recipes

The meals eaten by the Fat Club members at Gorse Hill were all devised by Sarah Schenker to provide maximum taste and nutrition with as little fat as possible. They were so popular that many members of the group asked for copies of the recipes to take home to try. Here are a few to inspire you.

RED PEPPER AND TOMATO SOUP

Serves 4
Per portion: 156 kcal, 2g fat

2 red peppers, halved, cored and deseeded
1 red onion, quartered
2 garlic cloves, crushed
2 sprays of Fry Lite oil
1 large potato, peeled and chopped
1 tsp ground cumin
1 tsp ground coriander
salt and freshly ground pepper
900ml vegetable stock
1 tin tomatoes
4 tbsp low-fat fromage frais

Heat oven to 200°C, Gas Mark 6.
　　Place the peppers, onion and garlic cloves in a non-stick roasting tin. Roast in the preheated oven for 40 minutes, or until the peppers have blistered.

Meanwhile, spray a saucepan with the oil, fry the potato with the cumin and coriander for a few minutes, season and pour in the vegetable stock. Add the tomatoes. Cover the pan and simmer for 30 minutes.

Remove the cooked vegetables from the oven. Place the peppers in a polythene bag. Tie the top and leave to cool (this will make it easier to remove the skin). Add the onion and garlic to the saucepan, peel the peppers and add to the soup. Simmer for 5 minutes.

Pour the soup into a blender and blend until smooth, then push through a sieve to remove the tomato skins and seeds. Return to the saucepan to warm if necessary. Spoon into 4 bowls and add a spoonful of the fromage frais to each.

BUTTERNUT SQUASH SOUP

Serves 4
Per portion: 145 kcal, 1g fat

1 butternut squash, peeled
few sprigs of rosemary
freshly ground pepper
150g red lentils, washed
1 onion, finely chopped
900ml vegetable stock

Heat oven to 200°C, Gas Mark 6.

Halve the squash and, using a spoon, scoop out the seeds and fibrous flesh. Cut the squash into small chunks and place in a roasting tin. Sprinkle over the rosemary and season. Roast in the preheated oven for 45 minutes.

Meanwhile, place the lentils in a saucepan. Cover with water, bring to the boil and boil rapidly for 10 minutes. Strain, then return the lentils to a clean saucepan with the onion and stock and simmer for 5 minutes. Season to taste.

Remove the squash from the oven, mash with a fork and add to the soup. Stir. Simmer for 25 minutes and ladle into 4 bowls. Garnish with extra rosemary.

CARROT AND CORIANDER PÂTÉ

Serves 4
Per portion: 84 kcal, 2g fat

500g carrots, grated
1 tbsp ground coriander
175ml freshly squeezed orange juice
300ml water
50g medium-fat soft cheese
30g fresh coriander
Salt and freshly ground pepper

Place the grated carrots in a saucepan with the ground coriander, orange juice and water. Cover with a lid and simmer for 10 minutes or until the carrots are cooked. Cool and transfer to a blender.

Add the soft cheese and coriander leaves; blend until smooth. Season to taste and blend again. Spoon into 4 small dishes and chill before serving with crusty bread.

THAI BEEF CURRY

Serves 4
Per portion: 128 kcal, 4g fat

300g lean beef fillet, finely sliced
1 red onion, cut into thin wedges
2 tbsp Thai green curry paste
125g mange tout, thinly sliced lengthways
1 green pepper, sliced into strips
1 green chilli (optional)
300ml water

Preheat a non-stick wok or large frying pan. Dry fry the beef for 2 minutes, then remove with a slotted spoon, leaving the juices in the pan.

Reheat the pan and stir-fry the onion for 1 minute until softened. Add the curry paste and stir-fry for another minute or so. Now add the mange tout, pepper, chilli if using and water. Return the meat to the pan and stir for a further 5 minutes. Serve with boiled rice.

COD FILLETS WITH A HERB CRUST

Serves 4
Per portion: 137 kcal, 1g fat

4 cod fillets weighing approximately 125g each
Salt and freshly ground pepper

For the crust:
50g wholemeal breadcrumbs
2 tbsp chopped fresh dill
2 tbsp chopped fresh parsley
2 tbsp chopped fresh chives
2 tbsp low-fat fromage frais
2 plum tomatoes (fresh or tinned), finely diced
2 tbsp lemon juice

Heat oven to 180°C, Gas Mark 4.
  Season the cod fillets and place in a foil-lined roasting tin, skin side down.
  In a bowl mix together the crust ingredients and spoon some on top of each fillet, patting down gently.
  Cook in the preheated oven for 20 minutes. Serve with new potatoes and French beans.

SINGAPORE NOODLES

Serves 4
Per portion: 340 kcal, 4g fat

250g Chinese egg thread noodles
1 spray of Fry Lite oil
1 bunch of spring onions, diagonally sliced
5cm piece of root ginger, grated
1 tbsp medium Indian curry paste
125g frozen peas

250g cooked peeled prawns
soy sauce to serve

Break the noodles into a large bowl. Pour over enough boiling water to cover. Stir and toss the noodles in the water and then leave on one side for 6–8 minutes.

Meanwhile, heat a wok and spray with oil. Stir-fry the onions and ginger until softened. Stir in the curry paste and stir-fry for a further 2 minutes. Stir in the peas and prawns. Reduce the heat, cover and cook for 3 minutes.

Drain the noodles and add to the wok, toss well to coat. Serve with the soy sauce.

MUSHROOM CRÊPES

Serves 4
Per portion: 112 kcal, 3g fat

For the crêpes:
50g plain flour
150ml skimmed milk
1 small egg, beaten
salt and freshly ground pepper
1–2 sprays of oil

For the filling:
300g chestnut mushrooms, chopped
1 bunch of spring onions, finely chopped
1 garlic clove, chopped
400g tin of chopped tomatoes
2 tbsp fresh oregano

Heat oven to 180°C, Gas Mark 4.

To make the crêpe batter, place the flour, milk, egg and seasoning in a blender and blend until smooth.

Spray a frying pan with oil. Heat the pan, pour in a ladleful of batter and cook for 1 minute. Carefully flip the crêpe and cook the second side. Slide out of the pan on to greaseproof paper. Make 3 more crêpes the same way.

For the filling, put all the ingredients into a small saucepan and heat gently, stirring occasionally, for 5 minutes. Divide the filling between the crêpes and roll up. Transfer the pancakes to an ovenproof dish and cook in the preheated oven for 20 minutes. Serve with a green salad.

SWEET POTATO AND LEEK FRITTATA

Serves 6
Per portion: 175 kcal, 3g fat

2 sprays of Fry Lite oil
800g sweet potato, peeled and cut into thin slices
200g leek, sliced
1 clove of garlic, crushed
1 tbsp chopped fresh sage
1 tbsp chopped, fresh parsley
3 eggs
3 egg whites
125ml skimmed milk
30g low-fat cheddar cheese, grated
Salt and freshly ground pepper

Heat oven to 180°C, Gas Mark 4.
Boil the sweet potato until just tender and drain.
Heat a non-stick pan, spray with oil and fry the leek and garlic over a low heat until tender. Stir in half the sage.
Spray a 25cm round flan dish with oil. Place half the sweet potato slices over the base of the dish, top with the leek mixture, then the remaining sweet potato. Combine the eggs, egg whites, milk, cheese and parsley. Season to taste and pour over the potato. Sprinkle with the remaining sage.
Bake in the preheated oven for 35 minutes. Serve with a green salad.

CHICKEN AND SUGAR SNAP PEA STIR-FRY

Serves 4
Per portion: 266 kcals, 3g fat

1 spray of Fry Lite oil
1 medium onion, sliced
1 medium red pepper, sliced
100g sugar snap peas
500g skinless chicken breast fillets, thinly sliced
2 tsp cornflour
150ml chicken stock
1 tbsp soy sauce

Heat the oil in a wok, add the onion and pepper and stir-fry over a high heat for 3 minutes. Add the peas and stir-fry for a further 1 minute.

Remove the vegetables from the wok, add the chicken and stir-fry over a high heat until browned. Return the vegetables to the chicken in the wok and add the cornflour, blended with the stock and soy sauce. Stir until mixture boils and thickens. Serve with boiled rice or noodles.

GINGERED PORK WITH STIR-FRIED VEGETABLES

Serves 4
Per portion: 198 kcal, 3g fat

500g lean pork fillets
1 spray of Fry Lite oil
1 medium onion, sliced
1 small carrot, finely sliced
1 courgette, sliced
2 tsp cornflour
150g snow peas, halved
100g beansprouts

For the marinade:
50ml soy sauce
2 tbsp red wine
1 tbsp brown sugar
2 cloves of garlic, crushed
1 tbsp grated ginger

Heat oven to 180°C, Gas Mark 4.

Combine all the marinade ingredients in a bowl. Add the pork and mix well. Cover and refrigerate for several hours or overnight.

Drain the pork and reserve the marinade. Dry-fry the pork in a non-stick pan, and brown all over. Transfer to an ovenproof dish and bake in the preheated oven for 30 minutes. Slice fillets diagonally.

Heat the oil in a wok, add the onion, carrot and courgette and stir-fry over a high heat until tender. Blend the cornflour with the reserved marinade and a little water and add to the wok. Add the snow peas and beansprouts, stir until the sauce boils and thickens. Serve with the pork, accompanied by boiled rice or noodles.

CHILLI CON CARNE

Serves 6
Per portion: 286 kcal, 4g fat

450g extra-lean minced beef
1 spray of Fry Lite oil
1 onion, diced
1 green pepper, diced
1 green chilli, deseeded and chopped
1 red chilli, deseeded and chopped
1–2 tsp chilli powder
2 tsp paprika
2 tsp cumin
400g tin tomatoes
1 tbsp tomato purée
225g tinned red kidney beans
Salt and freshly ground pepper

Dry fry the mince in a non-stick frying pan until fully browned. Remove the mince.

Heat the oil in the pan and fry the onion, pepper and chilli until soft. Add the tomatoes and tomato purée, the mince and the spices, stir thoroughly and cook over a medium heat for 20 minutes. Season to taste.

Add the kidney beans and cook for a further 5–10 minutes. Serve with rice.

VEGETABLE AND BEAN MOUSSAKA

Serves 4
Per portion: 146 kcal, 2g fat

115g black-eye beans, soaked or tinned
2 aubergines, sliced lengthways
450g courgettes, sliced lengthways
1 spray of Fry Lite oil
25g low-fat cheese, grated

For the tomato and bean sauce:
1 onion, diced
1 clove garlic, crushed
400g tin chopped tomatoes
1 tbsp tomato purée
150ml white wine
1 tsp oregano
1 tsp allspice
salt and freshly ground pepper

Heat oven to 180°C, Gas Mark 4.

If using dried beans, soak them for 1 hour in cold water, drain and cook them in fresh water for 30 minutes until tender.

Place the sliced aubergines and courgettes in a colander, sprinkle with salt and leave to drain for 30 minutes. Rinse well. Place the vegetable strips in a baking tray, spray with a little oil and roast in a preheated hot oven, for 10 minutes or until they start to char.

Heat a pan sprayed with oil, add the onion and garlic and fry until softened. Add the tomatoes, tomato purée, wine, oregano and allspice and bring to the boil. Reduce heat and allow to simmer for 20 minutes. Stir in the precooked beans or the drained tinned beans.

In an ovenproof dish, layer the aubergine and courgette

mixture with the tomato and bean sauce and top with the grated cheese. Bake in the preheated oven for 1 hour. Serve with a green salad.

BEAN AND POTATO STEW

Serves 4
Per portion: 282 kcal, 1g fat

3 x 200g of different kinds of beans, e.g. haricot, cannellini,
 borlotti, soaked or tinned
1 spray Fry Lite oil
1 onion, diced
1 clove garlic, crushed
2 carrots, diced
1 courgette, diced
1 pepper, diced
400g tin chopped tomatoes
1–2 bay leaves
2 tsp mixed herbs
bouquet garni
rosemary
300ml vegetable stock (or 150ml stock and 150ml red wine)
salt and freshly ground pepper
4 medium waxy potatoes, sliced

If using dried beans, soak them overnight; drain, rinse and bring to the boil in fresh water and simmer for 1 hour.

Heat oven to 180°C, Gas Mark 4.

Heat oil in a non-stick pan, soften onion, garlic, carrots, courgette and pepper. Add the tomatoes, all the herbs and stock. Boil until the liquid has reduced by half.

Add the precooked beans or the drained tinned beans, season and simmer for 15 minutes. Transfer to ovenproof dish, cover with potato slices and bake in the preheated oven for 45 minutes. Serve with a green vegetable.

MEXICAN CHICKEN TACOS

Serves 4
Per portion: 275 kcal, 5g fat

1 spray of Fry Lite oil
1 onion, diced
2 cloves garlic, crushed
1 red chilli, deseeded and chopped
1 green pepper, deseeded and sliced
400g skinless chicken, diced
paprika to taste
400g tin chopped tomatoes
1 tbsp tomato purée
225g kidney beans
4 taco shells
Half an iceberg lettuce, shredded
1 small jar spicy salsa

Heat oven to 200°C, Gas Mark 6.
  Heat oil in a non-stick pan and soften onion, garlic and chilli. Add the pepper, chicken, paprika, tomatoes, tomato purée and beans and simmer for 15–20 minutes.
  Warm taco shells for 2 minutes in the hot oven, then fill with the chicken mixture. Top with lettuce and 1 tsp of salsa.

STUFFED PEPPERS

Serves 4
**Per portion: 141 kcal, 5g fat (with mince); 193 kcal, 3g fat (with
            breadcrumbs)**

1 spray Fry Lite oil
1 onion, chopped
115g courgettes, finely chopped
115g mushrooms, chopped
450g tin tomatoes
1 tbsp tomato purée
1 tsp fresh thyme, chopped

247

1–2 tbsp French Dijon mustard
115g breadcrumbs (or extra-lean minced beef)
4 peppers, red, yellow or green, halved lengthways and deseeded
30g low-fat cheese, grated (optional)

Heat oven to 180°C, Gas Mark 4.

Heat a pan sprayed with oil, add onion to soften and lean mince beef if using. Add courgettes and mushrooms, tomatoes and purée, thyme and mustard. Cook for 20 minutes. Stir in breadcrumbs if using.

Spoon mixture into the pepper halves and sprinkle with the grated cheese if wished. Place on a baking tray and bake for 15–20 minutes. Serve with rice.

WARM CHICKEN SALAD

Serves 4
Per portion: 143 kcal, 5g fat

1 spray of Fry Lite oil
200g skinless chicken breasts
4 tsp balsamic vinegar
juice of half a lime
paprika to taste
150g rocket
150g lambs lettuce
12 cherry tomatoes, halved
50g sundried tomatoes, chopped
4 spring onions, sliced diagonally
8 black olives, pitted and halved

Heat oil in a pan and fry chicken until sealed. Add vinegar, lime juice and paprika and cook on low heat for 20 minutes.

Arrange salad ingredients in a large bowl, and add chicken mixture. Toss and serve.

MANGO SORBET

Serves 4
Per portion: 250 kcal, 0g fat

200g castor sugar
600ml water
1 cinnamon stick
3 strips of lemon peel
750g mango, peeled, stoned and diced
mint sprigs for decoration

Put the sugar, water, cinnamon stick and lemon peel into a saucepan. Slowly dissolve the sugar over a low heat and then bring to the boil. Cook over a medium heat for 20 minutes, until the mixture is syrupy.

Add the mango to the sugar syrup and cook for a further 10 minutes. Remove the pan from the heat and discard the lemon peel and cinnamon stick.

Purée the fruit mixture in a blender, then rub through a sieve. Allow to cool, then freeze for 3 hours until just frozen. Remove from the freezer and mash with a fork. Return to the freezer for a further 3 hours.

Remove the sorbet from the freezer 10 minutes before serving. Decorate with mint sprigs.

APPLE FLAPJACKS

Makes 12
Per flapjack: 245 kcal, 5g fat

75g low-fat spread
175g golden granulated sugar
100g golden syrup
5 tbsp skimmed milk
375g rolled oats
500g apples, peeled, cored and sliced
½ tsp ground cloves
2 tbsp lemon juice

Heat oven to 180°C, Gas Mark 4. Grease an 18cm shallow square tin.

Melt the low-fat spread in a pan with sugar, syrup and milk. Stir in the oats. Spoon two-thirds of the mixture into the greased tin and bake in the preheated oven for 20 minutes.

Meanwhile, place the apples in a saucepan with the ground cloves and lemon juice and cook until thick and pulpy. Spread the apple over the cooked oat base. Cover with the remaining third of the oat mixture and cook for a further 20 minutes. Allow to cool and cut into 12 fingers.

PLUM CRUMBLE

Serves 6
Per portion: 200 kcal, 4g fat

500g plums, halved and stoned
2 tbsp of honey
2.5cm root ginger, grated
pinch of cinnamon
grated rind and juice of 1 orange
125g unsweetened muesli
50g of low-fat digestive biscuits, crushed
50g plain flour
25g low-fat spread

Heat oven to 200°C, Gas Mark 6.

Arrange the plums in an ovenproof dish. Mix the honey, ginger, cinnamon, orange juice and rind and pour over the plums. Bake in the preheated oven for 15 minutes.

Meanwhile, put the remaining ingredients into a bowl and mix to make the crumble topping.

Remove the plums from the oven and scatter the crumble mixture over the top. Return to the oven and continue cooking for a further 20 minutes. Serve with low-fat custard or low-fat fromage frais.

MIXED BERRY FLAN

Serves 8
Per portion: 256 kcal, 3g fat

400g ricotta cheese
30g icing sugar
1 tsp vanilla essence
½ tsp nutmeg
25cm flan case
250g strawberries, halved
250g raspberries
250g blueberries
75ml water
75g castor sugar

Press the cheese through a sieve, stir in the icing sugar, vanilla essence and nutmeg. Spread over the base of the flan case. Arrange fruit over the top.

Put water and sugar in a small saucepan, bring to the boil and boil for 5 minutes until it forms a syrup. Pour over the fruit, and allow to cool before serving.

Further Information

SPORTS BRAS

Large breasts can make exercise uncomfortable. The solution is a good-quality sports bra with plenty of support around the back, cup and shoulders. At Fat Club we gave the female members bras supplied by www.sportsbras.co.uk. Another good source is Bravissimo, a company which specialises in bras for the larger bust. Find them at www.bravissimo.com or call 01926 459859 for a catalogue. They also specialise in swimwear for larger sizes.

PEDOMETERS

These calculate the number of steps you take in a day. The perfect target for an active person or for those trying to get fit is around 10,000 per day. They are widely available (we used some manufactured by Roche), but vary in quality, so buy the best you can afford.

HEART-RATE MONITORS

These are an important tool for monitoring your pulse rate as you exercise. If your rate is too low you will gain little from exercise; too high and you will tire too quickly and will not burn fat. At Fat Club we used the Polar Pulse Watch which is easy to use and water-resistant to 20m. The watch gives high and low target zones and works with Polar's compact (2 in 1) Waterproof Transmitter belt. The package costs around £40. Available from good sports shops, online from www.premiersportsandfitness.co.uk or call Polar UK on 01926 811711 for your nearest stockist.

BOOKS

Joyce L. Verdal's *12-Minute Total Body Workout* (£13.99, Warner Books) and *The Fat Burning Workout* (£10, Warner Books)
Rosemary Conley's *Low Fat Cookbook* (£12.99, Century Books)

Websites for support and advice on weight loss and exercise

The Internet is a rich source of information and we have selected a group of sites which have sensible advice for anyone wanting to lose weight and become fitter. By its very nature, however, the Internet has many sites which promise quick weight loss and other 'fad' diets – everything that Fat Club tries to distance itself from – and you should be careful which ones you choose to browse.

About.com: www.about.com/health/ with features on weight loss, fitness and well-being

BBC Online: www.bbc.co.uk/healthfitness/ Excellent advice on fitness for all ages

BodySmartUK: www.bodysmartuk.com

British Nutrition Foundation: www.nutrition.org.uk Go to nutrition facts in the index, then to slimming diets

FeelGoodUK: www.icircle.com

Food Fitness: www.foodfitness.or.uk Site includes food and activity tips and self-assessment,

Health Education Authority: www.hea.org.uk

Health and Fitness Magazine Online: www.hfonline.co.uk

Health in Focus: www.healthinfocus.co.uk

Health Net: www.healthnet.org.uk

Mind Body Soul: Health advice for 14–16 year olds

NetDoctor: www.netdoctor.co.uk/health_advice/facts/loseweight.htm

Think Fast: www.thinkfast.co.uk Health Education Authority advice to help you make the healthy choice at fast-food outlets, aimed at 15–34 year olds.

WeightDirectory: www.weightdirectory.com Good American site, with an online BMI calculator

WeightWise: www.weightwise.co.uk

Websites for advice on eating disorders:

The National Centre for Eating Disorders:
www.eating-disorders.org.uk

The Eating Disorders Association: www.edauk.com